The Life and Times of Gardiner Spring

VOLUME 2

AUDUBON PRESS
2601 Audubon Drive / P.O. Box 8055
Laurel, MS 39441-8000   USA

Orders: 800-405-3788
Inquiries: 601-649-8572
Voice: 601-649-8570 / Fax: 601-649-8571
E-mail: buybooks@audubonpress.com
Web Page: www.audubonpress.com

© 2008 Audubon Press edition
All rights reserved.
Printed in the United States
Cover design by Crisp Graphics

ISBN # 978-09820731-4-8

Original Publication:

In Two Volumes

Volume 2

New York:
Charles Scribner & Co., 124 Grand Street
1866

Original Publication Layout and Typography:
John F. Trow & Co.,
Printers, Stereotypers, & Electrotypers,
50 Green Street, N.Y.

CONTENTS OF VOLUME II.

CHAPTER I.
                                                   PAGE
HOPKINSIANISM, ... 5

CHAPTER II.
NEW HAVEN THEOLOGY, ... 23

CHAPTER III.
THE EXSCINDING ACTS OF THE GENERAL ASSEMBLY, . 44

CHAPTER IV.
EXTRACTS FROM MY JOURNAL, ... 59

CHAPTER V.
CONTINUATION OF MY JOURNAL, ... 73

CHAPTER VI.
FOREIGN TRAVEL, ... 96

CHAPTER VII.
THE SABBATH REFORM, ... 141

CONTENTS.

CHAPTER VIII.

	PAGE
MARY NORRIS, OUR ELDEST DAUGHTER,	150

CHAPTER IX.

THE SOUTHERN REBELLION,	177

CHAPTER X.

THE SOUTHERN REBELLION REPRESSED AND PEACE RESTORED,	205

CHAPTER XI.

THE PRESS AS WELL AS THE PULPIT,	216

CHAPTER XII.

FAMILIAR LETTERS,	234

CHAPTER XIII.

THE NINETEENTH CENTURY A PRACTICAL AGE,	267

CHAPTER XIV.

THE PAST AND THE FUTURE,	275

CHAPTER I.

HOPKINSIANISM.

UNTIL a comparatively late period in the theological history of New England, Hopkinsians were universally regarded as Calvinists. President Edwards, by his Treatise on the Will, and on the Doctrine of Original Sin; by his Treatise concerning Religious Affections; by his reply to Solomon Williams' book on the qualifications for Communion; by his Treatise on the nature of True Virtue, and his narrative of the Great Work of God in Northampton, took the initiative in those sharp distinctions and metaphysical investigations which led to the system of Hopkinsianism. He was not a Hopkinsian, but he was the teacher of Dr. Hopkins, and of many of the earlier Hopkinsian divines. In the year 1765, Dr. Hopkins published his inquiry concerning the promises of the Gospel in their relation to the exercises and doings of persons in an unregenerate state, and, in 1769, a treatise on the true state of the unregenerate. His views on this subject were controverted by the Rev. Mr. Mills, of Huntington, Conn., and by the Rev. Dr. Hart, of Preston, in the same State. It was on the publication of Mr. Mills that the disciples of Dr. Hopkins were first called Hopkinsians. On almost all other subjects there was perfect harmony between them and the old Calvinists; at least as much so as between Calvinists of the present day. Dr. Hopkins' dialogue on the nature and extent of true Christian submission was not then published, and was a posthumous publication. He himself professed to be a strict and consistent Calvinist; and the great aim of his ministry and his publications was to prove, illustrate, and harmonize the great principles of faith and duty, as exhibited in the confessions and catechisms of the Westminster Assembly. The late Dr. Miller, of Princeton, once remarked to me, " I should hesitate to *lay hands* on Dr. Emmons; but though I do not approve of all that Dr. Hopkins has written, I would ordain any man, otherwise qualified, who could honestly say that he believed *every word* of Dr. Hopkins' system." Dr. Hopkins was no Arminian, no Pelagian, no Sabellian, no Arian, no Socinian, no Universalist; no man, if we except the younger Edwards, has written more powerfully against these errors. On the doctrine of the Trinity; on the attributes, and purposes, and providence of God; on the native and total sinfulness of man by nature, and his responsibility as a free, moral agent; on the divinity and atonement of Christ; on the all-sufficiency of the Atonement, and the free offer of salvation to the race; on the present obligation of all who hear the Gospel to repent and believe in the Son of God; on the work of the Holy Spirit, and man's dependence on the power of God for the beginning and the continuance of the Christian's inner life;

on justification by faith in the Saviour's righteousness; and on the everlasting retributions of eternity, no Calvinist can express clearer or more convincing views than Dr. Hopkins.

I have heard it said, that scriptural views on these great subjects do not constitute a Calvinist, and that in addition to these, every thorough-going Calvinist regards Jesus Christ, as revealed in the covenant of redemption, as the *representative* of the elect, and the primogenitor of the human family, in the covenant of works, or by the law of Paradise, as the *representative* of the race. That this scriptural doctrine of *representation* constitutes the distinguishing feature of Calvinism, Hopkinsians do not deny. Where in the records of Hopkinsianism is to be found any repudiation of this great principle of the Christian faith? Even Dr. Emmons, who was an *ultra* Hopkinsian, affirms that "God placed Adam as the public head of his posterity, and determined to treat *them* according to *his* conduct; his first and single act of disobedience made all his posterity sinners." Elsewhere he says, "Our great progenitor was made the natural and *federal* head of millions of immortal beings." More explicit is the teaching of Dr. Hopkins. His language is, "By the constitution and covenant with Adam, his first disobedience was the disobedience of all mankind." So far as I am informed, Hopkinsians universally believe that the sin and consequent ruin of all was, by this covenant, infallibly connected with the first sin of the head and father of the race. The difference here between old Calvinists and Hopkinsian Calvinists is twofold. Hopkinsians regard this arrangement in respect to the imputation of Adam's first sin, as simply a procedure of *sovereignty*, while the old Calvinists regard it as a measure of *moral government*. I once thought it was a procedure of mere sovereignty; but on more full examination of the language of the apostle, "*judgment* was by one to *condemnation*," I became convinced that it was a procedure of moral government, and a judicial decision. *Judgment* and *condemnation* refer to judicial rather than sovereign acts.

The other point of difference relates to *mediate* or *immediate* imputation. The old Calvinists assert that the condemning sentence of the law falls upon all the posterity of Adam for *his sin alone*, and that they would have been justly condemned *for his sin*, even though they had remained sinless. The Hopkinsian Calvinists assert that there is an intermediate link in the chain that binds his posterity to the curse, and that is their own *sinful character*. Old Calvinists themselves are not agreed upon the question, whether mediate or immediate imputation is the doctrine of the Bible, or of the churches of the Reformation. I would like to know if it is not imputation enough, if the sin of Adam makes the race *sinners, and thus* brings them into a state of condemnation. To condemn them for his sin, themselves being righteous, is alike opposed to our natural sense of justice, and to that Law which declares, "He that doeth these things shall live in them." No matter how the taint of moral corruption is visited upon the race, nor *how small* it is in the new-born soul, all Calvinists believe that "*every sin* deserves God's wrath and curse, both in this life and that which is to come." Such is the view of leading Calvinists, and such is the scriptural view. "By one man sin entered into the world, and death by sin, and so death passed upon all men *for that* all have sinned." All have sinned and therefore all must die. The original ἐφ' ᾧ, translated *for that*, are rightly translated. The Protestant French Bible, made by the Professors and Pastors of Geneva, and Luther's German Bible, translate them *because*, the French "parce que;" the German, *diewal*. Calvin, Erasmus, Piscator, Tremellius, the Syriac version, Vatabulus, and Paræus, according to Poole's Synopsis, translate them *because*. McKnight says ἐπὶ with a dative case signifies *on account of*. Pickering's Lexicon says ἐφ' ᾧ signifies *wherefore, for which reason*. Calvin, in his commentary on these words, renders them *quandoquitor, because*. "Observe here," says he, "what *order* the apostle lays down; for he says that sin went before, and therefore death followed. There are, indeed, those who contend that we are so lost by the sin of Adam, as if we perished by no fault of our own, as if he only had sinned for us. But Paul expressly affirms that sin is propagated in all who suffer its punishment. And then he urges that more closely, when, a little after, he assigns the reason why all Adam's posterity are subject to death, 'and that is,' says he, '*quoniam omnes peccavimus*, because we all have sinned.'" In his Institutes, Lib. II. cap. I. sect. 8, he makes the following remarks: "Neque ista est alieni delicti obligatio; quod enim dicitur, nos per Adami peccatum obnoxios esse factos Dei judicio; non ita est accipiendum quasi insontes ipsi et immerentes culpam delicti ejus sustineremus, sed quia per ejus transgressionem maledictione induti sumus omnes, dicitur ille nos obstrinxisse." In plain English: "This liability to punishment arises not from the *sin of another;* for when it is said that the sin of Adam renders us obnoxious to the divine displeasure, it is not to be understood as if we, though innocent, were undeservedly loaded with the guilt of his sin, but because we are all subject to a curse *in consequence* of his transgression, he is therefore said to have involved us in guilt." On the subject of original sin, Calvin was a Hopkinsian. Dr. Hodge also affirms that "there are strong philological objections" against rendering the words ἐφ' ᾧ *in whom*, and that "our common version is to be preferred. All die *for that*, or because that, all have sinned."

But while we give free utterance to the preceding thoughts, we take leave to say that we have no sympathy with the two peculiarities of Hopkinsianism. The position that *God is the author of sin*, and the doctrine of *unconditional submission* to the will of God, as explained by Hopkinsians, and enforced by a willingness to be damned for his glory, as essential to true piety, appear to me to have been inconsiderately adopted. I myself was early educated in this belief, but, with all reverence for my early training, I could not retain it in my creed. Many are the discussions on these subjects I have listened to when under my father's roof, and I shall never forget the impression made upon my mind by listening to the outline of a discourse upon the words, "The wrath of man shall praise thee; the remainder of wrath shalt thou restrain." The *doctrine* of the discourse was, *There is no more sin in the world than God wants.* Though I was but a boy, the thought struck me painfully. My father disapproved of it, though he smiled; I felt it could not be true. Many a time has the thought occurred to my mind, that if God is the efficient cause of all the sin in the world, then is he the author of much more sin than holiness. I cannot believe it. Every intelligent being is created capable of sinning; if he sins, the sin is his own, and he himself is the author of it. " Every *good* gift, and every *perfect* gift, cometh down from the Father of lights." He is not the father of darkness. " He that committeth sin is of the devil."

In regard to a *conditional consent to be damned,* even if the hypothesis it involves be admissible, I have no confidence in it as a practical test of Christian character. The strong attachment to a particular system of theology, and the deceitfulness of the human heart, are too operative to allow any man to trust himself with such a test of character. The habitual submission of the soul to the will of God, an humble and confiding spirit under the daily dispensations of Providence, the self-denial that cheerfully takes up the cross and follows Christ, that comes out from the world and walks with God, that practises a steady course of obedience to his commands, and maintains an intercourse with God, its daily devotions; these form a safer and surer test of Christian character, than a supposed willingness to be damned for the glory of God. Hopkinsians thus believe and thus preach. Dr. Emmons himself, the strongest advocate for the notion we are combating, confesses that this is the way by which "all true believers may attain to the full assurance of hope," and that the "proper and sure way of attaining satisfactory evidence of a gracious state is to walk sincerely and closely with God."

But more than this: the hypothesis itself is inadmissible and absurd. It is *inadmissible*, because it contradicts the eternal and unchangeable attributes of the Deity, and makes God deny himself. It is *absurd*, because it makes the Christian character an absurdity, inconsistent with itself, opposed to manifest truth and the plain dictates of common sense. To be willing to be damned is to be willing to sin and suffer eternally. To be *damned*, in the scriptural acceptation of this word, includes the moral character and penal sufferings of the guilty inhabitants of the world of woe. Is it possible for a good man to consent to such a perfect abandonment to all wickedness? Can his *love* to God be such as to influence him to *hate* God, just as the devils and the damned do? Can his *penitence* be such as to influence him to *incorrigible and everlasting* wickedness? Can his confidence in the Son of God ever be so implicit as to induce him to deny the Saviour and unite with his enemies in blaspheming him forever? Can his *submission* ever rise so high, or sink so low, as to constrain him to be an *eternal rebel?* What would be thought of a man who professed to love God so fervently, that he was willing to hate him? or who professed to love his people, and the interests of his kingdom and his great glory, so much above everything else, that he was willing to be associated forever with his enemies, and in unsubdued hostility to his kingdom and glory? Are not all such hypotheses perfectly absurd?

Further: there is no small confusion of ideas and some sophistry in relation to the Hopkinsian dogma of *unconditional submission*. The divine attributes, although they are the objects of supreme love, reverence, and confidence, are never the objects of submission except when expressed and acted out. If I may so speak, God never comes in direct contact with man, except in his *commands* and *dispensations*. The *commands* of God are his revealed will, and constitute the only unerring, unchangeable, and perpetual rule of duty. Submission to them is of perpetual obligation, and is not limited by time, nor place, nor circumstances; it is of equal obligation in all worlds; it must be *unconditional*. The *divine dispensations* are the successive developments of His unrevealed purposes by events, both in the present and future world. They are the execution of His eternal purposes, and submission to them can only be exercised when the divine purpose is developed by the occurrence of events. In such cases the obligation to submission is complete, and must be unreserved, cheerful, unconditional. The error on this subject appears to be in requiring unconditional submission to events which have not occurred, and may never occur; thus substituting the *supposed* purposes of God for his revealed will. The doctrine of submission is well understood in civil government. No man is expected to pay obedience to an unpublished law; much less to submit to an unrevealed purpose. When a law is published, it is the duty of the subject to submit to it and obey. If he violates it, his duty is to submit to a trial, to a conviction, to a sentence, to imprisonment, and to be carried to the place of execution. To these successive dispensations of justice it is his duty to submit. But he has not yet submitted to the execution of the sentence. The fatal hour has not come. It may never arrive; he may be reprieved, or pardoned. He can submit only to *events* as they present themselves. Just so in the government of God. The will of God can be truly submitted to, only as events occur, and his will is acted out. A man can no more submit to what has never happened, than violate a law which was never enacted. As objects of voluntary exercises, they are both nonentities, and can exist only in a disordered imagination. If the Hopkinsian doctrine of submission be true, it amounts simply to this: that men are bound to submit to an event which God has not revealed, and which, on their own showing, can never take place. To maintain this doctrine, two things must be assumed: first, an event which God has not revealed; second, submission to it, as though it were present. The former is presumption; the latter is impossible. The obligation to supreme love and perfect obedience will exist to all eternity, even in the lowest abyss of despair; and there will all the incorrigible enemies of God be favored with the obligation and the opportunity for the complete exercise of unconditional *submission*.

Great and good men have been the zealous advocates of the views here animadverted on; nor are we among those who have called in question the excellence of their Christian character. As a class, I have never known more godly men. Men of greater humility, greater self-denial, greater devotedness to the interests and enlargement of Christ's kingdom, have never existed in New England, than the disciples of Dr. Hopkins. If their opposers had known them as well as I have known them, I am confident their prejudices would vanish. It was not Hopkinsianism that led to the decline of vital piety in New England. It was the semi-Calvinism, the Arminianism, the Pelagianism, that arrayed themselves, first against the Puritans, and then against all revivals of religion, from the days of Edwards to the present time. Nor was it Hopkinsianism that prepared the way for the Socinianism of Massachusetts. There never was a more unfounded calumny than this. It was the loose Calvinism of Boston, and the Moderation of other parts of New England, and the lax theology of eminent laymen, that opened the flood-gates of error. Nor did any class stand up so boldly to stem the flood, in its early rising, as the Hopkinsians. Calvinists of the old school have long since learned that Hopkinsians are their best friends, and that, in their collisions with Cambridge, New Haven, and Andover, they must look elsewhere for help than to a disjointed theology.

I am no enemy to Hopkinsianism, though I have no fellowship with its peculiarities. If it has done nothing else, it has so vindicated both the gracious and moral government of God, as to enforce the neglected doctrine of human obligation and responsibility, and demolish and cut up, root and branch, all the sinner's excuses. Some modern preachers would do well and plough deeper, if they ploughed with Samson's heifer.

. I do not look upon the Hopkinsian controversy with indifference. It made such men as Andrew Fuller, John Ryland, Timothy Dwight, Edward D. Griffin, James Richards, Asahel Nettleton, and Heman Humphrey, though they were not Hopkinsians. It contains errors, but it has elicited truth. It is delightful to inspect the wisdom of Divine Providence in the progress of theological thought, evincing, as it does, the scriptural declaration, "There must be heresies among you, that the truth may be made manifest." Truth never appears more in its divine excellence and beauty, than when it is held up and seen in contrast with error. It is the eldest-born of the Father of lights; and though soiled, and sometimes in tattered garments, yet it walks over the track of time, decked with the adornment of its native skies. Truth is not only the more illumined and brilliant for the darkness it penetrates and scatters, but its friends and advocates stand out before God, angels, and men, as heaven-appointed indices to Him who is "the way, the truth, and the life." The God of Zion appears in his glory, when he comes with his fan in his hand, to sever the wheat from the chaff, and to draw the line between those who receive and those who reject his word. The experience of the past is not only instructive, but full of encouragement: through all its conflicts with error, truth was evermore gaining some fresh laurels; it always gained more than it lost. Its early struggle was with paganism during the apostolic age, when Paul became its advocate at Rome and at Athens; nor would the world then have known the brutal degradation of paganism, but for his speech on Mars Hill, and the first chapters of his Epistle to the Romans. Celsus, though he "meant not so, neither in his heart did he think so," did good service to the truth by calling forth the elaborate work of Origen. Porphyry's assaults on Christianity drew forth the apologies of Methodius, Jerome, Eusebius, and Augustine. Athanasius, Basil, the Gregories, Ambrose, and those three master-minds, Origen, Chrysostom, and Augustine, would never have stood forth as such witnesses for truth, had they not been stimulated by solicitude for the Christian faith, and the fear that it was in peril. Men like these were raised up for the fall of heathenism in the world of philosophy and letters. And when, after a period of more than seven hundred years, dark ages of ignorance overshadowed new races of men, and when feudalism and Popery were staggering under the combined invasions of infidelity and Protestantism, and the work of Abelard, entitled "*Sic et Non,*" was productive of so much heresy, if not skepticism, God raised up that wonderful man, St. Bernard, to repel the advances of error, and lift up the standard of truth. The twelfth century was the most remarkable period of the Middle Ages, during which there were obvious advances in social government, and men like Thomas Aquinas, Roger Bacon, Frederick II., and Dante, gave new incitements to human thought; and then it was that Christianity, though it made little progress from without, made sensible progress from within. A century later, when the Mahometan literature and philosophy diffused so widely the disbelief of immortality, and the church endeavored to repress it by violence and the inquisition, then it was that the human mind asserted anew its rights of thought upon the truth God has revealed. The time was just at hand that would imperatively call for the exercise of this right, and Providence was preparing the way for it. In the fifteenth century, Rome had become the treasury of Europe, and her sovereign pontiff controlled its courts. Christianity was in danger. Philosophy, literature, and art became indifference to all religion, and it seemed to threaten a collapse of the truth as it is in Jesus. Poetry caricatured and satirized it, and great men were anti-Christian. The Catholic faith was found wanting, and led to infidelity. The change was decisive. "It was the earthquake which shattered forever the crust of error which had fettered thought." There were great revolutions, but they issued in the question asked by the Reformed churches, "What does the Bible teach?" The day had begun to dawn, in which neither the power of the state, nor the church, could repress intellectual or religious thought. About the close of the fifteenth century, and when the art of printing gave more general access to books, publications on the evidences of Christianity gave the conflict a more palpable form. The question was no longer submission to human authority, but to the divine authority of the Bible. The attention to experimental science which led to the inductive method of Sir Francis Bacon, induced a rigid examination, both on the part of friends and foes, not only into the grounds of belief in divine revelation, but into the principles of interpretation, and the canon both of the Old and New Testaments. The result was, that the word of God stood the test, and his truth was victorious.

English deism, taking its rise in the reign of the first Charles, at the close of the reign of George II. and the early part of that of George III., waned and sunk into the cold night of rationalism. Herbert, Hobbes, and Blount, Toland, Collins, and Shaftesbury, Woolston, and Hume, found their triumphant antagonists in Clarke, Butler, and Bentley; in Lardner, Sherlock, and Warburton; in Leland, Paley, Brougham, and Chalmers; when truth came forth from the conflict with a more wisely-adjusted panoply, and for renewed struggles and fresh laurels. The infidelity of the eighteenth century in France, while it challenged Christianity, demonstrated the strength of its high-born armor. Defunct in England, infidelity was indeed for a time pandemic in France, and produced that natural corruption which presaged its overthrow. England had sown the wind, and France reaped the whirlwind. Fontenelle, Voltaire, Diderot, Volney, the French encyclopedists, and Frederic II., of Prussia, seemed destined to desolate that fair empire, until their philosophy, their unbelief, and *soi-disant* philanthropy, were overwhelmed by the storm of the French Revolution. It was a practical development of the nature, tendencies, and results of infidelity, and convinced Europe and America of its destructiveness. It was the comment of Providence on the visionary philosophy of men who were without God in the world.

Religion was publicly declared obsolete by the national assembly, and a vile opera-dancer was led in triumph to the Cathedral of Nôtre Dame, and on the altar of God received the adorations of the people, as the "Goddess of Reason."

Germany, in our own day, with all its rationalism, has been made subservient to the progress of Christian truth. While, with great mental activity, great powers of endurance, and great advances in philosophical, historical, and critical science, it has thrown darkness and doubt over some of the essential facts and doctrines of Divine revelation; it has also, by the burnished weapons of offence and defence it has furnished to the friends of truth, done good service to the cause which it seemed for a time to put in jeopardy. Semler, Strauss, and Renan found more than their equals in Schleiermacher, Neander, De Wette, Oberlin, Tholuck, and Olshausen; and though the writings of the latter class are not all worthy of confidence, they furnish an important contribution to the treasury of evangelical truth. Viewed as a whole, and in their true perspective, they represent the daughter of Zion as "*coming up* from the wilderness, leaning upon her beloved." Vital Christianity has not died out in the churches of Germany; the land of Luther, where the enemy has scattered tares, is even broadcast with the finest of the wheat. The very errors of Germany have produced agitation that has resulted in more enlightened views of truth.

And this is true in relation to the theological discussions in this country. The Unitarianism of Cambridge, the semi-Pelagianism of some of the old Calvinists, the high-toned Calvinism of the Antinomian caste, and the metaphysics of the Hopkinsian school, have indirectly contributed not a little to build up the temple of truth. The agitations in the Presbyterian church, between Old and New School, have elicited earnestness, and effort, and caution, which were needed both by the Old and the New. We all know more and do more than we did before those commenced. Truth does not shrink from inquiry. Free and full discussion always, in the end, results in truth. There are differences of opinion even now, both among the brethren of the New School and the Old. For myself I say, let them be tolerated, and let them be discussed. I am no advocate for any test except that prescribed by our form of government. I do not ask that in every particular my brethren should subscribe to my creed. I only ask that they " sincerely receive and adopt the Confession of Faith of the Presbyterian church, as containing *the system of doctrine* contained in the Holy Scriptures." It is the *system* of Calvinism, as expressed by the Synod of Dort and the Westminster Assembly. Few, in this age of inquiry, believe *every word of it.* Nor did our fathers. I myself made two exceptions to it, when I was received into the Presbytery of New York, fifty-five years ago. Nor were those exceptions any barrier to my admission. I am no bigot, and no friend to innovations. Let our Confession and Catechism stand. I have no wish to alter them; the attempt would be hazardous. Witherspoon, Rodgers, McWhorter, Smith, Miller, and Richards were not men of strife, nor did they lend their influence to awaken jealousies, heart-burnings, and chilling alienations among those who ought to love as brethren. We have no Act of Uniformity to compel a perfect unanimity in every minute article of so extended a Confession. There are shades of thought and forms of expression, in regard to which men will not cease to think for themselves. I could specify many points in which not a few of our ministers and ruling elders do not exactly agree with our standards. Yet they are all HONEST CALVINISTS, and receive our standards as the most unexceptionable formularies ever drawn up by uninspired men, and receive them *as a whole* with all their hearts. The iron bed of Procrustes is not suited to the spirit of the age. Some modern Theseus will yet be raised up, and show to the church that there is small space for the couch of bigotry in the nineteenth century.

CHAPTER II.

NEW HAVEN THEOLOGY.

In the year 1829 a different turn was given to these discussions by the novel and unscriptural speculations of the Rev. Dr. Nathaniel W. Taylor, D.D., who occupied the chair of theology in Yale College. I had published a " Dissertation on the Means of Regeneration," an enlargement of the annual discourse preached before the directors and students of our own theological seminary at Princeton. I was requested by a large number of the students to publish it; and without the least thought of eliciting any new views upon the subject, acquiesced in their request. It was reviewed in the Christian Spectator in the spirit of fraternal kindness, and even commendation; but it gave rise to a full and unexpected development of some novel views from the pen of Dr. Taylor, that excited no small alarm among evangelical ministers, and that became the subject of a prolonged and sharp discussion. Dr. Taylor objects to the phrase, " using the means of regeneration," and does not understand by it any acts, which either precede, or are to be " distinguished from regeneration itself." Yet he affirms that regeneration " is through the truth, and implies attention to the truth, the sober, solemn consideration of the object which truth discloses, *prior* to the requisite act of the will or heart." Nor is the contradiction at all modified by " referring rather to the order of nature than of time." It amounts simply to this: that in the order of nature there are no means of regeneration. He frankly says that " the distinction between using the means of regeneration and regeneration itself is a theological, rather than a scriptural, distinction." He says, also, that " regeneration is an event which depends on the interposition of the Holy Spirit; and that some part of the process is *preliminary* to such interposition." He proceeds, therefore, to " designate those mental acts and states " which are thus preliminary, and which " constitute using the means of regeneration," and which " precede, as we propose to use the term regeneration, *that act of the will, or heart*, in which God is preferred to every other object." He then proceeds to say, that " before the act of the will or heart in which the sinner first prefers God to every other object, the object of the preference must be viewed or estimated as the greatest good. Before the object can be viewed as the greatest good, it must be compared with other objects, as both are sources or means of good. Before this act of comparing, there must be an act dictated, not by selfishness, but by *self-love*, in which the mind determines to direct its thoughts to the objects for the sake of considering their relative value, of forming a judgment respecting it, and of choosing one or the other as the chief good." That he may not be misunderstood, he afterwards says, "These acts of consideration and comparison of the objects of choice are dictated, not by selfishness, but by the desire of happiness or self-love, which in its own nature fixes on no definite object as the source of happiness. Self-love, or desire of happiness, is the primary cause or reason of all acts of preference or choice which fix supremely on any object." He regards regeneration as the mental preference of God as the chief good, instead of the world; as a *change* in the preference of the mind, dictated by the desire of happiness.

We cannot but inquire here, Is this the scriptural doctrine of regeneration? Do the Scriptures anywhere represent self-love, or the desire of happiness, as the cause of this change, or do they attribute it to the grace of God? Pelagius and Dr. Taylor may make depraved man the author of his own salvation: the Bible instructs us that this change in the moral state of the soul, is "not of blood, nor of the will of the flesh, nor of the *will of man*, but of God," and that from the first pulsation of the inner life, to its vigorous actings on the threshold of heaven, "he that hath wrought us for this selfsame thing is God." Is it so, that regeneration is simply a change in the governing purpose of the soul, or is it the transformation of the soul into the image of God, changing the moral character, and imparting new views, new affections, new principles, new pursuits? Is it merely a change from supreme selfishness to self-love; or is it a change from sin to holiness, and one in which self, in every form, is dethroned, and the God of heaven put in its place? Is it a change dictated by the love of happiness, or are its radical elements the love of truth and right, "the love of God, shed abroad in the heart by the Holy Ghost?" We revolt from the sweeping declaration, that "of all specific voluntary action, *the happiness of the agent is, in some form, the ultimate end.*" We have not so learned Christ. There is no moral rectitude in such a controlling motive; there is no obedience to the Divine law; there is nothing but that supreme selfishness which, while it may produce the piety that is sounding brass and a tinkling cymbal, may produce all that is abomination in the sight of God. Nor is the difficulty avoided by urging the distinction between self-love and selfishness, and supposing that, in the act of regeneration, there is a *suspension of the self-principle* in order to give self-love, or the desire of happiness, opportunity to decide whether or not the sinner will choose God for his portion, or the world. The Word of God assures us that the selfish principle maintains its controlling influence in the mind until it is regenerated. The agency of the Divine Spirit, then, results, not "in an appalling mental inertness and stupefaction," but in carrying the soul forth to God in holy love. The stream never rises higher than its fountain. No man, either from the principle of selfishness, or the natural principle of *self-love*, ever loved God *more than himself*. This every regenerated man does; and to suppose that he does it from the love of self, is to suppose that "he is bribed to hate a bribe." Many of Dr. Taylor's conclusions are drawn from *assumed* premises, of which he has produced no proof, and he has carried out his supposed arguments with much ingenuity, and much declamation. Three things have occurred to my mind in which he is in error. In the first place, he has wrong views of what the sinner does actually perform while under conviction. The scriptural history of the human heart, and the history of revivals, and the uniform testimony of the children of God, all show that the awakened sinner makes, in some sort, *desperate efforts*. But what are they ? The "heart is deceitful above all things, and *desperately wicked*." The sinner would not have been awakened and convicted, but for the intervention of the Holy Spirit. He ought to break off his iniquities by righteousness, and his transgressions by turning to God. He has no excuse for hesitating to do this, and no reason for hesitating but his unyielding wickedness. He has no reason at all. The most reasonable thing in the world for him to do, is to repent and believe the Gospel. But the depraved inclination of his heart is to break away from God, and neglect the momentous concerns of his soul, even under his strongest convictions. It is not true that he ever makes efforts towards returning to that God from whom he has so wickedly revolted. He breaks away, and God hedges up his path. He is anxious—he is distressed, because God is holding his conscience awake by the power of the Holy Ghost. And if the Spirit continues to strive with him, and his convictions continue, and he is not allowed to drop the subject, his restlessness, and conflicts, and distress increase, until God imparts his renovating grace.

In the next place, Dr. Taylor has also wrong views of the preaching of those who differ from him on the means of regeneration. There is no force in his arguments, unless he means that they do not address the conscience, and urge the impenitent to do their duty without delay, and unless, with their views of regeneration, they have no right thus to urge them. But they do preach, as plainly and as pungently as those whose tendencies are towards Pelagian and Arminian errors. We make our appeal to the church and the world, whether we do not set before the unrepenting the imperative claims of the Gospel, and urge our hearers to fall in with them "*now*, while it is called *to-day*." And we are consistent in so doing, inasmuch as the reason why they are dependent on supernatural agency, is their own perverseness, and because they "will not come to Christ, that they might have life."

In addition to this, Dr. Taylor has wrong views of the influence of the different methods of preaching. The most effectual way to awaken sinners, and increase their convictions, and lead them to Jesus Christ, is to show them their sinful character, and lost condition, and to let them see and feel that they are sinking to ruin. And how, under God, can we do this? Dr. Taylor will say, By showing them that there is a fearful uncertainty whether they will be saved or lost. But what is it that most clearly exhibits this uncertainty? Is it anything that savors of a smooth Pelagianism? We answer, unhesitatingly, No. All history, in the Bible and out of the Bible, answers, No. Though the impenitent ought to be urged to repent and believe the Gospel, and though there is nothing in their dependence that relieves them from this obligation, they like right well to think that they may make the efforts which Dr. Taylor speaks of, and in that very way they are induced to procrastinate, and until the Spirit ceases to strive with them, and their anxiety has vanished. Nothing shows more the fearful uncertainty of the sinner's ultimate condition, or contributes more to convince him that he has great reason to fear that he shall continue in his present character and be lost, than the five following facts: that such is his own perverseness that he *will die* unless God interpose; that continued impenitence tends to harden his heart; that no dependence is to be placed on present resolutions of future amendment, or a death-bed repentance; that God does not purpose to save all; and that none can tell whom he will interpose to convert and save. Truths and facts like these can be made to bear with tremendous weight on the conscience.

We would like also to know what is the meaning of the declaration that *God governs the mind by motives, and not by force.* Does he act upon the motives? if so, *how* does he act upon them? Does he in any way change them; or are they unchangeable, and always the same, and just as he revealed them in his Word? You say he makes them appear differently to the mind to which they are addressed. But how does he make them appear differently, if they never change? Obviously it is not on the motives that he acts, but on *the mind*, to which they are addressed. He opens the eye of the mind—he touches the conscience and heart, so that the unchanging truths of his Word are seen and felt. It was thus that he "*opened the heart* of Lydia, that she attended to the things that were spoken of Paul." He gives motives power only by opening the heart. If, then, it is the heart on which he operates, I ask, again, What is the meaning of the position that God governs the mind by motives, and not by force? *He always governs by force:* in the world of nature, by the force of natural causes; in the kingdom of providence, by the force of natural and moral causes combined; and in the kingdom of grace, by the power of his Spirit, acting not on the truth, but *through* the truth, and on the mind itself. It is all force; or, in other words, it is the will, the power of God, giving to natural causes and moral causes their appropriate place and influence. They have no place, no influence, independently of his will.

Some writers speak of the power of God as flippantly as they would of the action of natural bodies upon one another, and of the laws of the equilibrium and motion of solids and fluids, and of the forces by which they are made to act. But whence are these laws of nature? Who ordained them, and gave them their appropriate action, and gives it still? Newton discovered the great law of gravitation, but who first ordained and upholds it? Whose law is it, Newton's or God's? Our knowledge of the nature and properties of light and colors, and the changes they experience, when transmitted through other bodies, or reflected from their surfaces, or, in other words, the science of optics, may be traced to the celebrated Euclid, to the astronomer of Alexandria, and to the illustrious Newton; but the great laws which govern light are themselves the ordinance of the God of heaven.

It is his wise arrangement, his all-pervading decree, and his *omnipotent will* carrying this arrangement into effect, that gives their appropriate place to all natural and moral causes. It is the same force in nature, providence, and grace; it is all the determinate counsel and *executive will* of the Most High. " He speaks, and it is done." Is there no force here? " He doeth *all things* according to the counsel of *his own will.*" Is there no force here? " Thy people shall be *willing* in the day of thy power." Is there no force here? not of human mechanism, but of Divine efficiency; not of constraint, but of the omnipotent will upon the human will, working in men " to will and to do of his own good pleasure."

There is another error in the New Haven theology, to which my thoughts were directed, but with no intention that the discussion should be extended beyond my own pulpit. It relates to the great doctrine of NATIVE DEPRAVITY. Dr. Taylor denies it; Professor Stuart of Andover denies it; Professor Fitch and the New Haven School deny it; and so did Pelagius, Arminius, and Locke, and Dr. John Taylor, and Whitby, and their disciples. It is an important doctrine of the Calvinistic, Edwardean, Hopkinsian, Emmonite, and Princeton theology, and, as I deemed, from the " signs of the times," deserved the consideration of my own people. Having prepared with some care a discourse on this subject, I preached it to a large congregation, of which, in an unobserved corner of the church, Mr. Nettleton was one. Soon after it was delivered, he advised me to correct and enlarge it, and give it to the press. I hesitated long, but made up my mind to re-write it, and, after some valuable suggestions from his own instructive lips, gave it the form of a "Dissertation on Native Depravity." Very unexpectedly to myself, it occasioned no small controversy. On one of my visits to New Haven, I was requested to supply the pulpit of the College. I thought of this dissertation. I hesitated about preaching it. I read it to the Rev. Dr. Skinner, now of the Union Theological Seminary, and requested his views as to the propriety of so doing, at such a time, in such a place, and on so courteous an invitation. I saw that he hesitated. At length he smiled, and said, "Brother Spring, I think I would preach it." Whether wisely or unwisely, meekly or impudently, I did preach it, in the chapel of Yale College, in the presence of President Day, and the professors and students. I much doubt the propriety of so doing, nor do I now judge that I was prompted to it by the "meekness of wisdom." It created "no small stir." One of the professors in the medical department manifested his displeasure by abruptly and demonstratively leaving the chapel in the midst of the discourse. The dissertation was printed in New York in the year 1833. It was reviewed by the Rev. Professor Goodrich and others, in the fifth volume of the Christian Spectator, with needless severity, and little argument. The amount of their argument is, that "Dr. Spring is an Ishmaelite, and while he agrees with nobody, agrees more nearly with his New Haven brethren, than with any other class of theologians." I replied to these strictures, requesting that my reply might appear in the "Literary and Theological Review," then published in New York, and of which I was one of the editing committee. But my reply was rejected from its pages, and, I now judge, very justly. The Christian Spectator began its course under good auspices; but it had then degenerated into the repulsiveness of Taylorism. Its influence was more like the head of Medusa than the vivifying influence of the sun. The dissertation was subsequently reviewed by Dr. Tyler, of the "Theological Institute" at East Windsor, who understood the subject, and who set the New Haven gentlemen, and the author of the dissertation, in their true light.

In the biography of Dr. Beecher, it is stated, that "when Professor Goodrich came out with the notion that there is nothing sinful in infants," the Doctor remarked, "The moment I heard of that, I saw the end. I never felt so bad. I wrote a long letter to him and Taylor, telling them they must take that back."

The following communication from the late General Henry Sewall, a well-known officer in the army of the American Revolution, and a distinguished civilian in the State of Maine, and withal a profound theologian, is too valuable a testimony on this subject to be lost.

"AUGUSTA, ME., *June* 16, 1834.

"REV. AND DEAR SIR:

"By the courtesy of a friend, I have lately obtained, and read with interest, your Dissertation on

'Native Depravity.' This is certainly an important subject, and the controversy is not without its difficulties on both sides. But that view of it which Arminians and Pelagians give is so full of inconsistencies, and so much at war with Scripture and fact, that it cannot obtain my credence. I find it much harder to vindicate the justice of God in his course of conduct towards infants, if they are innocent, than if they are depraved.

"When my mind became first enlightened ' to discern both good and evil,' some fifty years since, I was surrounded by Arminian professors, who denied the doctrine of *native depravity*, and unflinchingly held that children are born as innocent as Adam was created. Notwithstanding the lapse of years, I still recollect distinctly a colloquial interview with one of those advocates for the *native purity* of infants, to whom I replied, that if they are as pure as was Adam, why are they not as holy and righteous? He readily granted the affirmative. 'Now, sir,' rejoined I, 'why was not Sodom spared? Were there not ten infants to be found there?' He was confounded. Several days afterwards he met me, and asserted that there were no infants in Sodom! Under these circumstances, I was of course led to examine the Scriptures on this subject—to compare my own experience and observation with this unerring standard—and to notice the progress of moral expression, as it became visible in my first child, who about this time, after a short sickness, was removed to the world of spirits, at the age of seventeen months. I afterwards lost another infant, before it had completed its seventh month. In both these I clearly discerned traits of moral evil. And I was necessarily brought to the conclusion that the Omniscient Creator viewed them from their birth as sinners in miniature. The very text on which you so justly base the argument (Rom. v. 12) brought irresistible conviction to my mind, that *death and sin* were co-existent, and that one was the wages of the other. This was further illustrated and confirmed by the providence of God, which has uniformly subjected infants to the same sufferings to which adults are exposed in this life. Nor was it, in my view, any satisfactory answer, that *lambs and doves* die; for this plain reason, that they are not *human*. I well recollect a conversation with the late Dr. Worcester, at Salem, in the year 1819, in which he gave it as his decided opinion, that the sufferings and death of infants were intended to impress us with the solemn truth that they were, in the sight of God, sinners. The objection frequently made by those who hold the doctrine of original sin, has no weight with me—that infants, on account of mental weakness, are *incapable* of sin; for if it proves anything, it certainly proves too much, viz., that they are *incapable* of regeneration; it being a plain axiom in divinity, that it requires no more strength of mind to be sinful than to be holy—to put forth wrong than right moral exercises.

" Although I would charitably hope that multitudes of infants will be saved by sovereign grace, I have not been able to adopt it as an article of my creed, that all infants, dying before they commit overt acts of sin, are *certainly, and for that reason,* saved ; because I do not find it revealed in the Bible. And secret things belong not to us. I conceive it to be revealed, that they are righteously *exposed* to punishment, which can be averted only by a change of character and an application of the blood of Atonement. All beyond this must be conjecture. With regard to those which I have been called to part with, it became my duty to surrender them without knowing or inquiring how they would be disposed of beyond the grave. A consciousness that the Judge of all the earth would do right, was to me sufficient. I had apparent ground of hope, however, in the case of my first-born, in view of the patience, meekness, cheerful resignation, and increasing intelligence manifested during the last twenty-four hours of his life, as indicating a change by regeneration. This alteration was obvious to others, and induced the physician to anticipate his recovery, without discerning anything more, for he had less skill in spiritual than in bodily malady. I have frequently heard my pious mother remark upon the text, ' of such is the kingdom of heaven,' that *some of such* will doubtless be subjects of that kingdom. And if I mistake not, the Presbyterian church have it among the articles of their creed, that *elect* infants will be saved. This is safe.

"In recent conversation with a gentleman who advocated the N. H. notion of human depravity, he asserted with confidence that infants were *incapable* of sinning. I told him that, on his principles, it behooved him to give a reason why the first moral exercise of which they *are capable*, is always and universally sinful? His reply was, that the wants of the *body* are necessarily in advance of the wants of the *soul*. I then inquired, how it was with the child Jesus? was he not nurtured in the ordinary way? Oh, that was a miraculous production, he said. But sir, said I, if nothing short of a miracle can produce a holy child of Adam, will it not follow, that all other children possess a sinful nature—as different from this special case, by your own concession, as holiness from sin? He demurred.

"While I deeply regret that there should be any schism in the evangelical churches, I am not so averse to controversy, but that I had rather see it checked by temperate scriptural argument, than that it should be permitted silently and covertly to gain such strength as to injure the cause of truth. For however sincere or confident the leaders of the N. H. speculations in divinity may be, I fear it will turn out to be little else than the old Pelagian heresy, new vamped and varnished, both as it respects *native depravity* and the *means of regeneration*. Some teachers in theology, whose conversion has been rather gradual and indistinct, are apt to speculate, and preach, and write in a manner corresponding with their own experience. Even the justly celebrated Scott is not without his defects in this particular. His Force of Truth is too indefinite and clouded for such a subject. He leaves his readers in doubt, not only of the time at which to date his moral change within the broad space of several years, but of the character assignable to his moral exercises, in his tardy passage from darkness to light. And this want of clearness and discrimination is apparent to the critical reader, in many of the notes and observations of his excellent Family Bible. Truth is precious, and, like gold, should be pure.

"With much respect and esteem,
"I am, Rev. and dear sir,
"Your most obedient servant,
"H. SEWALL.

"Rev. GARDINER SPRING, D. D."

There was a boldness in the speculations of the New Haven Theology which has given rise to irreverence for the character of God. It is driven to the alternative of limiting the divine *goodness* or the divine *power*. It asserts that it is *impossible* for God to regenerate, sanctify, and save a greater number of mankind than he actually does save; that he would save all if he could; that the only reason why he does not is that he is not able; and that he has done *all he can* for the salvation of all, and that they must do the rest. A late writer, and a disciple of the New Haven school, Benjamin W. Dwight, Esq., of this city, in an Essay on the Providence of God, in the July number of the Bibliotheca, for 1864, affirms that "it is the joy of God, at all times, to draw as *many as possible* of Adam's lost sons to himself." Elsewhere he says, "God has *no* ends of action, and, from the infinite perfection of his nature, and the absolute independence of his being, can have none but those determined by the present and *abiding* welfare of *each and all* his creatures."

This able and accomplished writer asserts, that "man, *each man*, was made directly for his God, for his gratification, company, smile, and aid, forever. For man, all for man,—this is the explanation, as tender as it is true, of everything done upon earth by God, or that he will yet do. Tenderly yearning at all times after the immediate and lasting good of each one of his great family of intelligent creatures, and with inexhaustible generosity educating them continually in *every way possible* for his own future company and communion forever; God's sovereignty is never to be thought of as being actively or *passively* set against *any man's* true interest, but as being only and altogether for him. He delights in the *widest possible* exercise of quickening and converting grace."

The *italicising* in these quotations is my own. How far the thoughts lead to downright Universalism, let any fair mind decide. The dissertation is an attractive one from its ability, and from the artful inmingling of error with so much beautiful truth. I read it, and asked myself, could the Apostle Paul, or the Spirit of God, stand at the side of the writer when he ventured thus to limit the power of God?

It would seem, in accordance with these speculations, that the God of heaven is a sadly disappointed Deity; disappointed in that he is unable to carry into effect the desires of his large and benevolent heart. Now, I put the question to every believer in the Bible, Is not this theory in direct contradiction to the obvious teaching of the Scriptures in relation to the divine omnipotence? Is it so, that the Almighty God, with whom all things are possible, who of the stones of the street can raise up children to Abraham; who has the same control over the hearts of men as the potter over the clay, to make of the same lump one vessel unto honor and another unto dishonor; who doeth according to his will in the army of heaven and among the inhabitants of the earth; who says of himself, "Surely as I have thought so it shall come to pass,"—" my counsel shall stand, and I will do all my pleasure;" who "hath mercy on whom he will have mercy, and whom he will he hardeneth;" who forms the light and creates darkness, and makes peace and creates evil; who hides the glories of his Gospel from the wise and prudent, and reveals them unto babes,— is it so, that this Omnipotent One, whose prerogative it is to sway the worlds of mind and control the views and form the character of men, as truly and as easily as he controls the laws and operations of the material world, is unable to gratify his own wishes, and fill the world with beings that are virtuous and happy? Can he not do all his pleasure? Has he mercy on whom he *can*, or on whom he *will*, have mercy? Is there no truth in the declaration that "what his soul *desireth*, that he doeth?" Is there no such thing as sovereignty in the dispensations of his providence and grace? Is there no efficacy in prayer for the conversion of those we love, or the conversion of the world, because God is unable to answer it? Is there no truth in his promises as the hearer of prayer, or is the strength of Israel no longer worthy of confidence? If he has not power enough to produce holiness wherever and whenever he wishes and chooses to do so, would there not be an element of confidence and joy subtracted from the song, "The Lord God *omnipotent* reigneth?" I would like to know if the sophistical reasoner of the dissertation to which we have referred, ever luxuriates, as the Apostle of the Gentiles did, in that highborn doxology, "Now unto him who IS ABLE to do *exceeding abundantly above all that we ask* OR THINK, *according to the power that worketh in us,* unto him be glory in the church by Christ Jesus, throughout all ages, world without end!" If there be in all our apostate race a single mind so shrouded in darkness that the truth of God cannot enlighten it; or, when enlightened, so obdurate and embedded in sin that the Spirit of God is unable to subdue and transform it; I see not but the divine glory is tarnished and the universe the loser. The philosophical objection that men are free agents, and that God cannot convert them except by a moral power and the urgency of motives, if it were true, is nothing to the purpose, because omnipotence is able to act upon the mind without infringing upon its moral freedom ; nay, by actually causing it, and making his people *willing* in the day of his power. I would like to ask the advocates of this false theology whether or not God did all in his power to make Pharaoh virtuous and happy, when he hardened his heart, and raised him up for the purpose of showing his power and declaring his name on the earth? whether or not he did all in his power to make ancient Israel virtuous and happy, when it is affirmed of them, "The Lord *hath not* given you a heart to perceive, and eyes to see and ears to hear?" whether or not he did all in his power to make Judas virtuous and happy, whose life and death as a traitor were foretold and ascertained by the determinate counsel and foreknowledge of God?

It appears to us that this writer cuts the Gordian

knots of theology rather than unites them. He gains nothing by so doing. We look over our earth, we study the history of the past, and we draw aside the veil of futurity, and are confounded at the extent of sin and misery that exist under the government of the Most High. There are mysteries in his government as there are in him : it is not our province to explain them, for his ways are not as our ways. If there are things in his administration which we cannot comprehend or unravel, it is just what we might expect. And what we ought to believe is, that, however dark to us, they are all perfectly accordant with infinite wisdom and goodness. We cannot see the end from the beginning. A voice from heaven says to us, "Be still, and know that I AM GOD." He has lived and will live a great while. His arrangements and plans are not accomplished in a day. He has wise purposes, noble purposes, vast and comprehensive purposes, and he accomplishes them in his own way; wise in heart and mighty in strength, able to do all that he desires, and that, in every view, and in all its relations and dependencies, all that he sees essential to the highest good of his universal and everlasting empire. In the language of Robert Hall, "It is *mind*, and mind alone, which is the seat of power. The power which the mind exerts over the whole of our corporeal system, may afford an apt illustration of that control which the Deity exercises over the universe. He has only *to will* the most important changes, and they are instantly accomplished. We have reason to believe that *all* finite minds are under the direction of the Supreme Power, who, without destroying their accountability, or interfering with their free agency, makes all their operations subservient to the accomplishment of his counsels. All created beings, in this respect, are but instruments in the hand of the Deity, whose will is sovereign over them. The very minds he has formed are kept in mysterious subordination, and can never overstep the bounds he has assigned them." These are Bible truths, and at a great remove from the presumptuous assertion, that there are minds which the Deity himself cannot control, whom he would fain renew and sanctify, but, after having done his best, finds it out of his power.

I care less for theories than ever, but I care more for God's word; its obvious meaning is its true meaning; and I submit to it, even where its teachings are most painful and humiliating. Why should man, who is a worm, sit in judgment upon the decisions of infinite wisdom? Make the radical error of New Haven theology the starting-point, and the Bible would have been a very different book. There is little of the Bible in this theology. Lord Bacon admonished one of his friends, who had just been appointed a Judge of the Common Pleas, that " he must draw his learning out of his books, not out of his brains "—a fitting admonition to the advocates of New Haven philosophy.

CHAPTER III.

THE EXSCINDING ACTS OF THE GENERAL ASSEMBLY.

The errors of the New Haven theology had begun to infect the Presbyterian church; nor was it unexpected that the professors in her seminaries, and the leading members in her judicatories, took the alarm. The Act and Testimony issued by the Assembly in the year 1836; the deposition of Mr. Albert Barnes from the sacred ministry, on account of what was deemed essential error; the strife for precedency and power in the two contending parties; the unhappy and unchristian collisions on the floor of the Assembly, and the well-grounded apprehension that what has since been designated the *New School*, were aiming at the control of the Princeton Seminary and invested funds, accelerated a measure which effectually divided the Presbyterian church. As the signs of the times indicate a strong tendency, in both departments of the church, towards a reunion, a full disclosure of the motives which introduced the division is not called for. During the heat of the controversy I was in Europe, and had nothing to do with those preliminary measures which issued in the final disruption. I was not a member of the Assembly in 1837, when the Western Synods were cut off; for although I resisted the policy, and had no sympathy with the errors of the New School, I was not convinced either of the moral or ecclesiastical rectitude of the Exscinding Acts. I had the confident assurance of such jurists as the late Chancellor Kent and Judge Spencer, that had the legal question been brought before the Courts in the State of New York, rather than the State of Pennsylvania, the decision would have been the reverse of that which was rendered. When the question came before the Synod of New York: To which of the two branches of the church will its members attach themselves? my own vote was cast in favor of the Old-School Assembly, not because I approved of the Exscinding Acts, but because the separation was made, and necessity was laid upon me to announce my future course. I say, *not because I approved the exscinding acts;* I had entered my *protest* against them, on the minutes of my own Presbytery, signed by Ichabod S. Spencer, Daniel Lord, and my own name. Nor have I ever regretted that I did so. That my confidence in the views of Old-School Presbyterians was not diminished by these discussions, is evident from the fact that on my departure for Europe, I left the pulpit of the Brick Church in the hands and at the control of the Professors of the Theological Seminary at Princeton, who kindly accepted the charge, and faithfully and acceptably performed the service. That my views of this whole matter were not singular, nor unappreciated by my brethren, will appear from the following letters.

Quite early in the discussion, I received the following from my honored friend and former co-presbyter, the Rev. Dr. Miller:

"PRINCETON, *December* 1, 1824.
"REV. AND DEAR BROTHER:

"It has been suggested that the editors of the Repertory ought, in their next number, to insert an article adapted in some measure to soften their opposition to the *ultra Old School*, and to prevent their being claimed, and unduly caressed, by the ultra New School.

"Now, my dear Brother, allow me to ask, how does this matter strike *you?* Do you think such an article *necessary*, or even *desirable?* If so, of what general character ought it to be? You would not think, I take for granted, of anything like a *retraction*, even in part, or of anything like saying *peccavi*. On what *points* in general ought we to dwell? In short, if you think that *anything* further ought to be said, you will greatly oblige me by communicating (in the most hasty and general manner possible) something like the topics which you think ought to be brought into view, or chiefly dwelt upon in a future paper.

"I hope, my dear sir, you will not cast this application by as a matter of mere form. I attach importance to your judgment in this case; and if it be expressed only in twenty lines (as much at length, however, as you *can*), I shall highly prize the reception of it.

"My own judgment *rather* is, that it is better to let the matter rest where it is, and say no more at present. Yet this opinion is not maintained *without wavering.* Sometimes I am of a different mind. I am anxious, for one, to know how you feel, and also to know whether you are acquainted with any opinions or *facts* which ought to have weight with us at this time.

"When you write (which I hope will be very soon), please to let me know when you think of sailing for Europe, and any other circumstance in relation to your enterprise which we ought to know.

"In haste, yours, very affectionately,
"SAM'L MILLER.
"Rev. Dr. SPRING."

"PRINCETON, *June* 10, 1831.

"MY DEAR BROTHER:

"I hope you got home in peace, and have recovered your healthful feelings after the *toils* and the *wonders* of the last three weeks. Such an Assembly, or one approximating to it, I never saw before, and most sincerely hope I may never see again. What the friends of truth and order and vital piety (for nothing less than all these are plainly implicated in the contest with a majority of the Assembly), ought in present circumstances to do, I am not certain; but of one thing I am very sure, and that is, that there are *certain subjects* on which we ought to make a very fice and vigorous use of the PEN for a year or two to come.

"In the mean time, and on the behalf of the conductors of the 'Biblical Repertory,' I would solicit from you, my dear sir, a contribution of this kind and for this purpose. We, of course, leave you at perfect liberty to choose your own subject. You know the nature and design of the work, as intended for the defence of evangelical truth and order, and you are also aware of the principal topics on which it is important that some portions of the public should be informed and *disabused*. The *radicals* of the present day wish to impress the public with the belief that they alone are the genuine friends and promoters of *revivals;* that NEW MEASURES and NEW HAVEN DOCTRINE have a wonderful and unequalled potency in this matter. Would you be willing to prepare a paper for the *next* number of the Repertory (which ought to appear on the 15th of July), the object of which shall be to show that the *new measures* of Finney, &c., are not really favorable to genuine revivals? But as I said, take any seasonable subject that occurs to you, and we shall be thankful for a contribution.

"Would you be willing to be one of twenty gentlemen, who should engage *each* to furnish twenty pages *per annum* for the Repertory? We are very desirous of forming such a *pledged body*, and we sincerely hope you will not object to becoming one of us. We are sensible that some of our number do not agree with you in doctrine as to all points. But we are persuaded there is no such difference as ought to prevent your coöperating with us in the present great crisis of our ecclesiastical affairs, and that we are entirely one in general *spirit* and *views*. And is it not time, my dear Brother, when persons come so *near together* in *everything*, and are so *entirely united* in spirit and general views—is it not time to unite together in support of our precious faith and order, when both are so vitally, and, I am sorry to be obliged to add, so *insidiously* assailed?

"I shall be glad to hear from you as soon as convenient, in reply to the particular request contained in this letter, and also in reference to any suggestions you may have to make respecting the *present crisis* and the *duties* growing out of it.

"With great respect and esteem, I am, my dear sir, your friend and Brother in Christ,
"Samuel Miller.

"Reverend Dr. Spring."

"Troy, *November* 22, 1836.

"Dear Sir:
"I have had it in contemplation for some time to write to you on the state of the church. I presume we stand nearly on the same ground, and I think it proper to look about, and see where I shall land, if set adrift by the dismemberment of the Presbyterian church. I apprehend the Rubicon is passed. Cæsar will go up to Rome. The purpose of the ultra Old-School men is fixed to secede. I think better of their doctrines than of their spirit. I cannot go with them. I cannot abandon the American Board. I think benevolent societies can be managed better by committees than by the Assembly. I am a New England man in feeling and doctrine; I agree almost entirely with Edwards and Fuller. I shall not be willing to be under Beman & Co., or Peters and his missionaries. I shall not go with them. Now, will there not be found enough to join, and make a respectable body, on Christian ground, equally removed from the

ultras of both parties? Not a few of the most respectable ministers have called on me this summer, and I should infer they were ready to take this stand. I think Princeton Seminary belongs to the Old School, and I am willing they should have it. And if, by remaining with the majority for a season, I can aid in bringing about that arrangement, I shall be willing.

"Dr. Corning, the bearer of this, is one of the oldest elders in the church. He was long associated with Dr. Coe. No man understands Mr. Beman better. His judgment is uncommonly good. He will have but little leisure; but I hope you will be able to see him. I wish you to communicate freely to me your views. I have given you mine. Can nothing be done? I am no party-man; I desire peace. We shall have Dr. Richards with us, and men of that stamp. If you can get a moment, let me hear from you by Dr. Corning.

"I should also be much gratified if you would, in few words, give me a history of your ministry—how you get *time* to study; what are your *hours* of study; how much you visit, and on what plan; how many sermons you *write* each week; how many you extemporize; whether you take up books, and lecture upon them in order. I feel myself a very unprofitable minister: I am anxious to learn of those who have been successful.

"Yours, affectionately,
"MARK TUCKER.
"Reverend Dr. SPRING."

My own people felt a deep interest in preventing

the apprehended division. Our Session, with one exception, were unanimous in counselling and sustaining the course pursued by their pastor. The *resolutions* referred to in the note of Mr. Lord, I greatly regret to say, have been mislaid. They were eminently wise ; and I introduce the note referring to them, merely to show the deep interest he felt in the whole subject, and his convictions, as a sound lawyer, that the final disruption might, with good conscience, have been avoided.

" DEAR SIR :

" I have presented my views in the shape of resolutions, which I submit for your use and consideration, to aid you in presenting better.

" They appear to me such as all fair Presbyterians may unite in, and render immaterial the abrogation of the plan of union, and allow of delegations from the excluded Synods, without the formalities of a repeal of the Act of Exclusion ; and proclaim the principle of justice which has been violated, so as to save it. I think they avoid the legal difficulties which ensue.

" Yours, truly,

" D. LORD, Jr.

"Reverend Dr. SPRING.
" *October* 15."

" NEW YORK, Monday evening, *January* 4, 1836.

" REV. DR. SPRING :

" DEAR SIR : Since attending the monthly concert this evening, my mind has been oppressed, in view of the several exciting subjects which threaten to rend and divide the Presbyterian church in the United States.

"I would take the liberty to direct your attention, in particular, to the decision of the Synod of Philadelphia, in the case of the Rev. Albert Barnes, with a view of eliciting your opinion in regard to it.

"Before your return from Europe, I heard your name associated frequently with the brethren who have sustained the appeal in his case, and since your return, an answer has been demanded to the question, 'How can Dr. Spring lend his influence to depose Mr. Barnes from the Gospel ministry?'

"I was happy to have it in my power to give a prompt and satisfactory reply; but I am strongly inclined to believe that there is a very general impression that, as regards the merits of the case, you coincide in opinion with those who sustain the appeal.

"I hope you will not consider me presumptuous in thus calling your attention to a subject of such deep and absorbing interest, and in respectfully suggesting to you the propriety of your expressing your views publicly as to the merits of this controversy. And I am urged to this the more, because I am satisfied that your opinions, though frequently expressed, are not generally known.

"It must be evident to all, that unless some expedient is devised to compose and settle these unhappy differences, our Zion will be rent and torn in pieces for years to come.

"In the hope that you may be able to suggest something which may lead to a satisfactory adjustment of this agitated subject, and towards promoting the peace and purity of the church, and at the same time satisfy the minds of your friends at home and abroad, as to your views in reference to Mr. Barnes' case, I have ventured to make this communication, knowing that your own better judgment and sense of duty will determine what course you ought to pursue at this interesting crisis.

"I am, with great regard, your friend and parishioner,

"HORACE HOLDEN."

In order to prepare the way for more harmonious action by the General Assembly, a proposition was made to call a Convention formed by Commissioners from Presbyteries, and the proposition came before the Presbytery of New York. I resisted it, and suggested a postponement, and the adoption of the following minutes:

"While the Presbytery appreciate the motives and honor the faithfulness which have induced their brethren to invite the Convention, referred to above; while they see nothing unconstitutional in such a procedure; while they deeply lament the errors in doctrine, which, though originally introduced into the church by a few designing men, are now, without any suspicion on the part of the great body of Presbyterians, extended by powerful associations, over which the church has no control; while they regard with deep regret the hostility extensively exhibited against the organized operations of the General Assembly for the extension of the Redeemer's kingdom in our own and other lands; while they look with grief upon the unconstitutional influence exerted by churches and ministers virtually Congregational, in very many of the Presbyteries connected with the General Assembly; and while, in all these things, they see cause for apprehension and alarm: they have confidence in God that he will still protect the interests of truth and righteousness in the church to which they are attached, without the painful resort which the Presbytery understand to be contemplated by, at least, very many of the friends of the proposed Convention. From the different documents issued by the brethren calling the Convention, as well as from views elsewhere expressed, the Presbytery judge that the design of the Convention is to mature measures, to be brought before the next General Assembly, that shall result in the deposition of ministers, whose theological views, though at variance with the standards of the church, are not at such variance as to exclude them from the sacred office. Or, should this be found impracticable, the Presbytery have reason to believe that the Convention will propose a division of the church. The Presbytery are free to confess, they are not prepared for either part of this alternative. They are not merely questions of doctrine, and measures, and ecclesiastical organization, which will agitate the Convention, but questions, if possible, of deeper and more extensive interest, and questions, the agitation of which the truest piety and the soundest policy require should be deferred for a long time to come. The Presbytery are well persuaded that not many years will pass away, before the most ardent friends of the Convention will look back upon it with regret. Error has never been eradicated from the church by the severe process of adjudication. Where errors are not essential in their character, it appears to the Presbytery that the most effectual means of opposing their progress is the diffusion of light and the exercise of love. A wise and powerful moral influence is more to be relied upon in this warfare, than the exterminating influence of ecclesiastical power. Let the church go forth unmanacled to the great work of converting the world; let churches and ministers who have never come under the common bond which unites the Presbyteries of this General Assembly be no longer recognized as having a place in her judiciaries; let men valiant for the truth call the advocates of error into the field of calm and dispassionate investigation, and we may yet be a holy and happy people. In this day of darkness and rebuke, God is calling on us to humble ourselves before him, and seek his direction in all that may conduce to purity and peace, rather than to chilling alienation and a final rupture. With these views, the Presbytery resolve,

"1. That it is inexpedient to appoint Commissioners to the proposed Convention.

"2. That it is expedient to concur in the recommendation inviting the churches to a day of fasting, and prayer to Almighty God for wisdom from above in the present crisis; and they do hereby appoint the   day of   for that purpose."

This motion was lost by a vote of twelve for and nineteen against it.

It is with unfeigned pleasure that I here record the fact, that notwithstanding the want of harmony in the Old School in these Exscinding Acts, once adopted, they were acquiesced in. There was no third party, as was proposed by Dr. Tucker and others. We were brethren. We submitted to that we did not approve, and hoped for the best. The two bodies have been moving on in their glorious work, and the New School with great and accelerated vigor. I do not think that our branch of the church give the dissentients the confidence they deserve; but this does not diminish our attachment to old-fashioned Presbyterianism. For myself, I was not a little gratified by the following communication from the Directors of the Princeton Seminary, indicating that, though I was no advocate for the excision, I was, in their estimation, sound in the faith once delivered to the saints.

"New York, *September* 9, 1852.
"Reverend and Dear Sir:

"The Board of Directors of the Theological Seminary at Princeton, held their adjourned meeting on the 7th instant.

"Having ascertained that the Rev. Dr. Humphrey had not yet accepted the professorship to which he had been elected, they appointed a committee, who, in conjunction with the Faculty, should make temporary provision for the performance of the duties of the vacant chair.

"Afterwards, at the request of the committee and of the members of the Faculty who were present, they *named* and *unanimously* approved the persons who should be invited to give instruction to the students on the subjects appertaining to the vacant professorship.

"Those persons were, the Rev. Dr. Spring, to give instruction on the *Composition and Delivery of Sermons;* Rev. Dr. Plumer, on Church Government; and Rev. Dr. Hall, on Pastoral Theology.

"The Board earnestly hope that your attachment to the Seminary, your desire to do good, the acknowledged claims of the Saviour and of a dying world, may constrain you to make the sacrifice which a compliance with their request will require at your hands. The service will not be expected without compensation, and may be performed at any time during the present session.

"In behalf of the Board of Directors,
"W. W. PHILLIPS,
"Chairman of their Committee.

"P. S. An early, and if possible a favorable, answer is respectfully requested.
"W. W. P."

After no slight deliberation, I was constrained to decline this appointment. I felt that I could not discharge its duties, without occupying the time devoted to the people of my charge. And, moreover, I did not feel qualified for the service without a measure of study and preparation which I could not devote to so important a service.

The two departments of the Presbyterian church, since the division, have greatly prospered. I am by no means sure that, in their united character, they would have accomplished as much for the kingdom of our adorable Lord, as they have accomplished, each in its own place and way. While I should rejoice to see them one harmonious whole, and would sacrifice not a little in order to attain so desirable a result, I am not so ardently attached to large and overgrown ecclesiastical organizations, as to desire this amalgamation, so long as there are found both in the Old School and the New any serious elements of strife. A few years at most, and the principal actors in this separation will have passed away, the attritions of party will be lost sight of, a more conciliatory generation will occupy the place of their fathers, and "the mountains shall bring peace to the people, and the little hills by righteousness." The Presbyterian family, in connection with the Congregational churches, has a great work to do in this land, if it were only to resist the encroachments of Rome and Prelacy; much more, in their united opposition to infidelity and science falsely so called, and the advancement of that kingdom which is "righteousness, and peace, and joy in the Holy Ghost." If we decline the honor, the joy, the reward of this service, we shall "leave our name for a curse unto God's chosen."

CHAPTER IV.

EXTRACTS FROM MY JOURNAL.

BETWEEN forty and fifty years of my ministry, I kept a journal. One of my ministerial brethren, and a co-presbyter, early advised me to include in these reminiscences my entire diary. Had he seen it, and known its extent and nature, he would have counselled me otherwise. I take leave, however, to include the following extracts, extending, though at widely separated intervals, from April, 1814, to August, 1864.

April 2d, 1814.—I have, of late, been somewhat impressed with the vast importance of the work of the ministry. I have been preaching and talking about the revival of God's work, and that it must begin in the hearts of God's people; and I am sensible that it can begin with no stronger propriety in any, more than in my own heart and life. I cannot preach as I have preached; I cannot live as I have lived; I *must* be more devoted to the service of my Divine Master. I have resolved to be so; yet I am afraid it is the height of presumption, and that the resolution here recorded will testify against me. But worm and sinner as I am, I am not satisfied with this prolonged lukewarmness. I have set apart this as a day of fasting and prayer; but it has been a cold, dull day, and very unlike the day set apart on my entering the ministry. I have no sense of my wants, and very little of the fulness there is in Christ. I would fain seek to attain to a greater eminence in that holiness which is the beauty and perfection of the ministerial character; but while I long to be useful, I fear that I am little better than a cumberer of the ground. I have not found my heart affected or enlarged in prayer, and have known to-day very little of what it is to have access with boldness into the holiest of all, by the blood of Jesus. Towards evening I took a walk round the battery, and enjoyed God's presence. To-morrow I expect to preach from Matthew xxii. 5, "And they made light of it." Oh! that God would make bare his arm, and plead his own cause!

April 3d, 1814, *Sabbath evening.*—This has been a good day. The God of Zion was with the preacher and the hearers. In the afternoon, Brother Daniel Clark preached to us a well-timed and affecting discourse. After the services of the sanctuary, I conversed with my sons Samuel and Edward, and prayed with them. "Oh! that Ishmael might live before thee!" Had sweet access to the throne this evening. May I be enabled to be more faithful in visiting my people! and not lose sight of the resolution of yesterday.

Saturday, April 9th.—In looking back upon the past week, I have much to bewail, and much to be thankful for. Woe is me, that I am so slow in crucifying my besetting sins! Every day I am debtor to restraining and preventing grace. My people appear solemn; they were so at the lecture on Thursday evening. Yet I hear of no awakenings. I should be more discouraged if I did not find the subtle adversary at work. I have no fears from the mere calling of hard names. "The Lord is with you, if ye be with him." There is a stronger than the strong man armed. Oh! to stand still and see the salvation of God! I exchange pulpits to-morrow with Dr. Richards, of Newark. Should it please God to make this beloved and honored Brother the instrument of a work of grace among this people, I should have no ground for boasting. May the Spirit of Jesus be with us both! " The mercy of the Lord endureth forever." I shall never be weary of this song.

Saturday evening, April 16th.—How rapidly the weeks pass away! With me, the past has been almost a blank. I have written nothing except a little ode to my dear wife, now at New Haven, and the skeleton of a sermon for the Sabbath. I have read little, and made no religious visits. Would that this evening could bear testimony to *something* I have done for Christ this past week! Would that it could bear testimony to more godly sorrow for the past! Oh! my heart! Oh! wretched man that I am! who shall deliver me from the body of this death? I could not complain if God should cast me out of the vineyard.

Shall I ever drag out another useless week? I see God's law to be holy, just, and good; but I see another law in my members warring against the law of my mind, and bringing me into captivity to the law of sin which is in my members. How just and right in God to hide his face from me! I have felt that it is solemn mockery to approach God as I do, while I thus regard iniquity in my heart. This week has been almost as unhappy as it has been sinful. Besides the conflict in my own bosom, there has been conflict in the Presbytery, in which I have had my full share. The call of the church in Rutgers-street upon Rev. Ezra Stiles Ely, has been before us, and we have refused to sanction it. Thanks to the Head of the Church, that, in the face of public clamor, the Presbytery had the firmness to do their duty. Yet there is a root of bitterness which, I fear, will bear bitter fruit.

May 7th, Saturday evening.—How rich are God's mercies! My dispersed family are once more at home. It was pleasant to meet once more at our domestic altar, and read His Word, and sing His praise together, and seek His face. I returned this week from New Haven with my wife and our dear babe. God has showered his blessings upon us, in our going out and our coming in. Externally, I am prepared for the Sabbath; may God prepare my heart! I expect to preach from the narrative of blind Bartimeus, and to show " wherein blinded sinners are like him, and wherein they are not like him."

June 4th.—During the past month I have been reading the Life of Harriet Newell, and it has been a blessing to my soul. Her short and sweet life, and her triumphant death, are, instead of a thousand arguments, in favor of foreign missions. I have just returned from the General Assembly, greatly encouraged by the reports of the churches on the state of religion. Truth is advancing, and Christ's kingdom is beginning to triumph in the end. I preach to-morrow from the text, "They have made their faces harder than a rock; they have refused to return." I was gratified, and yet ashamed, to see such men as Dr. Griffin, and President Davies, among my hearers. I have had refreshing interviews this week with Brother Beecher, of Litchfield. We conferred on the subject of revivals, and prayed together for one among my own people. I feel the need of such ministerial friends.

June 11th.—Brother Beecher and Brother Blackburn have been laboring abundantly among us this week, and there seems to be a shaking among the dry bones. My own heart is somewhat awake; Christians are waking up, and a few among the thoughtless begin to inquire what they must do to be saved. Household visitation begins to be attended with God's blessing. God seems to be coming in gentle influences among the people, and Christians are greatly encouraged.

Saturday, June 18th.—To-morrow will be our Communion Sabbath, and this Saturday is a day of fasting and prayer in the church, with the view of imploring the effusion of the Holy Spirit upon us as a people. It has been a pleasant season; the prayers offered were to an unusual degree for Christian growth and usefulness. There was some anxiety for those who were perishing in their sins; I myself shared it, and felt and rejoiced that the work is all in God's hand. My heart trembles, but I can cast this dear, dying people on the arm of almighty grace. This is my resting-place; this my encouragement to preach, to pray. The Lord can clear the darkest skies. A part of the afternoon I spent with the Female Praying Society, and in the evening met the church in the session-room, where we enjoyed a sweet season of prayer.

June 25*th*.—The last Sabbath was a solemn day, and an unusually precious Communion. Not only was it a feast of fat things to the children of God, but a solemn day to impenitent sinners. I preached on Monday evening to a very solemn audience at my own house, and on Thursday evening in the session-room. Several persons are deeply convinced of sin; one poor girl, Miss Goldsmith, seems ready to sink under her burden, and one young man, who bitterly reproached himself for having so often called upon God with his lips, but not with his heart. These are tokens for good. We cannot hope too much from God. I am sorry to say that my health begins to fail. Dr. Porter, of Andover, once told me that a revival would be the death of me. I do not think so. " As thy days, so shall thy strength be." Duty is mine; events are

God's. It would not be unpleasant to die in the midst of a revival. If I could feel, and act, and preach like Brainerd and Edwards, it would be Christ for me to live, and gain to die. I hope I am willing to be subjected to any discipline that shall make me more spiritual while I live, and, when I die, more meet for heaven. I have some trials, but they are few. God gives me all things richly to enjoy, "honey out of the rock, and oil out of the flinty rock." Shall not the goodness of God lead me to repentance? I am sometimes afraid lest the better God treats *me*, the worse I shall treat *him*. What I need is, a deeper and more habitual sense of the *realities* of eternity, permeating my conduct, my studies, my sermons, my prayers, my visits, that I may not labor in vain, nor spend my strength for nought.

Saturday evening, July 16*th.*—I have found that God has been working when I least expected it. Sabbath before the last I preached to children; and this week heard of a society of little girls in Mr. Picket's school for reading the Scriptures, prayer, and praise. On Monday evening I preached to crowded rooms, at Capt. Haven's, in Pearl Street, and on Thursday evening to a more solemn audience in the session-room.

September 25*th, Saturday evening.*—Eight weeks ago I left home on account of my health. Returned in safety, and in company with my brother and sister Taft, but have come back with a dissipated mind. *The war with England* is the absorbing topic, and there is no seriousness among my people. I am greatly embarrassed on the subject of praying for the war. I cannot do so conscientiously. My congregation are chiefly of the Democratic party, and expect their minister by his pulpit services to fortify their hostility to Great Britain. The most and the best that I can do, is with all my might to *pray for peace.* There may be trouble near, but " the Lord liveth, and blessed be my rock!"

Saturday evening, January 13*th*, 1815.—Several scenes of interest during the last three weeks. On the first Lord's day of the year our religious services were unusually solemn. The prayer-meeting at our little Bethel in the evening was never more full nor more interesting. The Lord was there, and especially manifesting himself to my own soul. I do not recollect that my own hopes were ever more strong and bright, and the consciousness of pardoning mercy ever sweeter, than when I returned home this evening. God may be preparing me for some great trial; yet who can tell but that it may be for some blessed work in the ministry? Strange as it is to myself, and more strange as it would seem to others, did they know the hidden evils of my heart, I am habitually free from embarrassment on the great question of my own interest in the great redemption. My chief anxiety relates to my work as a minister of Christ. I fear I am presumptuous. Search me, O God, and try me. The state of things in the congregation, notwithstanding the war, is looking up. Our public meetings and our social gatherings are more full and more solemn; preaching, I hope, is more faithful, visitations are more frequent. There are eight or ten among the men of the world whose minds are deeply impressed.

February 24th, 1816.—This is my birthday. I have lived in God's world thirty-one years, and can sing of mercies and judgments. Mary, Hannah, Walton, Lewis! Alas, how families crumble to the dust! Who hath made me to differ? I have thought much of my dear parents to-day. They are mourners, and their hearts bleed. But they have a refuge in this time of trouble. Saviour of Israel, be thou near, very near my dear parents in this dark hour! We are a dying household. It is with me a day of fasting and prayer; but it has not been one of fitting humiliation. With what emotions of adoring thankfulness ought I here to make the record, that this birthday witnesses what I have so long desired, *the outpouring of God's Spirit upon this dear people.* "Return unto me, and I will return unto you," saith the Lord. In reviewing what a gracious God has done for us, I trace it as far back as the latter part of last summer. During a journey for the health of my dear wife, we were thrown into the midst of a region where God was giving efficacy to the word of his grace. We saw so much and enjoyed so much, that we could not return home without renewed effort and hope for our own congregation. Nor did we. We returned on the 10th of September, and I told the people what God was doing elsewhere. The waters of the sanctuary were at so low an ebb, that we all felt that they must begin to flow. And they did flow in streams of salvation. It was the time of Jacob's trouble, but he was delivered out of it. God gave us the Spirit of grace and supplication. We felt the inspiriting import of those sweet words, "O thou that hearest prayer." From day to day we heard of instances of awakening, and conviction of sin, and some of conversion. There was a private prayer-meeting in Church-street, and an evening lecture in the session-room following it, which were emphatically days of the right hand of the Most High. The promise was fulfilled, "Before they call I will answer; and while they are yet speaking I will hear." The month of January was such a month as we never saw before. God appeared in his glory to build up Zion. Scoffers were silenced, and doubters were constrained to acknowledge, "This is the finger of God!" At the close of an evening service appointed for the youth, more than one hundred spontaneously remained after the benediction to inquire what they must do to be saved. Within ten days of this time, the solemnity was almost universal; scarcely a family in the congregation remained unmoved. It was like the trees of the forest when moved by a mighty wind. There was a blessed ingathering of more than a hundred souls.

February 24th, 1819.—Still in this world of hope. In defiance of all the sins of the past year, and a guilty life, I am permitted to see another birthday. I have been often surprised that I am suffered to live. Blessed be God, I am not afraid to die, and often more afraid to live. I am an abject sinner, and it will indeed be wonderful grace if I ever sit down with Christ at the Supper of the Lamb. That gràce is my strong refuge; Calvary is my hiding-place. There is the munition of rocks. I hope in the grace and guardianship and faithfulness of that omnipotent Redeemer, to be kept from falling and presented faultless before the presence of his glory with exceeding joy. This text has often comforted me, when I have been afraid of trusting in the divine mercy: " The Lord taketh *pleasure* in them that fear him, in those that *hope in his mercy.*" It affords me unutterable pleasure to feel that I am not denied the privilege of laying my own soul beneath the droppings of the same blood I have for nine years recommended to my dying and guilty fellow-men.

Among the mercies I am bound to record, are the recovery of my dear wife from a very dangerous illness last June, and the most merciful dispensation of Providence towards my dear brother Samuel, in his attention to a course of studies with a view to the Christian ministry. This brother became hopefully a pious man soon after the death of our departed Lewis, and is now preparing for the ministry. A youth of promise devoted to this work is always an interesting event; but much more so is this devotement, from the relation it sustains to me as his brother. One brother, at least, a fellow-laborer in this glorious harvest! Bless the Lord, O my soul!

My dear Susan's illness was most severe. After a most trying pregnancy, she was permitted to become the mother of a lovely daughter on the 29th of May, 1818. About ten days after her confinement, she began to decline. Incessant faintings left us with very little hope that she would survive more than a few days. I insert a sketch of some conversation with her here lest it should be lost. I remained at her bedside during the greater part of the time, and was much comforted by the happy state of her mind. On a Thursday morning, as I sat by her, I laid my head by hers and wept. She perceived it; and to anticipate any painful remarks my excitement might cause, I said, "Oh, my dear, I have confidence in God. *You have, I trust.*" "*I hope so,*" said she, "*I have all along considered it very doubtful whether I should recover from this sickness. Death appeared very near to me before my confinement; but I could not say I was willing to go and leave you all.*"

"But," said I, "if we are Christ's, we shall soon meet again." She replied, "*Yes, if I am Christ's; but that I cannot say.*" She wept. Just after this, I took her in my arms and held her up in the bed, observing, "This makes us feel like very little creatures." "*Yes,*" said she, "*I feel fit for nothing but to be here in the hands of God.*" I replied, "It is a precious privilege to be in the hands of God." She answered, with emphasis, "It is."

Soon after this, she said to me, "*Take care of these dear children; I cannot bear to leave them in the care of nobody better than a mother-in-law. I fear they will be neglected.*" Here we wept.

The next day her danger was evidently increased. It became necessary to cover her body almost entirely with the most exciting stimulants, and the physicians began to despair of giving her any relief. I had previously told her I would watch every symptom, and give her the first intimations of her danger. On Friday evening I went to her bedside and sat down. She saw my solicitude, and I disclosed it by saying that we all feared she would never recover. She made no reply, but remained calm and unmoved. I could not but observe that her mind was very clear, and astonishingly calm. I said, "You hope you have been born again?" "*Yes*," said she, "*but I have always more doubts than hopes. But in my doubts I have seen nothing but grace to flee to. Christ has been my refuge, and is now, and I hope will be.*" I said, "You have seen the sinfulness of your heart?" She answered, "*I have, and it is* AWFULLY *sinful. This has sometimes discouraged me, but there is enough in Christ to cleanse.*"

I left her, and returned to her chamber after tea. The danger was hourly increasing, and I had resolved to bring it near. I told her plainly we thought she would die. She was aware of it, and said, "*My wish is that God would glorify himself by me.*" I remarked, "It is a precious truth that God will glorify himself by such insignificant and vile creatures as we are." "*Yes*," said she, "THAT *has been my sweetest thought, that God would glorify himself in me and by me.*" Here she seemed to hesitate, and added, "*unless it be some sweet views of the way of salvation by Christ.*"

·On Saturday morning no tokens for the better. I took the little babe, and said it was not improbable that this dear babe would live to see the Millennium. "This," said I, "is worth suffering for;" she added, "*yes, and dying for.*" She smiled when I gave her a view of *Emerson's* calculation as to the proximity of that glorious period, and spoke of the babe as born for such a season.

On Sabbath morning, no more hope and no less calmness. I enjoyed a very precious season of communion with her at the throne of grace, such as I hope never to forget. I thought it an anticipation of our everlasting fellowship in a brighter world. I read the 73d and 86th Psalms, in which she appeared to take much consolation. Before we prayed, I asked, " What shall we pray for ? " " *Pray,*" said she, " *that I may be* MEET *for heaven; that I may be made* HOLY. *Everything else appears of little importance compared with this,—and for my dear children; they will need everything.*"

Sabbath was a trying day; and towards evening, I saw that the physicians began to *hope.* She *lived.* After a tedious and long-continued debility, *she lives still,* the comfort of my heart, and more endeared through the severity of her trial, and the greatness of God's mercy. " His mercy endureth forever."

CHAPTER V.

CONTINUATION OF MY JOURNAL.

February 24*th*, 1820.—Another year has fled, and another birthday anniversary has come. The past year has been marked with some most solemn providences: during that year, both of my dear and honored parents went to their rest.

I have prayed for and written to my brothers Pinckney, Charles, and John Hopkins, none of whom, I fear, are the children of God. Oh, that our father's God, their covenant God, would sanctify and bless them!

February 24*th*, 1824.—I perceive I have made no entry in these pages for four years past. My dear brother Pinckney, whose name is mentioned above, died on the 9th of September, 1820, of a typhoid mania. His illness was most distressing, and during the last few weeks I was with him. Some months previous to his death he became hopefully pious.

From August to December, in 1822, I was abroad in Europe; a voyage and a tour much to the benefit of my health, but nothing to the growth of grace in my soul. I bless God I *was* kept from *all outward* sin; but this is all I can say. My heart most awfully departed from the Lord. To the present hour my *imagination* is poisoned by the scenes of splendor, and of folly, and of sin, which I witnessed in the Old World.

February 24*th*, 1825.—I have at length arrived at the age of forty years,—thirty-three years younger than my beloved father when he died, and nineteen only younger than my dear mother at her death. This is an age I have scarcely ventured to hope I should ever see. I know not how to express myself in view of the amazing rapidity with which the tide of human life is ebbing away. I am surrounded now by a family of eleven children, the oldest twenty-two years younger than myself, and the youngest thirty-nine. No breach has ever yet been made in my large family! Who can speak of such undeserved goodness?

I have never known more of the power of indwelling sin, than I have the past year; never so much of the conflict between the flesh and the spirit, God and the world, self and Christ's kingdom and glory; and never so much of the burden, the severity, the *meaning* of the spiritual warfare. I have never had so many fears lest, after all, I should descend into the eternal pit, and never more clearly have seen the wisdom and goodness of God in lighting the fires of hell in full view of his people all their way, and perpetually pointing them to the quenchless flame and the gnawing worm. Frequently, these few months past,

I have been awfully afraid of lying down in hell. I see I must part with sin or part with heaven. And I bless God it is so. I would not desire it otherwise. I used to think it desirable to see more of my sins; but I see now that the way in which God makes me to know my transgression and my sin, is by suffering me to indulge my sinful heart. God be praised that I have not yet acted it all out.

The year has been one of great outward mercy. My public labors as a minister still have the confidence of my people, and to a great degree. I am alarmed at it, particularly when I find the men of the world, the enemies of God, so well satisfied with me. I fear I have been unfaithful. But by God's grace enabling me, I will still throw commotion into their camp, and disturb both their sins and their hopes.

Amid these mercies my trials have increased. First of all, my own sins stare me in the face. Next, I think of my family, and cry, "Turn away ungodliness from Jacob!" I have trials which shake my nerves, hold my eyes waking and weeping, and almost break my heart. Oh, that those dear sons might become the sons of God! My plans for their usefulness in the church and the world seem all defeated, and my heart is desolate. God of Abraham, forgive the sins of their poor father, and remember thy covenant.

It is a solemn time now in our city. More disease than I ever knew prevailing. Forty thousand persons, it is supposed, are now sick. Among those who have fallen is my respected and beloved Brother, Dr. John B. Romeyn. He is to be interred on *this my birthday!*

New York, August 19th, 1825.—This morning I returned from Fairfield, Conn., where my wife and nine children have been residing for several weeks, to avoid the heat of the city, and particularly on account of our dear Julia, whose health had been for some time declining. Day before yesterday we left her in the field of graves—alone—in the cold bosom of the earth—sixty miles from us, away in a land of strangers.

This is a new scene. This is the first breach made in our large family, and I feel that God has made it. The youngest, and perhaps the loveliest scion, has been torn from its parent stock. But I see and adore God's hand. Oh, that sweet babe! The last time I saw her living, I left her with the prayer on my lips, "God take you, dear babe, to his own bosom!" My soul is sweetly comforted in the thought that God has taken her. My child has a better Father now. At least *one* of my dear family is in the bosom of unchanging love. Earth was too uncomely and untoward a world for her; our bosoms too faithless and cold; our nurture too unkind and injurious. Dear babe! I rejoice God has not left you here to encounter the hazards of this ensnaring world, and that you will now be trained up by Him and for Him, and that that dear mind, of which there were so many and so sweet indications of loveliness, is committed to the care of untiring faithfulness in a better world. God has given us eleven children. Sometimes I am tempted to feel that we have but *ten* now. No; we have eleven still, eleven *living* children; one lives in a sweeter and higher world. I have new ties to heaven. I feel that I have, and fewer to earth. Let the fruit of this affliction be to take away sin. It has come just at the right time; the very time I have needed it. It is no dismaying blow; but so tender, so melting, that my soul flows out in reaching it. It is *good* for me to be afflicted. May the hand that sends the arrow bring the healing balm!

My dear daughter, *Julia Lynch Spring*, died at Fairfield, Conn., August 16, 1825, about one o'clock, A.M., and was there buried.

New York, February 24*th*, 1830.—Since writing the above, I have survived the dangers and mercies of five years, and am now, to my surprise, *forty-five years old*. My sun begins to go down.

The past five years have been years of great mercy, —and great sin. The last year, 1828-9, God again visited the people of my charge with the influences of his Spirit, and about sixty souls, I hope, were brought to Christ, within the space of about three months.

In one particular the last year has been peculiar. I have had some difficulties with some of my brethren in the ministry, with whom I have hitherto been on terms of great intimacy. Our little weekly prayer-meeting, consisting of four ministerial brethren, has been reduced to two. One of them has been suddenly called out of the world—an affecting admonition to me! I have scarcely known, till the past year, what it was to be in a condition to exercise the spirit of forgiveness. From humbling experience, I find that to return good for evil is a hard work for such a heart as mine. And this conviction sometimes alarms me. I fear I have not the spirit of Christ. God grant that

I may institute a rigid and impartial scrutiny into my heart in this matter to-day! In his light may I see light. I find my heart strangely *suspicious*. Sometimes I am resolved to withdraw from the Missionary and Education cause, because I foresee they will be scenes of contention. But then, again, I know they are exposed to evils, and the church is exposed to evils, through the mismanagement of these excellent institutions, which perhaps I may prevent. But I now feel very much disposed to put myself far away from all strife. My spiritual welfare greatly suffers from this state of things.

New York, May 25*th*, 1856.—This is the Lord's day, and to me and my people a day of intense interest. Doubly so to me, because, fifty years ago, my beloved wife and myself became one. We were married on the 25th of May, 1806. It should have been celebrated as our "golden wedding;" but it was the Lord's day, and no one thought of it. It is the memorable day, also, on which I delivered the closing sermon in the old Brick Church in Beekman-street. "We have thought of Thy loving-kindness, O God, in the midst of Thy temple; that ye may tell it to the generation following; for this God is our God; He will be our guide even unto death." This was my text. It was a solemn day. The audience was immense. God was with us. I obtained the key of the church from the sexton, yesterday morning, and spent some time alone in the pulpit, and in thanksgiving, confession, and supplication, and greatly enjoyed this season of prayer. Oh, how much I have enjoyed in that precious old pulpit! What Sabbaths! what communion seasons! what years of the right hand of the Most High! Dear old church, I have preached my last sermon there, and shall enter it no more! How wonderful God's goodness towards me! How rich the streams that have flowed here, and in what gladness in the city of our God! As I stood in the pulpit to-day, I seemed to stand amid generations that are past; my imagination peopled those seats with forms and faces that are no more. God's voice to me is, "Arise, and depart hence, for this is not your rest." I obey it, but with strangely-mingled emotions. Dear old church! of this and of that man it may be said, "He was born here." Farewell, thou endeared house of God, companion and friend of my youth, comforter of my pilgrimage, scene of my many infirmities and God's abounding grace,—farewell! Sweet pulpit, farewell! Throne of grace!—no, the promise stands good, " *Wherever* I record my name, I will come unto thee, and will bless thee." I go to a distant part of the city; but " if Thy presence go not with me, carry me not up hence." The winter of life has shut in; its snows are already upon me; I know not what a day may bring forth. These mutations will soon be over. The Lord liveth, and blessed be my Rock. The Root of Jesse stands as an ensign to the people, and his rest shall be glorious. While I live, I ask no greater joy than to preach the Gospel to this beloved people. Many sheaves it has been my privilege to gather from this field of labor. God grant that in the great and final ingathering, they may be to the praise of His glory who made them meet to be partakers of the inheritance of the saints!

New York, August 7th, 1860.—This morning, at half-past 8 o'clock, my sweet wife was released from this scene of debility and suffering, and departed for the rest that remaineth for the people of God. She had been confined to her chamber for two years; the last six months, for the most part, to her bed; the last week almost unconscious; the last forty-eight hours wholly so, except on one occasion returning her husband's caresses. She was the mother of fifteen children, six in another world, nine in this. She died in the presence of her husband and eight children, all of whom ministered to her with constant care, great love and tenderness, and unsleeping assiduity. Her husband was rarely absent from her bedside, and, at her request, closed her eyes in death. Her funeral is now arranged for Thursday next; the services to be conducted in the Brick Church, and her body to be deposited in a vault, generously prepared by the Trustees for the family of their minister, and there deposited, at her request, until the resurrection.

Of her religious character I can say, that it was made up of strong principle, self-sacrificing devotement to every Christian duty, great cheerfulness in suffering, implicit and strong confidence in what she called the " glorious redemption of the Son of God," a stern attachment to truth and right, and a life of unostentatious consecration to higher interests than her own. She was a stern and unsparing rebuker of wickedness, and a loving friend of the good.

I have been her husband and she my wife, for four-and-fifty years; our attachment has been mutual, and strong and sweet to the end. I had no friend on earth in whom I had such reliance; no counsellor so wise; no comforter so precious. For the last thirty years we have rarely differed in opinion; when we did, I generally found she was right, and I was wrong; and when I persevered in my judgment, she knew how to yield her wishes to mine, and would sometimes say, with a smile, " God has set the man above the woman. You are *king*, my husband; but I am the queen." In all my ministry, in sickness and in health, at home and abroad, by night and by day, I never knew her own convenience, comfort, or pleasure, take the place of my duty to the people of my charge. There are few such women in these strong features of her character.

In her person, she was beautiful even to old age; in youth, I have never known a more attractive woman. She had a fine intellect, combining clear conceptions, strong reasoning powers, a lively and poetic imagination, keen wit, and abounding pleasantry, all cultivated by extensive reading and unusual researches in history. Her colloquial powers were of a rare order, and interesting to all classes; men of eminence, and plain men of business, and even servants, deemed it a privilege to spend a leisure hour in her society. In this particular she was the charm of the now bereaved house. The cheerfulness which she threw around the circle in her sick-chamber was perfectly beautiful. There was not a servant in the house who did not regard it as a treat to sit by her bedside. When she was pensive, it was touching pensiveness. She saw the dark hour approaching, told her daughter where she would find her apparel for the grave, and when her daughter wept, she said, with unutterable tenderness, "Oh, never mind!"

She was fond of music, and her voice, in sacred song, gave sweetness to our daily praise. Our evening worship was always conducted at her bedside. The last Lord's-day evening but one before she died, we sang the hymn,

> "My God, the spring of all my joys,
> The life of my delights," etc.

She had partially lost her powers of utterance, and we did not expect to hear her voice in praise again, this side the song of heaven. But wonderful to us all, her sweet soprano notes broke forth, and we united, though not continuously, in our last song of praise on the earth.

The last week of her life she was speechless; yet there were some sweet tokens of recognition which I shall never forget. She knew my voice, and smiled when I spoke. When I took her hand, she smiled. When I sang to her, there was an inexpressibly beautiful smile upon her lips, calm and heavenly.

I bless God that I had such a wife—that I had her at all, and that I had her so long. I bless him that I had so much joy in attending upon her last sickness, and so many tokens of her love. I bless him that her course is finished, and that she will never shed another tear. It was joy to me to watch her last breath, and to have the consolation that, through Him who loved us both, she has gained the victory, and now wears the crown. Oh! how I should love to see it on that sweet brow!

But, alas for me! My darling wife, I give you joy; but what shall I do without you? I look on that lovely corpse, and say, Yes, that is my beloved wife; this is all that is left of her now. Those sweet lips will speak to me no more. That laughing eye is dim. Those hands I have pressed so often are cold in death. That sound judgment, that wonderful discrimination of character, which so often guided me, will instruct me no more. We shall no more pray, and sing, and read God's Word together. Alone! alone! Ah! I have but the shadow of the solitude *now*. I can look upon her cold and lovely form, and feel that she is with me still. Yet will not God remember the words on which he has caused me to hope, "Even to old age I am he, and to hoar hairs will I carry you?" "The Lord gave, and the Lord hath taken away; blessed be the name of the Lord." Oh! for a sanctified improvement of this affliction to my dear children, to my own soul, and to my beloved flock! I think of this trial, and many coming sorrows, and I need *her* to enable me to bear them; I think of multiplied and unexpected mercies, and say, what are they without *her?* Sweet Susan, it is well it is so. I hope, through that same grace, to be with you yet, where HE is, and both of us to be like him, because we shall see him as he is. I cannot look to earth; clouds darken on my pathway now.

This beloved woman was the mother of fifteen children: *Samuel, Edward, Mary Norris, Gardiner, Susan Barney, Lindley, James Walton, Anna Town-*

send, *Elizabeth, Augusta Murray, Julia Lynch, William Maxwell, Hannah Hopkins, Sarah Fulton,* and *Lucius Lewis.* Six of these beloved children have been removed by death. *Julia* died at Fairfield, Conn., August 22d, 1825, and rests in the graveyard of that beautiful village. *Hannah* died in Bond-street, July 6th, 1831, a precocious child, and early fitted for heaven. *Sarah* died in Bond-street, January 8th, 1832. *Dr. Edward,* as we used to call him, died at sea, near the Cape of Good Hope, on the 13th of February, 1850. He married the daughter of the Hon. Richard Riker, of New York, and left a widow and three children. He was a practising physician of high promise ; but his health failed him, and he was cut off in the midst of his days, while on his return voyage from San Francisco and China. *James Walton* died in New Orleans, on his return from the Island of Cuba, on the 19th April, 1851. He was an enterprising merchant, married the daughter of the Hon. Harmer Denny, of Pittsburgh, and left a widow and three children. His dust rests in the family-vault of Mr. Denny, near Pittsburgh. *Mary Norris* died in New York at the house of her sister, Mrs. Spofford, March 21st, 1856, and was buried by the side of her husband in my family-vault, where their two children preceded them. She was married to Johnson P. Lee, whose sudden death from an accident on the railroad crushed her earthly hopes beyond recovery. She was an eminently lovely Christian. In New Orleans, at Bloomingdale, in New York, in the social circle, in the female prayer-meeting, in her extensive correspondence, her influence was felt, and " her works follow her." Samuel, Gardiner, Susan, Lindley, Anna, Elizabeth, Augusta, William, and Lewis, are still living, all of them married except Lindley and Anna. Of my departed children, I might say much to the praise and the glory of matchless grace. Of the living and their families, paternal partiality bids me be silent in these pages, while impartial love often constrains me to wrestle for them at the throne of grace. All my daughters are professed Christians, and two of my sons. May their father's God enable them to appreciate the promise, "to him that overcometh." The grace of perseverance alone cannot be counterfeited. My chief solicitude for them is, that those who are afar off may be brought nigh, and that those who are no more pilgrims and strangers, may honor their Christian discipleship.

> The names here recorded, oh! are they on high,
> In the Lamb's book of life, "up there" in the sky?
> This fountain of joy, will its streamlets flow on,
> And mingle with crystal from under the throne?
>
> This garden of pearls and amaranth flowers,
> Whence blossoms have wafted to Eden's fair bowers,
> Shall it wither and melt, and never more bloom,
> And childhood and manhood be lost in the tomb?
>
> Oh, may these blossoms expand in fragrance on high,
> And these waters flow, unmixed with a sigh;
> These trees, too, be fair, yielding fruit unto God,
> And these plants be laurels on the brow of their Lord!
>
> When pass'd the cold river, to tread earth no more,
> May the feet of these loved ones reach Jordan's bright shore;
> Stand firm on the Rock where the ark of God stood,
> Far, far from the dangers of the boisterous flood!

The joy of our hearts, may they go up to dwell
Where angels and saints the loud chorus shall swell;
Where the arches with infantile voices shall ring,
While " to God and the Lamb " they eternally sing!

Oh, that all might be ransomed from sin and the grave,
And washed in His blood who is mighty to save!
And, made pure by his Spirit, bow down at his throne
Together, their Lord and Redeemer to own!

For the dearest on earth, where nothing is dear,
At the throne of his Maker, a father bows here;
And bows for the children whom God has thus given,
That the Giver would guide them to Christ and to heaven.

October 16th, 1860.—Last evening witnessed the celebration of the fiftieth anniversary of my pastorate. I had been the pastor of the Brick Church for fifty years. Many a time I thought to have been brought down to the grave, and from year to year have felt that the thread was a very brittle one which bound me to the work of the ministry. As a Christian church, the people to whom I have ministered for so long a period, felt a deep interest in the fiftieth anniversary of my pastorate, and, unknown to myself, resolved to celebrate it in a manner highly honorable to themselves, and not a little gratifying to their pastor. Few congregations and few ministers can look back upon so prolonged and pleasant a relationship. Our progress, from the commencement, has been marked with signal tokens of the Divine presence and favor; our sanctuary has been the birthplace of immortal souls, and the consecrated habitation of more than two generations, now in the solitude of the grave. We cannot forget the past, nor shut our eyes upon the light it still sheds upon us, nor harden our hearts against the claims of the Divine faithfulness, nor refuse to speak one to another of his loving-kindness in the midst of his temple. We have changed our location, and knew not what other changes might follow; but we can gratefully set up our Ebenezer, and inscribe upon it in deep and legible characters, "Hitherto the Lord hath helped us." It was an eventful hour, the evening of this celebration. It quickened the pulse of the old, and brought a fresh coloring to the cheeks of the young. Fathers were there with their sons, mothers with their daughters, the bridegroom with his bride, and many a stranger within our gates, and genius, and taste, and clerical dignity, and scholarly accomplishment, and judicial and medical science, in indiscriminate thanksgiving, were assembled to " bid us God speed." One was absent—the pride of my household, and one who would have enjoyed the occasion more than any other—she was reposing beneath the tower of the church where we were assembled. To myself, as well as to many others, the whole scene was one of touching interest. The house was filled to overflowing. Horace Holden, Esq., the most prominent of our ruling elders, and than whom no man was more beloved and respected in the congregation, was called to the chair, and the Rev. Dr. Phillips, pastor of the First Presbyterian Church, opened the meeting with prayer. Addresses were made by Mr. Holden, Daniel Lord, Esq., Jasper Corning, Esq., the Rev. Dr. Krebs, by the appointment and on behalf of the Presbytery of New York; by my own mother's son, the Rev. Dr. Samuel Spring, of East Hartford; by the Rev. Dr. Rodgers, of New Jersey; by my old classmate, the Rev. Dr. Humphrey, of Berkshire, Massachusetts; by the Rev. Dr. Murray, of Elizabethtown; by John G. Adams, M.D.; and by the Rev. Dr. William J. Hoge, my associate pastor. The address of Mr. Lord was accompanied with the presentation of a valuable service of silver plate, as a tribute of the congregation for " laborious services so long enjoyed ; " a " gift of intrinsic value," putting honor upon " the ministry as a lofty calling ; " a " costly testimonial laid before their pastor." Mr. Lord then read the letter of presentation, in the following words:

" REVEREND AND DEAR SIR:

" The people of your charge unite with you in thanks to God, for having enjoyed with you the fiftieth year of your ministry among them.

" They gratefully acknowledge the faithfulness of your services to their fathers and themselves, in preaching to them the Gospel of Christ, with sincerity and singleness of purpose, with prayer and labor, not having in your view the fear or favor of man, but the honor and glory of God in advancing the kingdom of his Son; and having before you chiefly the consecration to him of the love and service of those who are committed to your charge.

" They cannot, as they ought not, forbear to express to you their thanks and love for your sympathy in their joys and prosperity, and in their afflictions and bereavements; nor can they fail to acknowledge you as the tender friend, as well as the counsellor to sacred duties, and the minister of heavenly consolation.

"They, with the Christian multitudes of our country, look upon you as having an honorable place in its sacred literature, whose printed words will continue to advance the object of your ministry after you shall have entered into your rest.

"They also bear witness to your usefulness as a public-spirited, Christian man, in the councils of the church at large, and in the literary, religious, and benevolent institutions of your age, bringing not only thoughts of wisdom, but words of peace.

"As a slight mark of their esteem, they now ask your acceptance of a durable expression and memorial of their friendship and love, and of their sincere and abiding reverence."

To this presentation and address, I could make but a brief reply. The different addresses were sufficiently complimentary, and, while they greatly gratified me, they made me ashamed of my shortcomings, and feel deeply that I am not worthy of such commendations.

I may here add, as I transcribe, at a later date, the preceding paragraph from my diary, that a small octavo volume of three hundred pages, issued by the committee of arrangements, and entitled, "Brick Church Memorial," publishes at length the narrative of this celebration, and contains the discourses delivered on the closing of the old church in Beekman-street, and the opening of the new church on Murray

Hill, together with the discourse delivered on the fiftieth anniversary of my installation, the proceedings of the memorial meeting, and the discourse on the occasion of the death of my beloved Mrs. Spring. In a very kind review of this volume, in the January number of "The American Theological Review," for the year 1862, edited by Professor Henry B. Smith, of the Union Theological Seminary, the writer is pleased to say that "the whole volume is of no ordinary value," and narrates the story "of one of the most honorable and successful pastorates in this country, extending through more than half a century." I cannot express my obligations too emphatically to this reviewer, forming, as he does, no part of our congregation, and employed in a distinct and different sphere, and in the other department of the Presbyterian church, for the great kindness with which he has spoken of this volume, and of the Brick Church and its unworthy pastor.

It may well be believed that this anniversary was to me a solemn day. It made me feel that here, on the very battle-field where, half a century ago, I girded on my armor, and where the word of the Lord had free course and was glorified, I must soon retire from the conflict with the powers of darkness. By their formal vote, the congregation had given me this liberty, at the same time requesting me to remain on the field so long as God should give me strength to wield the sword of the Spirit. I have remained upon it, not so much the leader of the Lord's host, as the shattered ensign on the mountains of Israel. The Lord's name be praised, if I may even stand still and see the salvation of God, and shout my feeble Alleluia as the tribes of Israel wend their way towards the promised land. What the destiny of the Brick Church is to be hereafter, I do not know. What it shall be, depends, under God, upon the self-denying piety of its members, upon the fidelity of its eldership, and upon its pulpit ministrations. Her place among the churches of this city and land ought to be no matter of doubt. Let her make the cause of truth, the cause of godliness, the cause of Christ, her own; and though she may be called to renewed conflicts, unwearied effort, and undiscouraged prayer, she will not travel through a starless midnight, but will look forth "fair as the sun, clear as the moon, and terrible as an army with banners." I love the Brick Church; I am jealous for its usefulness, and jealous for its honor. It would be a grief of heart to me, on my pillow of death, if its sun should go down in darkness, or even wane in twilight.

April 13*th*, 1865.—The foregoing extract is the last entry in my diary. My sweet wife was too valuable a woman ever to be forgotten. The preceding sketch furnishes but the outline of her excellencies, which I have presented more at large at the close of the sermon commemorative of one who was my first love. I never thought I could love another. But I was advanced beyond my threescore years and ten, partially blind, and needed a helper fitted to my age and condition; no one needs such a helper more than a man in my advanced years. I sought and God gave me another wife. A few days only more than a year after the death of Mrs. Spring, on the 14th of August, 1861, I was married to Abba Grosvenor Williams, the only surviving child of the late Elisha Williams, Esq., a distinguished member of the bar. She is the heiress of a large property, and retains it in her own hands. She is intent on her duty as a wife, watchful of my wants, takes good care of me, is an excellent housekeeper, and instead of adding to the expenses of my household, shares them with her husband. Not until after our mutual engagement was entered into, did we know that we were descended from the same stock, and that our grandmothers *were sisters*. Mrs. Spring's grandmother was *Jerusha Porter*, the daughter of the Hon. Eleazer Porter, of Hadley, and my grandmother, *Sarah Porter*, was also his daughter, and was the wife of my grandfather, Samuel Hopkins. Jerusha married Colonel Ebenezer Williams, of Pomfret, whose son, Elisha Williams, was the father of Mrs. Spring. Jerusha Porter, Mrs. Spring's grandmother, and Sarah Porter, my grandmother, were the children of a sister of Jonathan Edwards.

In preceding pages I have alluded to the death of my brother Pinckney. The following letter I received from him, while he was a teacher in the Grammar School at Andover, and a few weeks before an epileptic fit which ensued in his derangement and death.

"ANDOVER, *March* 20, 1820.

"MY DEAR BROTHER:

"I have taken my pen, to attempt to give you some idea of my feelings on the subject of religion.

But how shall I commence? You probably expect that it will be with some heartless acknowledgment of its importance, and some unfeeling expression of my own sinfulness. But no, dear brother; it is, I trust, with some realizing sense of the vast importance of the subjects which relate to a future life, and an earnest desire to make them the business of this.

"God, in his infinite mercy, has seen fit to arouse me, as I trust, from a state of stupid indifference, and direct my attention to the concerns of my immortal soul. He has allowed me to see, in some measure, the great ingratitude of my former life, and to feel against what a Being it is that I have been sinning all my days—One who has placed me in a land of Christian privileges and advantages—has given me parents who have worked, counselled, and prayed for me, who have agonized at the throne of grace, that I might feel my lost, undone condition, and fly to the cross of Christ for mercy. Yes, it is against a Being who has granted me all these privileges that I have *fought* my way to this time in life. And this is not the worst of my case: I have crucified the Lord of glory, and put him to an open shame; I have resisted the strivings of his Spirit to a most aggravated degree. How many times has my attention been momentarily excited, and soon these feelings passed away like the morning cloud or the early dew! Oh! dear brother, against what great light and great privileges have I constantly been sinning! What an act of infinite mercy, that He has not long ere this cut me off, and consigned me to the pit of eternal woe. Oh! dear brother, where am I? what am I? Can it be possible that I am still in a state of probation—that I am on this side of a miserable eternity? 'What shall I render unto the Lord for all his benefits toward me?' Thanks be unto his name, that he has styled himself a God of mercy, 'who delighteth not in the death of the wicked, but that they should turn to him and live.' To him would I desire to go and entreat for mercy. I would plead the merits of his dear Son, and throw myself at the foot of the cross, and beg for mercy. 'Lord, I am vile, what shall I answer?' Ever praised be his name that there is an INFINITE atonement, sufficient for the whole race of man. The blood of Christ is amply sufficient to wash pure from their iniquity the vilest of the vile.

"Oh! the riches of sovereign grace! 'God so loved the world, that he gave his only-begotten Son, that whosoever believeth in him should not perish, but have everlasting life.' I would cry with the father mentioned by the evangelist, 'Lord, I believe, help thou mine unbelief.' I feel as though I could go to Christ and say, 'Here am I, Lord; what wilt thou have me to do?' I would resign myself into his hands as clay in the hands of the potter.

"'Jesus, we come at thy command;
With faith and hope and humble zeal
Resign our spirits to thy hand,
To mould and guide us at thy will.'

"This language of the immortal Watts is, I trust, the language of my heart. Oh! there is an inexpressible sweetness in bowing at the foot of the cross, and looking up with an eye of faith, and imploring His mercy. There would I desire to keep and prostrate myself low in the dust, and cry for mercy. You tremble, dear brother, lest I am building on a false foundation. Oh! pray, if that is the case, that I may be aroused to a view of my awful condition. Thou searcher of hearts, who knowest and triest the reins of the children of men, 'Search me and know my heart, try me and know my reins, and see if there be any evil way in me, and lead me in the way everlasting.' Pray much for me, dear brother, that I may keep humble, that I may have free access to the throne of grace, and enjoy much of the light of God's countenance and communion with him.

"My feelings would lead me to write sheets, but my limits compel me to close by requesting an early answer to this. I want your counsels and your prayers. Do not withhold them. May I not, with feelings of closer union than ever, subscribe myself your most affectionate brother,

"PINCKNEY."

CHAPTER VI.

FOREIGN TRAVEL.

During the summer of 1822, some repairs and alterations were made in our church edifice, which allowed me a season of repose and absence from the city. At the earnest solicitation of Capt. Samuel Candler, one of the members of the church, I embarked, with my son Edward, and the family of Capt. Candler, on board the ship London, for a voyage across the Atlantic. Both the outward bound and the return passage were altogether free of charge, and the kindness of Capt. and Mrs. Candler, together with the splendid accommodations of the ship, and fine weather, rendered the voyage, in every view, delightful. After employing several weeks in London and its vicinity, and accompanying Capt. Candler on a visit to his family friends at Colchester, I left my son, Edward, to the care of Mrs. Candler, and crossed the Channel, for France. After a deliberate survey of Calais, I took the diligence for Paris, where I was the guest of Mr. Wilder's family, and was received, not only with Christian affection, but with the generous hospitality for which that amiable and accomplished family have ever been so justly distinguished. Here I met the Rev. Dr. Jonas King, the beloved Missionary of the American Board, who had been pursuing his studies in Paris, with a view to his mission in Greece. He had just recovered from a dangerous attack of typhus fever, and so slight was the hope of his recovery, that his American friends had actually selected the ground in the cemetery of *Père-la-Chaise*, for his interment. A kind Providence restored him to be a blessing to a degenerate people, an honor to the American church, and a noble advocate, both by service and by suffering, for the truth of the Gospel in opposition to the corruptions of the Greek church, its ridiculous ceremonies and absurdities, its slavery and thraldom, and its deplorable ignorance. Our intercourse in Paris was exceedingly pleasant, every way unembarrassed, and profitable to us both. We visited the Catacombs, and employed many hours on Mont Calvaire, passing from station to station, and witnessing the farcical shows and hypocritical disguises by which the Catholic priesthood had so long and so completely deluded vulgar minds. There had been a far-famed nunnery on Mont Calvaire, which was suppressed by Napoleon, and where in breaking up its subterranean passages, they were found, notwithstanding all the vestal vows, to be paved with the bones of infants. It was not the most sacred fire that perpetually burned upon their altars. The hymn to Venus does not include the Vestal goddess among the three that escaped the power of the queen of love. The vow of chastity was violated on Mont Calvaire without the danger of being buried alive in the

Campus Sceleratus, or scourged to death in the *Forum.* The Confessional of the Catholic priesthood, if the facts narrated to me in Paris are reliable, is too often the chamber of licentiousness. There is a remarkable fact in relation to the Fine Arts in Paris, which made a deep impression on my own mind. It is that the finest products of the pencil are of two opposite classes: the sacred and the profane; the moral and the immoral; the professedly religious and the professedly obscene. These last, from all the degrees of cautious indelicacy to the most vulgar and unblushing effrontery, and impudent impurity of representation, like the Venus de Medici, are either entirely naked or slightly clad. They are the Devil's work. Many a time have I wished that I had never seen them.

Dr. King was making his arrangements for his departure for Greece, and through the Arabian Desert for Jerusalem. Under the reign of Louis Philippe, no private assemblage for Protestant religious worship was allowed, where the number of worshippers exceeded seven. We were very solicitous to celebrate the Lord's Supper before Dr. King's departure; and four of us, Mr. and Mrs. Wilder, and Dr. King, and myself, employed a Sabbath morning in that delightful service in the boudoir of Mrs. Wilder. We went through the entire service in the form and manner in our American churches. It was a most solemn and affecting scene. One of the company was just about to direct his course to Jerusalem, not knowing the things that should befall him there; another was just about to embark for the Western Continent; two were to remain. I preached from the words of our blessed Lord, "I will not henceforth drink of this fruit of the vine, until the day when I drink it new with you in my Father's kingdom." We read God's holy word; we prayed; we sang; we brake the bread; we took the cup, under the deep impression that we should never meet again, until we met in the upper sanctuary. And thus we parted. Nor will the day ever be forgotten. The Saviour was there; his blessing was there; his promise was there, " Lo, I am with you always, even unto the end of the world." I met Brother King in New York, in December, 1864, and he said to me, "I want to see the man who preached in Mrs. Wilder's boudoir, and dispensed the Lord's Supper there just as I was starting for the Holy Land." The following letter from Dr. King to Mr. Wilder, kindly furnished me by the latter gentleman, has a reference to this pleasant scene.

"MT. CALVARY, *May* 7, 1823.

"DEAR MR. WILDER:

"How shall I express to you the emotions I now feel within my bosom. The hour has come—the hour about which we so often conversed and prayed in the garden of Nanterre, and in the little consecrated room at Paris. My feet now stand on that awful hill where our dear Lord and Saviour poured out his soul unto death, and finished the work of man's redemption. Here the arms of everlasting love were extended on the cross, and here the meek and tender heart of the Son of God was pierced with a soldier's spear! Here flowed that precious blood in which our polluted souls must be cleansed, or lost forever! Here do I weep, and pray, and confess my sins! Oh, that you could be with me, that we might weep and pray together! Oh, could I see you to-day, it would be like the meeting of Jacob and Joseph in the land of Goshen. I pray God that I may see your face before I die, and that we may rejoice together, and praise the Lord for all his goodness, and for all his wonderful works towards us, and towards the children of men. Oh, praise the Lord, for he is good, and his mercy endureth forever!

"I suffered much in the wilderness from scorching winds, which were sometimes indeed dreadful to bear, and also from want of pure water. For several days I was obliged to drink water which was full of sand and gravel, and which smelt and tasted so bad that it almost occasioned vomiting. All this, however, I, as it were, forgot, the moment I entered within the limits of Canaan. Thus will the soul, redeemed from sin, forget all the trials of its earthly pilgrimage, as soon as it enters the heavenly Canaan.

"I arrived here with my dear brethren, Messrs. Fisk and Wolfe, just one week before the Passover, which we celebrated on the anniversary of that sorrowful night, when our Lord was betrayed into the hands of sinners, and when he agonized in the garden of Gethsemane, and 'sweat as it were great drops of blood falling down to the ground.' Oh, how often did I think, on that evening, of that solemn and precious season in your closet, when a little before parting, you and I, and Mrs. Wilder, and Dr. Spring, celebrated together the death and sufferings of our Lord.

"We partook of the sacrament here in a little upper room, on Mount Calvary, where I lodge. Some of the bread and wine which you presented me on parting at Paris, and which I had preserved until my arrival here, we used as the emblems of that body which was broken, and of that blood which was shed for the remission of sins.

"Last Monday we kept our first monthly concert of prayer on the Mount of Olives, after which we went down to Bethany, the town of Martha, and Mary, and Lazarus, whom Jesus loved, and whose house the blessed Saviour used to visit. Oh, it was to me a delightful place, for it brought to mind all those delightful hours of Christian intercourse and heavenly conversation which I enjoyed at Paris. If we, who are so unholy, had so much pleasure in conversing with each other, what must those visits have been at Bethany, where the meek and lowly Jesus took part in the conversation, and talked with Martha, and Mary, and Lazarus, about the things of another world!

"That the Lord Jesus Christ may love you, and come unto you (John xiv. 23), and make his abode with you, is the sincere desire and prayer of your unworthy Brother and missionary on Mount Calvary,
"J. KING."

I hope I shall not be severely judged if I also add the following from the same source:

"JERUSALEM, *May* 19, 1823.

"DEAR DR. SPRING:
"What shall I say to you? Shall I open my bosom

and pour out the fulness of my heart, and tell you how much joy I feel at the remembrance of those happy, interesting days spent with you at Paris and Nanterre, when we used to bow together with our dear Mr. Wilder, and when I used to sit and listen to your speech, which 'distilled as the dew and as the small rain upon the tender herb,' while you talked of faith and hope, the efficacy of prayer, and the joys of heaven? Shall I mention that precious season when, as we were about to part for different climes, not knowing the things that might befall us, we met together, and in a little upper room celebrated with tears the death and sufferings of our Lord and Saviour? Never, never, shall I forget that moment when you turned to me and uttered those melting words, 'Dear Brother, let not your heart be troubled!' In that hour I do think we were favored with a little foretaste of what the saints enjoy in the world above.

"Oh, that you could be with me here on Mount Calvary, where I am writing, and hear the roaring of the Turks from the minarets, and see the deep iniquity with which this Holy City is polluted! Mine eyes run down with tears at the desolations of Zion! Every thing around me seems blasted and withered by the curse of the Almighty. Before this curse shall be averted, there must be offered up many 'prayers and supplications with strong crying and tears unto Him' who has 'cast down from heaven to earth the beauty of Israel;' such prayers as you and your beloved flock had been offering when the Holy Spirit came down upon your congregation 'like a rushing mighty wind,' and multitudes were converted.

"Had I your spirit within my body, and your hand to wield my pen, I would send a message to all the churches throughout Christendom, beseeching them for Zion's sake not to hold their peace, and for Jerusalem's sake not to rest, 'until the righteousness thereof go forth as the brightness of a blazing torch, and the salvation thereof as a lamp that burneth.' I never felt, so much as I do now, the importance of praying that God would glorify his great name among all nations, and cause the name of his Son, Jesus Christ, to be adored throughout all the earth. I sometimes pray that He would arise and shake terribly the earth, that the people may know that there is a God in heaven, and that Jesus Christ lives and reigns over all, 'God blessed forever.'

"The Jews here have all the blindness and stubbornness and stiff-neckedness of their fathers. Some of them tell Mr. Wolff that, were they in power, they would calmly judge him and put him to death. The Catholics threaten with excommunication any one who shall receive from us the Holy Scriptures, and pronounce a curse upon every one who may in any way aid us. The Mussulmen walk about in pride, and if any one of them should leave his religion, certain death would be his portion. So strict are they here, that I dare not even purchase a Koran, lest I should involve myself in difficulty. Any *native* Christian who should presume to purchase it and read it, would instantly lose his life. The Greeks and Armenians have a name that they live, and that is nearly all. They are, however, more noble than the other Christians, for they gladly receive the Word of God.

We have had sometimes thirty a-day calling on us to purchase the Holy Scriptures.

"Best regards to Mrs. Spring and your children, and accept for yourself the assurance of the affection and esteem of

"Your unworthy friend on Mount Calvary,

"J. King."

During his visit to our city, in 1864, I requested Dr. King to give me, in writing, his recollections of our intercourse in Paris. He replied that his Journal would furnish the best outline of those pleasant days, and sent me the following:

"Extracts from my Journal at Paris, Sept., 1822.

"*Sunday*, 15*th*.—Rev. Dr. Spring preached a very solemn and impressive sermon to our little circle at Nanterre, from Deut. viii. 2. * * *

"After the divine service was concluded, Dr. S., Mr. W., myself, and some others, set out on a visit to Mount Calvary, about a mile and a-half distant from Nanterre, and which, for nine days during the month of September, is the resort of pilgrims, some of whom come sixty, eighty, or a hundred miles on foot, to pay their devotions. Having filled our pockets with tracts, we began to ascend the mountain, distributing them on the right hand and on the left, among the thousands that were ascending and descending. * * *

* * * "The sides of the mountain, particularly on the east, south, and north, are thinly covered with shrubbery and trees, among which wind about, in various directions, numerous footpaths, leading to the convent on the summit. At different distances, on the sides of these paths, stand little buildings, open in front, which are called stations. In them are images of Christ, and the Virgin Mary, &c. Before them the pilgrims stop, kneel down on the ground, and worship. One, I observed, was a station to pray for the dead. We visited several of these stations, and distributed the tract entitled, 'Le Sermon de Notre Seigneur sur le Montagne.' This was received with much avidity, and with gratitude. We even gave them to those who were on their knees, in the act of adoration, who would arise and come after us to thank us. Frequently they would all leave their devotions and flock around us to receive this precious gift; and when our tracts were all gone, some inquired when we should come again. We left them giving us thanks, and made our way back to Nanterre, where we dined.

"In the evening, Mr. Wilder, Dr. Spring, and myself, went into Paris, and had a delightful season of prayer with each other, at the Rue de Petit Carreau, No. 18.

"*Thursday*, 19*th*.—Called on the Baron de Staël * * * * Introduced to him Dr. Spring, whom he received with much pleasure. * * * * Went to Nanterre, where we arrived a little after mid-day. Mr. and Mrs. Wilder and Miss Berteau, and Mr. Storrow's children, had gone to Mount Calvary to distribute tracts and Testaments. Dr. Spring and myself, having filled our pockets, and hats, and hands, with tracts and Testaments, set off with the hope to find them. Just as we began to ascend the mountain, we saw them coming at a distance. On meeting them, they informed us that they had been stopped by the Commissary of the Police, and that a *gendarme*, by order of the Missionaries (Rom. C. M.) had taken away their tracts and Testaments, and prohibited them, in the name of the law, to distribute any more on Mount Calvary. Mr. W. advised us not to proceed with the intention of distributing those which we had. We, however, went, giving to every one we met, till we came in sight of the *gendarmes*, when we ceased giving, but occasionally let some fall from our pockets, which the wind, which was very high, scattered in all directions, and were gathered up by the crowd. At length, we arrived at the top of the mountain, took our stand on the highest elevation near the cross, and there, in our own language, offered up, each of us, a prayer to the God of heaven for direction, and to have mercy on those tens of thousands that we saw around us, bowing before graven images. I then felt in some degree strengthened to go on, and, taking a tract from my pocket, presented it to a lady who stood near me, and who appeared to be a lady of some distinction.

"She received it with thanks, and I was not noticed by the *gendarmes*. Dr. S. let some fall from his pocket, and we made our way down to one of the stations. There he laid some on the charity-box, while I stood before him to hide what he did. We then went to another station, and I gave ten or twelve to a lady, whom I charged to distribute them. She was immediately surrounded by a number, to whom she distributed, while we made our way to another station, and finally we took our way home, and distributed till we came to the foot of the mountain, when we found we had no more to give.

"Some took me for one of the missionaries, to whom I gave a number, and charged them to go on to the top of the mountain and distribute, which they reverentially promised to do. The tracts we distributed were 'Christ's Sermon on the Mount,' and 'St. Paul's Defence before Agrippa.' We gave about four hundred of these, and some New Testaments, which were received by nearly all with gratitude and joy. Occasionally we were refused.

"In the whole, we have distributed, since last Sabbath, seventeen hundred tracts. I should judge there were on the mountain and around it, twenty thousand people.

"*Sunday*, 22*d.*—Went to Paris with Mdlle. Berteau, to hear Dr. S. preach at the *Oratoire*. After sermon, went to Mr. Wilder's. Mr. and Mrs. Wilder, Dr. Spring, and myself, retired to the boudoir, and there spent a most solemn, affecting, and interesting season in celebrating together the Lord's Supper. Dr. S. first delivered one of the sweetest, tenderest sermons that I ever heard on a similar occasion, from St. Matt. xxvi. 29: 'But I say unto you, I will not drink henceforth of this fruit of the vine, until that day when I drink it new with you in my Father's kingdom.' I felt as though it were probably the last time we should ever drink of this wine till we met at the marriage supper of the Lamb. We were celebrating an ordinance which our Saviour had instituted just before he was to enter upon the scene of his greatest sufferings; and we were celebrating it on the occasion of my departure to that land where he died, and where I might, with reason, expect to pass through scenes of trial, in which I should need all the consolatory promises he had left to support me. The time, the place, the occasion, the little company, so dear to my heart, all tended to fill my heart with the deepest emotions. We could not refrain from weeping during the whole time we were together. I did not weep through fear of danger, but in view of past sins, and fear that I should not have strength and grace to support me in persecutions and death, which I might be called to pass through. Dr. S. turned to me, and, with ineffable tenderness and kindness, said, 'My dear Brother, let not your heart be troubled: I feel as though God would go with you and support you.' After supper, we sung a hymn, together with the doxology, took each other by the hand, saying that this season would long be remembered by us all. * *

" * * * In the evening, about twenty of our friends came in, among whom was Gen. Macauley, and the Rev. Mr. Mann, from England. Mr. Wilks explained a part of the 4th chapter of St. John, and Dr. S. followed him with a very interesting address and exhortation.

"After the company had retired, we sat up till twelve, conversing and listening to the gracious words which proceeded out of his mouth. We then united in prayer, and retired. Oh, how delightful is such a season, after having been so long from communions, from Christian friends, in this great city, this land of the shadow of death, and at a time, too, when I feel the greatest need of it!"

My *second* visit to Europe was in the year 1835, under the appointment of the *General Assembly of the Presbyterian Church*, as their delegate to the *Congregational Union of England and Wales*, and as a fraternal response to the deputation of the Rev. Dr. Andrew Reed and the Rev. Dr. James Matheson, who had visited the American churches the preceding year. The narrative of their visit to this country was published in London, " respectfully dedicated to the churches of England and America, with the earnest desire that it may promote their mutual affection, and their united devotedness to the salvation of the world," in two beautiful octavo volumes. After a special season of prayer at Zion Chapel in London, and at the house of Dr. Raffles in Liverpool, they embarked in the ship Europe, and after a prosperous passage, " sprang on the landing at New York, and realized the presence of a country which had long dwelt as a picture of interest and hope in their imagination." They were received with great cordiality, and their narrative presents no unfavorable view of the American character. They were present during our Anniversary Week, and gave interest to all our meetings. They speak of them as " delightful," with " more spirit and efficiency in them than they had been taught to expect, in no way inferior to their own, and in some respects perhaps superior." They preached with great acceptance in many of our churches, and left impressions by no means unfavorable to the land of our fathers. They attended the meetings of the *General Assembly*, and speak of "this body as next in importance to the Congress itself." It was at a period of sharp discussion between what are now designated as the "Old and New School." Dr. Reed says: "For my own part, I was glad of an occasion of observing the conduct of such a body under very trying circumstances, and the result was unfeigned *admiration*." Very extensive were his visits through the Northern, Middle, Southern, and Western States, and, among other places, the cradle of the Pilgrim Fathers. Of Plymouth Rock he says: "I stood on it and trembled. I know of no spot more sacred on earth, except the one spot where the Holy One suffered, the just for the unjust."

I have no room in these pages for more extended reference to the narrative of these excellent brethren. It was a most responsible office to respond to this acceptable and useful deputation. My friends in New York, well knowing my straitened circumstances, had made ample provision for my wants, and, very unexpectedly to myself, had put into my hands a purse containing twenty-five hundred dollars. At the same time I was furnished with letters of credit on Liverpool, London, and Paris, from Brown, Brothers & Co.; from the late John Adams; the late James McCall, and the late Jacob Halsey, whose private letters of introduction to distinguished mercantile houses were of essential service, and whose kindness to me will not soon be forgotten.

But there were other preparations not less indispensable to an honorable discharge of the duties of my appointment. The state of our churches, their efforts and their prospects, the cause of missions and education, our literary institutions, the Bible cause, the condition and prospects of our slave population—the wide West, and especially the Valley of the Mississippi, containing nearly a million and a half of square miles, and more than one-twenty-eighth part of the entire land-surface of the earth, and then containing nearly five millions of souls; of these and other statistics I endeavored to possess that accurate information which would qualify me for those off-hand addresses which would be expected of me. Then there was my speech before the Congregational Union; the British and Foreign Bible Society; and the Paris Bible Society. This latter troubled me. I was utterly ignorant of the French language, and employed two French teachers to qualify me for my work. I had three months before me, and, by God's blessing upon my determined purpose, made such proficiency in the language as to read it with ease, to write it without difficulty, and to pronounce it almost without any foreign accent. I regard this acquisition as no unimportant design of Providence in my ministerial career. It opened to me the French character, the French literature, and the French theology.

With these preparations, humble indeed compared with the work before me, in company with my daughter Susan, now Mrs. Spofford, I embarked on the 26th of February on board the ship Poland, Capt. Anthony, for Havre, London, and Paris. They were new emotions that filled both our bosoms; we were novices, launching upon untried scenes. My sons, Edward and Gardiner, accompanied us to the Narrows, and when they bade us adieu, we felt that we had indeed left our own dear home. A fair but light breeze soon bore us away from the waters of New York, and we felt, if we did not exclaim, "My native land, good night!" Our noble ship, with all her canvas spread, like the corsair's bark,

"Walked the waters like a thing of life."

We had eleven passengers, all American except one, and he a German. We watched the retiring hills until dear America cast her last shadows upon us, and then retired, well knowing that "if we take the wings of the morning and dwell in the uttermost parts of the sea, God is there." The fourth day after our departure was the Sabbath, ushered in by a radiant sun and a clear sky. There had been high winds, and sleet, and snow; but now it was a Sabbath morning, and all was joyous and happy. The ocean seemed to know that it was the day of rest; its storms were hushed, and its glad waters spake only of praise. We, too, assembled for praise and prayer. Susan was quite sea-sick, yet she came on deck. The day was cold, and she sat with a hot potato in each hand to keep her warm. The restless agitation of the boundless ocean—its ceaseless heavings—what grandeur in this expanse of waters, stretching away and yet away, and on all sides mingling with the sky, rolling and tumbling, and blending with the very verge of the distant horizon! And there is but a frail plank between us and this vast ocean, and all the living tribes, and floating carcasses, and coral groves beneath. The dark *blue* sea; I could almost charge it with having stolen its beautiful coloring from the skies, so light and almost fading do they appear. The sea-green tinge vanishes, and the cerulean line darkens according to the depth of the water.

March 5th.—A week to-day since we left our beloved home. We are crossing the southern edge of the Grand Banks of Newfoundland. Mr. Van Rensallear assists us greatly in our French, which adds not a little to the pleasure of our voyage. We gazed this evening at the sun setting, and what a glorious sight it was! As the golden orb sank into the sea, its disc became oblong, and its splendors flashed across the waves, tracing a pyramid of light of the brightest hue. Its disc was tinged with various colors, assuming a thousand fantastic forms, as, gradually quenched by the billows, it sank to rest. The moon, too, greets us wanderers and cheers these desolate tracks of ocean with her smiles. I have stood upon deck to see the evening stars go down, and the moon plunge her cold orb in the sea, veiling herself in a silver drapery of clouds that float attendance on the queen of night. And that sheet of burning gold, those trains of phosphoric light the ocean summons from her realms to bespangle her billowy surface with the jewels of the deep, those stars of fire that seem to rival the little twinklers above, dashing, and foaming, and sparkling in very exuberance of beauty—who will not say, in view of such scenes as these, "Marvellous are thy works, Lord God Almighty, in wisdom hast thou made them all." We have as yet wandered alone—quite alone—not a distant sail, not a porpoise, or whale, or fleet bird, has flitted across our path, or flapped his dark wing over us.

March 8th.—Again it is the Sabbath, when we held religious worship on deck, and distributed tracts to the seamen. Our ship belongs to the temperance society. Everything is quiet, labor is suspended, and not even the decks are washed on Sunday. Everything is like clock-work on board the Poland. Punctuality and subordination are the law. We are now on soundings and looking out for land.

March 15th.—It is a beautiful day, and we had religious services as usual at noon. Just at the close of the service, the cry of *Land ahead!* greeted us from the mast-head. They were not the green hills of Old England, but the *Lizzards*, on the English coast, a promontory on the south coast of Cornwall, the most southern point of land in England, and at the north entrance of the English Channel. At evening we passed the coast of Normandy, on the French side of the Channel, lined with the ruins of ancient castles, and tumbling to decay. Early the next morning the pilot came on board, but we lay at anchor the whole day for want of the favoring tide. The next day we landed at *Havre;* it was a terrible day, the wind blowing and the rain pouring in very fury. We were soon surrounded by a bevy of boats, a motley group, so chattering their almost unintelligible jargon, that I felt as though we were in an aviary of magpies. We at length quitted our little prison of three weeks, not without some feeling of regret that we bade adieu to our courteous captain, and the noble ship that had so safely borne us over the perils of the deep. He who holds the waters, carried us also in "the hollow of his hand." Once more we boldly trod on terra firma, and felt thankful and happy. Havre seemed to me a dismal place, with dark, and dirty, and narrow streets, and no side-walks. We visited the Catholic church, and listened for a while to the mummery of the priest. We visited it from curiosity, and left it for our edification.

March 18*th*.—We took the diligence for Paris; stopped at Balbec for breakfast, pursued our journey through the valley of the Seine, a perfectly level agricultural country, lined with small villages, where the women were performing the more menial offices, and the lazy men sitting calmly by and smoking their pipes, and the loaded donkeys, more like a caravan destined to Mecca or the Holy Land, than a stage-coach for the metropolis of France. We reached Rouen about four o'clock, where we had about two hours to look round the city, the capital of Lower Seine, and before the Revolution the capital of Normandy. The town is two miles long, and one broad. Here is the statue of the celebrated Maid of Orleans, Joan d'Arc, who was burned by the English as a witch, in 1430. The principal edifice is the Cathedral, built by William the Conqueror, and which is considered the finest specimen of Gothic architecture in France. Here are the tombs of Rollo the Dane and William of the Long Sword. A little circumstance occurred here that was somewhat amusing. Mr. Van Rensallear, in order to procure some little relic of the place, instead of gathering some flowers, broke off the *nose* of one of the marble saints! He hoped to escape the detection of the guide, but unfortunately, on leaving the Cathedral, we had to pass the mutilated statue, and were charged with the sacrilege. It was a lady-saint whose sanctity our gallantry had thus violated, and we had to meet the most terrific volleys of abuse. A few glittering coins, however, obtained absolution for us, but neither entreaty nor cash could procure *the nose*. We took the diligence at six o'clock, rode all night, and the next morning reached Paris.

We entered it by the Barrière l'Etoile, and were set down at the Messagerie Royale, amid vexations and chatterers more wearisome even than on the quay at Havre. We took lodgings at the residence of Madame Bonfils, on the Rue Rivoli, immediately opposite the gardens and the Palace of the Tuileries. We walked out the next day under the escort of an American gentleman, Mr. Stoddard, of Boston. As we passed the narrow, dirty streets, we could not but exclaim, "Can this be Paris? that perfect Elysium? that earthly Paradise?" Yet portions of it are most beautiful; and many a magnificent column, and bronze statue, and superb edifice, and stately dome, and adorned boulevard, bear testimony to the taste and enterprise of Napoleon I. On the next evening we attended a meeting for prayer, composed principally of Americans, and all *young men ;* and it was like a sunbeam breaking through the clouds. The next day, which was the Sabbath, we heard Mr. Grandpierre; and in the afternoon I preached in the same pulpit, to about one hundred Americans, and in the evening heard the Rev. Frederic Monod. We had letters to Hon. Edward Livingston, the American Ambassador; and through the kindness of Daniel Lord, Esq., of our own church, John Jacob Astor had given us letters that introduced us to persons and families of distinction. The following week we spent in visiting the works of art that once embellished Rome, and where a lady would scarcely wish to linger. Visited also the Chamber of Deputies, which is said to be the finest hall in Europe. Through the politeness of Mr. Livingston, I had a seat with the Foreign Ambassadors, whence I heard the debates, but no good speaking. We dined with Mr. Lutteroth, and in the evening met several strangers at his residence, where we had a prayer-meeting conducted in the French language. The next day was the Sabbath. We bent our way towards the small Eglise Protestant, searching in vain for some token of this day of rest. We met nothing but confusion and noise, and gay shops with busy customers. It was a gala-day; everything was gaudy and gay, while shouts of laughter issued from the crowd. It was anything but a Sabbath. The place of meeting was a small room; we heard Rev. Mr. Audebez in the morning, and I occupied the pulpit in the evening. The next day we dined with our New York friends, Mr. and

Mrs. Adams, where we met a delightful circle of Americans, and it was quite like a day at home. The next day we went again to the Louvre. I have not words to transcribe the scene minutely; it was enchanting—more like enchantment than reality. The marked difference in the coloring of the French and Italian schools the most superficial observer could not help noticing. In anatomical exactness and boldness of perspective, the French surpass other artists; but in some instances their glaring, gaudy colors seem laid on with a trowel, and are wanting in that harmony, softness, and delicacy which distinguish the schools of Italy. From the gallery of paintings we went to the Palais Royal—a little world in itself, comprising all varieties of character, occupation, and amusement, from the highest to the lowest—portions of it appropriated to the vilest uses, and from the whole of which the Duke of Orleans receives an immense revenue. In the afternoon we dined at the Café de Paris with a few friends, and in the evening attended a concert of instrumental music, which I have nowhere found excelled. The next day we visited the "Carousel," where is the triumphal arch erected by Napoleon, after the model of Septimus Severus at Rome. The bronze steeds, guided by a figure of Napoleon, were brought from Venice, and once adorned the car of Nero, and had but exchanged the greater tyrant for the greater man. This wondrous man has been reviled, and many a rude hand has defaced the memorials of his brilliant career; but a voice from the massive ruins still seems to say, "I am the work of Napoleon."

The next day Mr. Livingston introduced us to the Gobelin Tapestry. We saw the workmen sitting, like so many painters before the canvas, weaving in a thread at a time in imitation of the painting which is placed behind them. These pieces of tapestry occupy years of labor, and are intended only for the palaces of kings. On the Sabbath we went to the Eglise Protestant, and heard that noble man, Mr. Grandpierre, at whose request I again preached in the afternoon. The next day we dined with Mr. Wells, our banker; and on Saturday rode the whole extent of the Boulevards, which, like a belt, encircle Paris. Here we saw the Place de Grève, and the Guillotine, and the spot where Louis XVI. was beheaded, and that scourge of humanity, the Bastile. We visited also the Palace of the Luxembourg, and the Place Louis XV., where the marriage of Louis XVI. was celebrated, and where the volcano burst forth that shook all France to its centre; Nôtre Dame, too, that most ancient church in France, standing on the site of an old heathen temple, which was erected during the reign of Tiberius, and dedicated to Jupiter. We visited, also, the Hôpital des Invalides, erected for the invalid soldiers of France, where these sons of Mars find a quiet retreat; a noble monument to the genius of Henry IV. and of the munificence of the nation.

Again it is the Sabbath. We went to the Oratoire in the morning, and heard Mr. Monod; in the afternoon Dr. Codman, of Dorchester. On Monday we visited several of the Catholic churches, and among the rest the Chapel Expiatoire, where there is a small building erected over the grave of the Swiss who fell in defending Louis XVI. and Marie Antoinette from the fury of the mob. The ashes of this hapless pair now lie in the tomb of St. Denis with the kings of France. In a niche, encircled by marble columns, there is a beautifully executed statue of Louis. Faith, with a ministering angel, hovers round his couch, while Religion supports in her arms the dying monarch. Here also rest the bones of the Swiss; a plain marble slab covers the spot, adorned with the simple inscription, "The faithful Swiss."

But I must have done with Paris. The Sabbath in Paris, alas! what is it? If France is like Paris, it does not know what sin is—sin against God; they do not seem to know there is any such thing. Protestantism in France, notwithstanding its Unitarianism, has many good features, and some redeeming qualities. It has some excellent men, who are like the salt of the earth. Once on the Lord's day I attended the Catholic church—the celebrated church of St. Roch. Perhaps I did wrong in so doing; but I desired to see Romanism with my own eyes, and to hear with my own ears. It was the aristocratic church, where the queen and her daughters worship. I saw the *high mass*, or that special service of the Romish church which is used at the celebration of the Lord's Supper, and the consecration of the bread and wine. The wine was taken by the priest, but was withheld from the people. As I left the cathedral, I could not but exclaim, "Oh! the nonsense! the jargon! the Babel of trumpets and tongues! What madness, to put such stuff in the place of our affectionate remembrance of the death of the Lord Jesus." It is an awful curse upon our world that the Man of Sin has so much power over cultivated minds. We did not leave Paris without visiting the Pantheon, which was seventy years in building, and to the top of which we ascended by four hundred and sixty-four steps. At a Protestant service, we saw thirty young persons received into the church. They were dressed in white, and with white vests; the young men with a white ribbon on their arms. They are received to the communion at a certain age, and after a course of cathedral instruction. The early part of the following week I visited the "Institute of France," and through the politeness of Dr. Hosack and Dr. Francis, of our city, was introduced to some of the *savants*, and in the evening attended a meeting of the French and Foreign Bible Sociey. This week we also visited Versailles, in company with Dr. Codman, and in the evening I wrote to the young men of the Brick Church, giving them the names of all the kings of France that were entombed in St. Denis, from Clovis to Louis XVI.

It was now the week of the religious anniversaries, and I began to prepare for my departure for London. After a delightful prayer-meeting on Monday morning, in view of the exercises of the week, Tuesday brought us to the annual meeting of the Tract Society, where I made an address in English. On Wednesday I attended the meeting of the Evangelical Society, and on Thursday of the Foreign Missionary Society, and was called upon to make the closing speech. Friday, May 1st, was the anniversary of the French and Foreign Bible Society, to which I was delegated, for which I had prepared my speech in the French language, and which I was enabled to deliver without mistake, and without embarrassment. The press said some complimentary things concerning it, and my countrymen who were present congratulated me. At six o'clock the same day we started in the mail-post for Calais, and the next evening took the steamer for Dover, and arrived at four o'clock, A. M., stopping at Worthington's hotel, and in the enjoyment of a quiet Sabbath, away from the noise and bustle, the frolic and fun, of a French holiday.

Early the next morning we started for London, and arrived in time to attend the anniversary of the British and Foreign Bible Society, to which I was an appointed delegate. Much has been said, and deservedly said, of this blessed institution, of its patrons, and of its vast assemblies in Exeter Hall. I heard some truly excellent speeches, and delivered a very poor one. I became acquainted with many excellent men, both clergy and laity, both in and out of the Establishment, received the customary compliment to dine with Lord Bexley, the President; then, after a couple of days of sight-seeing and shopping, took the stage for Scotland. We visited Glasgow, a commercial city, which reminded us of New York more than any other city we had visited. Here I became acquainted with Dr. Ewing and Dr. Wardlaw, both professors in their theological school, and men of great eminence. Scotland was the scene of my romantic reading. Walter Scott was "Scotia's Star," and Mary its "murdered queen." Little did I think, when reading and talking of the "dinna forgets" of Old Scotland, and when entering into the wild enthusiasm of the poet's pen in his Lady of the Lake, that I should ever tread upon the soil of the martyred Covenanters, and look upon that lake's bright bosom.

July 2d.—We left Scotland for Ireland, and after a night's terrible tossing in the Irish Channel, arrived in Belfast, whence, after a walk over the town, we took the stage for Ballymena, stopped at a wretched inn, but spent the night and part of the next day with Mr. and Mrs. Gihon, to whom I had letters from Mr. James Brown, of New York. We were received most courteously, and there found Mrs. Gihon, of New York, a ladylike woman, whose civility was the more acceptable, in that we could converse so freely of home. The next day we came to Ballymena, where was pointed out to us the house in which Mr. Brown was born—a wretched Irish hovel, which, contrasted with his residence in University Place, made us think of the kind Providence that had so wonderfully smiled upon self-made men. Amid rain and every discomfort we reached the Giant's Causeway, a curiosity worth visiting, but which in no small degree disappointed us. I felt ashamed of my disappointment, when no less a man than Sir Humphrey Davy walked over it three successive summers, in order to solve the problem of its formation. The Irish coast is magnificent; its caves, which we entered in a small boat, were deep and solemn, and almost made us tremble. The hand of the great Architect was there, and there his voice was heard. The Causeway raised its bold front, and stretching out miles into the sea, seemed divinely commissioned to say, "Hitherto and no further!" Our little bark, on emerging from the cavern, bounded over the glassy billows which had proved the grave of thousands. It was here that the Rothsay Castle, the Invincible Armada, and our own Albion, were lost. It was here that the lamented Fisher, of Yale, left the deck in despair, went down into his berth, and calmly wrapped himself in his winding-sheet. The subterranean waters on the north coast of Ireland are perfectly beautiful—the caves arched, as it were, with a ceiling of diamonds, of every color and every shade of color. We seemed lost amid a labyrinth of rainbows, while the deep water was so transparent that we could see the least pebble on the bottom. It seemed one bed of emeralds. It was quite late when we landed, but we were in haste for Dublin. We passed the night at Coleraine, and as we awoke in the morning—it was the morning of the 4th of July—we felt sad that on that day we were in a foreign land. My fellow-traveller, my daughter Susan, thought of home and of Bond-street. Nor could she well restrain her poetic tendencies, but gave utterance to them in the following lines:

> O had I the wings of a dove,
>   I'd fly o'er the dark blue sea,
> And come with my warm, fondest love,
>   To spend this bright day with thee.
>
> But thought—it has wings, and I send
>   Mine o'er the deep, deep sea;
> On its pinions are loves which blend
>   With prayers to my God for thee.

> May it bring to thee bliss and mirth
>   As I waft it o'er the sea;
> The brightest hopes and joys of earth,
>   The blessings of Heaven on thee.

We left Coleraine about ten for Dublin. Our coachman was an Irishman, who said that "America was the country for him, where a man might vote twenty times at an election if he wished. America would not have been what it is but for the Irish. Its greatest President was an Irishman, born in a little Irish village." "And what was his name?" I inquired. "Why, President Jackson, to be sure!" We reached Londonderry at two o'clock, and at ten arrived at Armagh, a wretched, impoverished, filthy place, where we passed the Sabbath, and where, in the absence of the Presbyterian clergyman, I volunteered to preach, and did so from the words, "Ho! every one that thirsteth," etc. We dined with Mr. Buchanan, the brother of the British Consul in New York. We started early on Monday morning for Dublin, through fields of flax and bogs of peat, and by many a castle of the lord of the village, rioting in luxury while his dependants are starving before his eyes. Oh! the miserable policy of the British Parliament towards Ireland! We reached Dublin in the evening, where we found a party of New Yorkers, and where we, with our American friends, procured the large parlor, and all that could accommodate us in a first-class hotel. We were under obligations to Mr. Wolfe and Mr. Simeon Draper of our city, and their parties, for many kind attentions. Dublin is a beautiful city, and its public edifices an honor to old

Ireland. The whole party—eighteen of us—left on the 9th in a steamer for Holyhead in Wales, and after a rough passage, landed again on terra firma. The next day we went to Bangor, passed through the beautiful vale of Llangollen, through Wrexford to Chester, where we visited Eaton Hall, the seat of the Earl of Grosvenor, one of the most beautiful spots in the kingdom. From the ancient town of Chester we rode about six miles, and a short sail landed us at Liverpool. Here we were the guests of the late Sir William Brown, a most delightful family, by whom we were treated with unostentatious but princely hospitality, and where we remained some days, during which we visited the lions of the city and several adjacent places of historic memory and interest. Here I became acquainted with Lord Brougham, and, while I was instructed by his various learning, was charmed by the simplicity of his character. In company with Sir William Brown and the late Judge Irving of our city, it was my privilege to hear one of this great orator's best addresses.

We left Liverpool for London, and passed a day at Burnslem, where is the largest earthenware manufactory in Europe, and where I purchased a beautiful dinner-set for Mrs. Spring, and shipped it for New York. The next day we left Burnslem for Newcastle-upon-Tyne, took the stage for Worcester, passed through Cheltenham, one of the fashionable watering-places in England; thence to Bath, where I had an interesting interview with Rev. William Jay, and thence to Salisbury and Southampton, where we spent the Sabbath in the family of the Rev. Mr. Adkins, and where I preached at the morning service. On Monday we took the boat for the Isle of Wight, passed through Ryde and Reading, and visited the grave of the "Young Cottager." We plucked a flower from her grave, and copied the lines inscribed to her memory.

> " Ye who the power of God delight to trace,
> And mark with care this monument of grace,
> Tread lightly o'er the grave, as ye explore
> The short and simple annals of the poor.
>
> " A *child* reposes underneath this sod,
> A child to memory dear, and dear to God;
> Rejoice, yet shed the sympathetic tear:
> *Jane*, the young cottager, lies buried here."

We proceeded to New Port, where we visited the Dairyman's Cottage, and whence that lovely spirit, the "Dairyman's Daughter," took its flight for the heavenly world. We visited her grave; a sleeping group lies there, a whole family of beatified spirits.

> Sacred to the memory of
> Elizabeth Walbridge,
> who departed this life in the year 1801,
> Aged 21.

After visiting Carrisbrook Castle, where Charles I. was confined previous to his execution, we left New Port for Brighton, a beautiful spot fronting the English Channel, the summer residence of the King. The next day we left for London, where we found letters from home in the very hand-writing and the well-known style of the dear writer. Here we spent the Sabbath, and I preached for Dr. Morrison, and on

Wednesday we left London for Holland. We passed through Rotterdam and the Hague, visited the cathedral at Delft, saw the monument of the great William, Holland's liberator, and also the monument of Grotius; breakfasted with the American minister, and the next day started for Haarlem. We saw nothing here to interest us but the magnificent and world-famed organ. I gave the organist a sovereign for an hour's entertainment, and all I can now say of it is, that it was cheaply purchased. I had no conception of the *varied* power of the organ till I heard the great organ at Haarlem.

We left in the diligence for Amsterdam, where we spent the Sabbath, with no very favorable impressions of the religious observance of this day of God. On Monday we visited the palace and the museum, and taking a carriage to Nimegen, rode through the "Black Forest" to Cologne. We embarked for Cologne with some of our Rotterdam passengers, and reached Cologne about three o'clock the next day, where we found a good hotel, and saw the old Roman Cathedral, and the old Roman bridge. Cologne is distinguished for its paintings; paintings of the 13th century, of the 14th, and of the 15th, for, like the Roman empire, the art has had its rise and fall. There was one painting by a modern artist that is exquisitely beautiful, "The weeping of the Jews by the rivers of Babylon." The whole group seemed to say, "How shall we sing the Lord's song in a strange land?" At the church of St. Pierre, we saw the last and greatest piece of Rubens—the crucifixion of St. Peter, represented with his head downward, and his crucifiers in the act of nailing him to the cross. Oh! it is a masterly piece, and he might well lay his easel by. We left Cologne for Bonn, the distance about fifteen miles, and the famed seat of one of the Universities.

The next day we started for the passage up the Rhine. I had heard and read so much of the scenery of the Rhine, that for the first fifteen miles I was disappointed. But the disappointment soon gave way to admiration—luxuriant vines, mountain piled upon mountain, rocks in exquisite confusion kissing the very clouds, and on the topmost summits ancient castles frowning upon the plain below, here and there a distant village, as the mountain gradually sloped away. We reached Coblentz about seven in the evening, and resumed our voyage the next morning for Mayence, where we took a post-chaise for Frankfort-on-the-Main, which we reached about noon, and where we were glad to enjoy the repose of the Sabbath. Here we found our old friends, Mr. Wolffe and family, and passed a pleasant evening with them. We left Frankfort for Darmstadt and Heidelberg, where I had valuable letters to one of the theological professors. From Heidelberg we went to Carlsruhe, where we spent the night; the next morning we started for Basle in Switzerland, through Berne to Geneva. We found the city very full, it being the centennial celebration of the arrival of Calvin after he was driven out of France. We spent several days here on the borders of the Lake Leman, and under the shadow of Mont-Blanc, and amid the instructive ministrations of the Geneva pulpit. We passed up the valley of the

Chamounie to Mont-Blanc, charmed by its beauty, and wrapt by its wonders. We returned to Geneva on Saturday, heard Dr. Malan on the Sabbath, and on Monday left for Lyons. Here we were entire strangers. I knew there was an American Christian lady buried there, the wife of James Brown, Esq., of New York, at whose request I visited and repaired her dilapidated grave. A large willow weeps over her dust, and she sleeps as sweetly there, and as near to heaven, as she would have slept beneath her native land. We left Lyons for Chalons. It is the grape-harvest in France, and it is a joyous sight. We spent a Sabbath in Chalons, heard a sermon in French, and on Monday, Tuesday, and Wednesday pursued our way without much rest, till we were once more in Paris. We were welcomed by our American friends, who met us most joyfully, and we all had quite a jolly time of it at a social dinner in the Café de Paris. In this city we spent the Sabbath, in the morning hearing Mr. Grandpierre, and in the evening our excellent countryman, Dr. Robert Baird. We employed several days in shopping and visiting. We left Paris for London, thence for Liverpool, where Mr. and Mrs. Brown received us with their wonted kindness, where we spent the Sabbath, and where I was for the first and last time the hearer of the lamented Raffles. We did not leave Liverpool until the following Friday.

Farewell to Europe! Some painful, but many more delightful memories are associated with this pleasant and instructive tour. When I left England, there were about five thousand evangelical clergymen in the Established church. Better and more devoted men than some of these I never expect to see this side the Celestial City.

But there are evils in the churches of England, and not those of the Establishment only, but in all denominations of Christians, which I fear will be cured only by the slow and heavy progress of time. Could the mass of British preachers and British Christians be diffused throughout the American churches for a single year; could they inspect the peculiar framework of human society in the Western world; could they witness the *kind* of religion which prevails, especially in many sections of this fair land; could they stand still and see the salvation of God as it has been displayed abroad for ten years past before this youthful people; while they would find much to rectify, much to censure, much to lament, they would also find much to admire, and not a little which they would cheerfully imbibe and imitate. I have often said, would that multitudes of those godly men and godly women who have stood so long the brightest ornaments of Old England, and through whose prayers and piety she has survived the rude shocks that have assailed her, could be transported to these shores, and be the eye-witnesses of what God has wrought in this highly-favored, though in some respects misguided, country, and then return with all the spoils of their observation and experience, to enrich their native and much-loved land!

I need not say that the United States have been sufficiently slandered by English travellers. Aside from a series of well-digested letters, which were written by Mr. Hodgdon, of Liverpool, almost every page which I have had the opportunity to read on this subject, from the pen of Englishmen, is foul slander. Not many years since, at New Haven, I fell in with a masterly work, said to have been written by the late President Dwight, which I could not help wishing might come in the way of several of the travellers and literary journalists who, either from ignorance, thoughtlessness, or depravity, have caricatured and abused the American people. The work to which I refer is entitled, "Remarks on the Review of Inchiquin's Letters, by an inhabitant of New England," in which this writer deprecates, with characteristic severity, the ungenerous efforts to alienate countries that are naturally friends.

Old England, distinguished as it is for the beauty of its scenery and fertility of its soil; for the freedom and firmness of its civil and religious institutions; for its wealth and influence, its honor and arms; and preëminent as it is in talent and genius, in learning and piety; is but a small part of the terraqueous globe. It is well for a man to creep out of the pinhole of his early associations and spheres of action, if it were for nothing else than to learn that he himself is smaller, and the world larger, than he had supposed them to be. After having traversed the immense waters which separate the Old World from the New, after having surveyed mountains and valleys, lakes and rivers, cities and villages, states, churches, and men, scattered over this vast territory, it is very possible he may have conceptions of the magnificence of the world he inhabits, to which he has been hitherto a stranger. He may perhaps feel as a very little thing, while at the same time his heart is enlarged, his thoughts expand, and in every progressive discovery he sees new motives for admiration and praise.

Among my loose papers relating to foreign travel, I find the following, by whom written I know not:

"It has been my privilege to occupy the past ten years in the cities and villages of the United States extending from the Potomac on the south, to the Lakes and St. Lawrence on the north. Here I have formed connections which will remain as long as I am permitted to dwell among men; here I have become interested in the growing plans of Christian benevolence in which America seems destined to bear by no means an ordinary part; and here I have been permitted by the constituted authorities of the Church of God, to become a minister of the everlasting Gospel, and to testify to my fallen and dying fellow-men the unsearchable riches of Jesus Christ.

"I was led to this country by a singular incident. In the autumn of 1822, I was present at an evening service in the Methodist church in Colchester, in the County of Essex, where I understood an American clergyman, the Rev. Mr. Spring, of New York, was requested to present some narrative of the recent revivals of religion in the American churches. The house was full, and I was deeply interested in the exercises of the evening. Before the service I had procured an introduction to the preacher, and was prepared to listen with perfect confidence, and even partiality, to his statements. I had formed an early desire to become acquainted with the state of religion in the New World, and this opportunity only confirmed it. The following morning, in company with Mr. Spring, I took breakfast with the Rev. Mr. Marsh, of the Established church; held much conversation with him about the religious and moral condition of France, and also hinted my design of visiting America. In the course of the morning I accompanied the American preacher to the Castle, St. John's Abbey, St. Butolph's Priory, and accepted an invitation to dine with him at the house of the Rev. Mr. Saville, the minister of the dissenting congregation. Here I also hinted my purpose of going to America, and was heartily cheered in my project. In the evening of the same day I had the pleasure of meeting a party of ladies, at the request of a lady who was the Superintendent of a female school, where I also met the gentleman from America, who was desired to attend a religious meeting with some of the young ladies of the school. I was interested in the meeting, and before the night passed away, formed a definite purpose to cross the Atlantic, as soon as I could make preparations for so long an absence as I intended."

My *third* voyage to the other side of the Atlantic was made merely for the sake of rest, and the benefit of the sea-air. My congregation had, from the first, granted me six Sabbaths' furlough during midsummer, and I resolved to employ these weeks of relaxation on the ocean. Six Sabbaths would give me almost seven weeks of absence, and I engaged my passage on board the ship Ashburton, belonging to Messrs. Grinnell &

Co., R. L. Bunting, master. I preferred a sailing ship to a steamer, because it was less expensive, and a longer passage. By taking the steamer on my return, I hoped to be in my place without loss to my people of a single expected service. I engaged my passage, and a state-room " a little abaft midships, and on the starboard quarter." I am told that this entry was not a little to the amusement of the owners, more especially when they found that instead of coming from an "old salt," it was from the Rev. Dr. Spring. The voyage was an exceedingly pleasant one. Capt. Bunting, the first officer, and all the crew, did all in their power to serve me; we had religious services on board; I had my morning bath in the salt water; my daily exercise at the rigging, and tried my hand in keeping the *reckoning* of the ship. I instructed the seamen, and distributed religious tracts, not only without obstruction, but with their hearty concurrence; and when I left the ship, I am satisfied that I had the good-will of all hands. I left the ship in the Irish Channel; it was in a violent thunder-storm; the wind ahead; and I feared it would be some time before she would reach Liverpool. There was a large fishing-boat that came alongside while the ship was *in stays*, and I gave the man a guinea to take me ashore. He was true to his charge, and in less than an hour I was on the Emerald Isle, alone, a stranger in a strange land. It was at noon on Saturday, and I made for the nearest town, Waterford, six *Irish* miles distant, where I might " rest on the Sabbath-day, according to the commandment." Early on Monday morning I started for Dublin, where I remained but a single day, and whence I took the steamer for Liverpool. In Liverpool I remained but three days, calling upon no individual except the Rev. Dr. Raffles. On the fifth day after my landing in Ireland, I took the steamer for New York; arrived at Jersey City about 10 o'clock on Saturday morning, and was in my pulpit the next day, without the loss of a day beyond my time.

My health was greatly benefited by this voyage, my nervous energy was invigorated, and I had courage for my work. I have often asked myself, What has become of that company of noble seamen? Two of them, the captain and the first officer, I know, have passed from time to eternity. The ship's crew, where are they? Gone, probably, all gone! It is a satisfaction to me to know that I had personally their confidence, and had proclaimed to these hardy sons of the ocean the way of life through Jesus Christ. Mr. Williamson, the first officer, whose physical frame seemed impervious to all disease, died but a few years since. Capt. Bunting sickened and died in New York, but a short distance from my own residence. Mrs. Bunting was a member of the Presbyterian church in Rutgers-street, and on their removal to the upper part of the city, became a member of my own pastoral charge. She is living still, and a very lovely Christian woman. She took great interest in her husband's religious character, before his sickness. One evening, on ship-board, I saw him reading the Bible. "Dr. Spring, my wife and I are reading this chapter together this evening." "How is that? She is in New York, and you are here, on board the Ashburton." "Why, sir," said he, "before I left home we made a selection of chapters, and engaged to read the same chapter on the same evening; and she is now reading the same chapter." "Oh," said I, " Capt. Bunting, that is *beautiful, most beautiful!* God is now speaking to you both, at the same time, and in the same words, and you are thus holding sweet communion with one another." " Yes," he replied, " and we have marked out the chapters for every day for the whole voyage." Capt. Bunting, before he died, I trust became a true Christian. His sickness was prolonged many weeks. I often saw him, and saw him at peace with God, through our Lord Jesus Christ. He had never been baptized, and I baptized him a few weeks before his death. He did not live to commune with us; but on my report to the Session of the state of his mind, he was received, and died a member of Christ's visible church. Oh, what sweet influences a truly Christian wife can exert on the character and destiny of the husband she loves! The social affections are among the most winning and attractive means of grace and salvation. When Andrew had become a follower of Jesus, the first thing he did was to make the Saviour known to his own household. " He *first* findeth *his own brother*, Simon, and saith unto him, we *have found the Messias*, which is being interpreted the Christ." The discovery was too valuable to be preserved in silence, within his own bosom. " Out of the abundance of the heart the mouth speaketh." He would not eat his morsel alone. It was glad tidings of great joy, and he would proclaim them. They spread like the electric fire, from the family, through the *" city* of Simon and Peter." Philip findeth Nathaniel, and saith unto him, "We have *found him* of whom Moses in the law and the prophets did write, Jesus of Nazareth, the son of Joseph."

These three voyages across the Atlantic were of great service to me in more respects than one. They made me acquainted with men of eminence, godly men, men of cultivated minds and large hearts, and opened a correspondence which resulted in lasting benefit. I was not a stranger to the sea; I had in my early days made two voyages to the Island of Bermuda, and now greatly enjoyed the ocean. The iodine of the sea was what I needed. And the lessons of the sea, oh, how full of God! How it speaks for God! I never felt the beauty and sublimity of those many declarations of the Bible where the glory of Him who "maketh the clouds his chariot and rideth upon the wind," who hath "measured the waters in the hollow of his hand, and meted out heaven with a span," until I was on the ocean. I was a spectator of the scene of which the prophet Habakkuk says, "the deep uttered his voice and lifted up his hands on high." That voice of storms must be heard on the wide waters, and those ocean billows, lifting up their hands, must be seen in order to be felt. They are scenes which to the present hour stand out before my imagination, and never will be forgotten. I have more than once been lashed to the taff-rail, that I might not lose sight of them. There is power, there is eternity, there is the immensity of the Godhead in the ocean, unbounded, bottomless, immeasurable, encompassing the earth on every side, underneath it, cementing and holding it together. I love to look at the spacious firmament and the shining heavens; but nowhere do these bright lights, so richly scattered by the hand of God through the vast expanse, display such illuminated magnificence and beauty as when gazed at from the placid bosom of the ocean. Oh, it is grand! It brings the Eternal One, the living and true God, surprisingly near. The universe subsists in him, as in a boundless ocean. The fishes of the sea are not so truly encompassed by the deep waters, as are all creatures by the omnipresent Deity.

There is one thought on this general topic which may be worthy of the consideration of the Christian geologist. I say *Christian* geologist, because I have nothing to do with that class of geologists which set the discoveries of natural science above the Mosaic record. It is a conceded fact that the ocean surrounds the earth on all sides. The Pacific, the Atlantic, the Northern, Southern, and Indian oceans, constitute but one immense sheet of waters, occupying a space on the surface of the globe at least three times greater than that which is occupied by the land. According to the latest computations, the whole surface of the earth, including land and water, comprehends an area of 197,552,160 miles. The ocean occupies two thirds of this surface. The great objection of modern geologists to the Mosaic record is, that the geological formations which prepared this globe for the reception of man, antedate the epoch of its creation, as given by Moses. The effects of the Deluge, it is affirmed, cannot account for these formations. They must be traced to geological movements far back of "the beginning," according to the received chronology. Though not altogether unacquainted with the subject, I confess to no small measure of ignorance of the great results which have arisen from the operations of geological laws. This one fact I well know, that geological formations are more or less rapid in proportion to the degree of heat or cold to which they are subjected. This earth, "standing in the water and out of the water," is surrounded on all sides by a sheet of water three times greater than the land itself, where these geological formations are going on. The problem, which has not to my knowledge been solved by modern geology, is, What length of time is occupied in these geological formations under the combined action of fire and water? The smith whirls his wheel, iron-bound and red hot, two thirds under water, and in a few moments it becomes cool; the geological formation is perfect. Why is it not thus with the geological formation of this earth, heated as it is in its internal strata, and cooled as it is by being thus inundated with water? Or does it require unknown centuries back of the Mosaic record to perfect its most ancient geological formation? "Who is this that darkeneth counsel by words without knowledge? Where wast thou when I laid the foundations of the earth? Declare, if thou hast understanding, who laid the measures thereof, if thou knowest? or who hath stretched out the line upon it? Whereupon are the foundations thereof fastened? or who hath laid the corner-stone thereof?"

CHAPTER VII.

THE SABBATH REFORM.

As has been intimated in a preceding chapter, I was early taught to "remember the Sabbath-day and keep it holy." I never can be sufficiently thankful for this early training. In a volume entitled "The obligations of the world to the Bible," there is a chapter in relation to the influence of the Sabbath; and in a subsequent volume, entitled "First Things," there is a chapter on the First Sabbath; in both of which my convictions of the value of this sacred day are expressed much better than I can now express them. When I first came to New York, Sabbath desecration was by no means so flagrant as it became at a later period. Carriages and carts were not allowed to run wild by our churches; an iron chain was stretched across Nassau and Beekman-streets in order to protect the church, at whose altars I served, in the quiet enjoyment of its religious services. There were not wanting those who complained of this restriction as an infringement of their liberty; but the leading minds of our fellow-citizens strongly favored a decent observance of the Lord's day. Their avowal was frank and open, that while they would impose no legal restraint on those who neglected the house of God, they insisted upon the right of legal protection in their own religious worship.

But the men and the times changed; a stream of corruption set in, which bore down the protecting barrier to which allusion has been made, and which threatened to inundate the city. In the year 1827, when the lamented Stephen Allen was Mayor, and magisterial integrity and authority were not without their influence, I preached in his hearing five discourses upon the obligations of the Sabbath. The first was upon the divine institution and the perpetuity of this day of rest; the second was upon the change of the day and the time of commencing it; the third was upon the manner in which it ought to be observed; the fourth was upon its prevalent desecration; the object of the fifth was to show that the Sabbath is a blessing to mankind. In this last discourse Mr. Allen took so deep an interest, that he sent me a kind note, requesting that it might be published. It was published, and received with favor. I was greatly encouraged by the countenance and support which Mr. Allen gave to my humble efforts, and I had a private interview with him at his residence in Beekman-street, with the view of enlisting him in some general effort for Sabbath reform. Nor was he slow of heart in acquiescing, but engaged to preside at a public meeting of the citizens in the City Hall, summoned through the daily press, for the consideration of this important subject. I was warmly zealous in the cause, and felt that the friends of the Sabbath were able so to present its claims, that even its enemies could no longer resist them. The meeting was called; able speakers, both clergymen and laymen, saw the importance of the discussion, and the city was in a glow of excitement. But long before the appointed time, the place of meeting was *preoccupied* by those who had taken the alarm at this supposed, and clerical, invasion of their civil rights. Mr. Allen did not come to the meeting, and, as I afterwards learned, for the best of all reasons. Peter Radcliff, Esq., a firm friend of the Sabbath, and General Bogardus, presided, and with the sole view of tranquilizing the popular excitement, and protecting the abettors of the movement.

It was not without difficulty that we got into the Hall; our friends earnestly entreated me not to attempt it. Those on whom we relied to advocate our cause, one after another deserted us, and the Rev. Alexander McLeland and myself were left alone, of the ministers of the Gospel, to face the storm. We forced our way through the crowd, and found ourselves in the midst of an indignant assemblage, passing resolutions *requesting the ministers to mind their own business.* We were marked men. The excited multitude looked daggers at us. They would not listen to us. Our persons were in danger, and we left the Hall without the opportunity even of bearing our testimony for God and the Sabbath. There was more zeal than wisdom in this movement. It was a failure.

Other efforts were made, but without success. There were frequent conferences among the friends of the Sabbath; the difficulties to be encountered were great, and no organized effort of a permanent character was made until the spring of 1857. It was a wise thought, that if a successful effort were made to arrest the evil, it must be in the hands of *Christian laymen*, men of character and standing in the city, of all religious denominations, and whose efforts would be unembarrassed by the prejudice against clerical interference. Isolated effort could accomplish little. Even the most glaring Sabbath nuisances could not be abated, while the abettors of these efforts met a storm of reproach from the press.

On the first of April, 1857, at a large meeting of Christian citizens, a "Committee to promote the better observance of the Sabbath" was appointed, who were connected with eight Christian denominations, and of which Norman White, Esq., the leading spirit in this enterprise, the unwearied laborer, was the chairman. The church of God in this city, in this and other lands, the bar, pulpit, and our courts of justice, are under great obligations to the Sabbath Committee. They began their work by an investigation of the *extent* of Sabbath desecration. They found that nearly *ten thousand places of business*, including more than *five thousand dram-shops*, were open to the public on the Lord's day; and that thousands of men, women, and children were gathered on that day, in the different places of public amusement, "for the purpose of diversion, dissipation, and sin." In one of their documents, that Committee say: "These evils have existed so long almost without rebuke, they were so entrenched in the avarice of some classes, and in the love of sensual pleasure in others; they were so strengthened by Old-World training and prejudice, and were pandered to so industriously by the German and English Sunday press; and ignorance or indifference as to their nature and extent were so profound on the part of the Sabbath-keeping community, that exposure and reformation seemed to border on the chimerical, if not the impossible."

Yet under all these disheartening circumstances, they persevered in their work. As the chairman remarked at the National Sabbath Convention at Saratoga: "We are only upon the threshold; it is a life-long work." The subject enlisted the pulpit, the press, and personal influence. The daily press, "without fee or reward," was their ablest and most effective advocate. Party politics, personal abuse, theological differences, varying views of church polity, they have not cared for; nothing has so absorbed them as the onward movement of this great enterprise. They have carried it into railroads, into Congress, into the army and navy. Nor have they labored in vain. They have suppressed the vociferous cries of the Sunday newsboys, that offence against public peace and order, and nuisance to our religious community, and they have done it in defiance of the most violent ribaldry and abuse. They have suppressed the Sunday pageant of the fire department, so that it has fallen into disuse under the weight of its own folly. They have rectified the abuses of the Sabbath in the Central Park. They have suppressed the Sunday liquor traffic, so vast in its extent, so lawless, and so productive of pauperism and crime, and driven it into corners. They have suppressed the Sunday theatres and beer gardens, and the Sunday concerts of the German population, where crowds of all ages and both sexes assembled for purposes of varied and degrading wickedness. They have done much to protect the sanctity of the Sabbath amid the horrors of the late civil war, to promote its observance in the army, and to secure God's blessing upon our arms. They have given a fresh impulse to the pulpit, and able discussions and stirring appeals from the ministers of the Gospel have diffused light and stimulated effort throughout the land, for the more sacred observance of this day of the Son of Man. They have carried the reform into our canals, our steamboats, our flouring establishments, our salt establishments, our fisheries, and originated Sabbath Associations in foreign lands, with the promise of fruitful results.

It is a glorious work which this committee has performed, if it were only to call up the attention of the churches and the nation to the moral power of the Sabbath in preserving and perpetuating our religious and civil liberties. No nation can live and prosper without the Sabbath. Their observance of the Sabbath is the index of their morality, their religion, and their prosperity. A nation, a city, a family, that tramples upon the law of the Sabbath, tramples upon every other law. They become practical atheists, and say unto God, "Depart from us, for we desire not the knowledge of thy ways." A Sabbath-breaking man, a Sabbath-breaking community, is an ungodly man, an ungodly community, and leads an ungodly life. To violate it is to invade the rights of God the Creator, God the lawgiver, God the preserver, God the Redeemer, God the judge. Men have their rights, which God gave them; but they have no right to do wrong—no right to violate the fourth commandment. God never gave it to them, and if they presumptuously assume it, he will make them the losers. God gave them the Sabbath as a nucleus of unnumbered blessings, as the *envelope* which wraps up all the means of grace and salvation; nor is there any duty more incumbent upon human governments, than to guard this sacred deposit, given alike to the rich and the poor, to man and to beast. This is God's arrangement, and woe be to the people that violate it. *Hooker* made the declaration, "We are to account the sanctification of one day in seven a duty which God's immutable law doth exact forever." *La Place* said, just before his death, "I have lived long enough to know what, at one time, I did not believe, that no society can be upheld in happiness and honor, without the sentiments of religion." *Adam Smith* expressed the sentiment that "the Sabbath, as a political institution, is of inestimable value, independently of its claim to Divine authority." *Coleridge* remarked, "I feel as if God had, by giving the Sabbath, given fifty-two springs in the year." *Isaac Taylor* affirmed, that "a Sunday given to the soul, is the best of all means of refreshment to the mere intellect." The great *Blackstone* declared that "a corruption of morals usually follows the profanation of the Sabbath." *Montalembert* expressed his conviction that "there is no religion without worship, and no worship without the Sabbath." Lord *Macaulay* said, "If Sunday had not been observed as a day of rest during the last three centuries, I have not the smallest doubt that we should have been at this moment a poorer and less civilized people than we are." *Edmund Burke* said, "They who always labor can have no true judgment; they exhaust their attention, burn out their candles, and are left in the dark." Archbishop *Leighton* said, "The very life of religion doth much depend upon the solemn observance of the Sabbath; consider, if we should but intermit the keeping of it for one year, what a height of profaneness would ensue in those that fear not God." *Walter Scott* said, "Give to the world one half of Sunday, and you will find that religion has no strong hold of the other." Sir *Matthew Hale* declared, that "the more faithfully he applied himself to the duties of the Lord's day, the more happy and successful was his business during the week." These thoughts do but give emphasis to the Saviour's declaration, that "the Sabbath was made for man;" appointed for hallowed and benevolent ends, fitted to man's nature, necessary to his physical, intellectual, moral, and immortal well-being, and pointing as with the finger of its Divine Author to the "rest that remaineth for the people of God." Next to the unspeakable gift of his Son, is the gift of his Sabbath. His Word would have been disregarded, but for the Sabbath; but for the Sabbath, his church would have had no place among men, or had been a disfranchised exile in a strange land. I rejoice to have lived to see the "Sabbath Reform." I know that it is a "life-long work," but its results are not doubtful. The language of him who is the Lord of the Sabbath-day, to the laborious and honored committee who are so successfully extending it, is, "The Lord is with you, if ye be with him." His promise is sure, that "it shall come to pass that from one new moon to another, and from one Sabbath to another, shall all flesh come to worship before him."

CHAPTER VIII.

MARY NORRIS, OUR ELDEST DAUGHTER.

THERE is one name in a preceding enumeration of our beloved children, that deserves more than a bare inscription on these pages: the name of our departed daughter, Mary Norris, the wife of Johnson P. Lee. She was well known in this community, and, to some extent, her womanly bearing and her gentle, active Christianity. I make the following extracts from her journal:

July 1st, 1837.—I have left my father's house, and am quietly located in Franklin House. What can I do for God and the souls of men here? Very little, except by my prayers and example; watchful, lest the latter do more harm than good. Day before yesterday was the anniversary of our marriage. Seven years! It seems a brief dream. A review of God's mercy to us melted my heart. I had a precious season of prayer with and for my husband.

Sabbath evening, July 2d.—What a vile, guilty heart is this! so full of spiritual pride, thinking myself something when I am nothing. At church this morning, and especially while walking home, a flash of light, I believe from the Spirit of God, showed me the depravity and vileness of my heart to a dreadful degree. I saw a selfishness, a pride, an envy, in the state of my mind for the last few weeks, that surprised and shocked me. Indeed, every hellish passion seemed to have a resting-place in my heart, and I knew it not. How have I deceived myself and others! I have wished to be an idol—to be bowed down to and worshipped. I would appropriate to myself all the love and esteem of the good and great, and because I do not receive it, consider myself wronged. Wretched one that I am! These sins, they must be crucified. How shall they be slain? I can only go and say, "Lord, if thou wilt, thou canst make clean." Yes, let them be slain in *any way*, by suffering, by shame, by poverty, by disappointment, rather than they should still live in my heart. Oh! this weary conflict! Shall I ever hold out to the end? I feel the blighting, withering influence of sin. The valley of weeping is my place, not the top of Pisgah. I am sad—unusually sad. I have great fears lest I am deceiving myself with vain hopes, and lest all my prayers and duties are performed to keep up the delusion. There is one Being who knows, and to Him will I go; and though all my past hopes may have been delusion, yet will I ask grace to live to his glory, and leave my soul in his hands.

Monday morning.—My mind is in a strange state at times, dead and cold to spiritual things, and then, again, the fire of love is enkindled, prayer and praise flow spontaneously, and then a stupor seizes me, and I can neither think, nor pray, nor sing. This state of mind distresses me. Do I possess any portion of the spirit of the Gospel? It may be, in some small degree; but it is very small. Blessed Saviour! if thou hold me up, I shall be safe. I have no life but in thee.

Monday.—Some sweet, precious hours alone this morning. My hour for Zion is becoming my most precious hour. There I can pour forth all the best affections of my soul without fear or reserve; for I know that when the Lord builds up Zion, he appears in his glory. Felt some sinking of heart this morning, for the first time, at the prospect of poverty; but all vanished at the mercy-seat. All is sunshine when God is on the throne. How precious is the Word of God! I never enjoyed it as I do now.

Wednesday.—Father gave me some of his mother's letters. I have been reading them with great interest. Everything from grandmother's pen touches my heart. If she were alive now, I think I should profit by her counsel and prayers. But I would not call her back to this cold, sinning world. And in that blessed world are my beloved children, too. Does she not know and love them? and sweet Hannah, and Sarah, and Julia, and some of her own? is she not happy now? When shall I join their songs?

Monday, October, 1837.—How fearful is this conflict with Satan and my inbred sin? I seem to see him, to hear him, and am almost tempted to feel that it is useless to contend with him. And my Saviour hides his face, and seems to leave me alone. Yet he will not leave me; has he not promised? I shall perish, and that justly, if his arm does not hold me back.

Sabbath evening, October, 1837.—The enemy has been aiming all his arrows at me to-day. The conflict has been fearful, but he has not prevailed to drive my heart from God, though he has driven me from the mercy-seat again and again. When I have bowed my knees, and begun to lift my voice in prayer, such floods of sinful thought have overwhelmed me, that I have risen in haste, and felt that I was mocking God. Again and again would I return, and still he prevailed against me. I never felt so truly another law in my members warring against the law of my mind, and that it was no more I, but sin that dwelleth in me. I took to the Ceylon school; I prayed for others, but my heart was stone. Yet I did not yield. I walked the floor a long time, and gained some glimpse of my Saviour's face. He will not cast me off forever. Rejoice not against me, O mine enemy! When I fall, I shall rise again; when I walk in darkness, the Lord shall be a light unto me.

February 28th, 1838.—It is now three months since I have been able to write in my journal. Amid all changes, goodness and mercy have followed me. I have enjoyed much peace of mind. We have had some special meetings in our church, and in the various churches of the Presbytery, and some tokens of the presence of God with us.

Monday morning.—Can it be, that such a sinner as I, does indeed enjoy so much of the light of God's countenance? My soul has been full to overflowing. Everything is full of joy. Prayer, the Word of God, the ordinances of his house, all, even my temporal mercies, the light of the sun, food, rest, friends, all seem so many streams of pure joy from the fountain of everlasting bliss. My Saviour says, "He that drinketh of the water that I shall give him, shall never thirst; but it shall be in him a well of water, springing up to everlasting life." The morning service yesterday was one of the best I ever heard. It was on the text, "Hath not God made foolish the wisdom of this world?" I thought I knew something about the Bible before; but I came home oppressed with my ignorance. I took it into my hands, and was so affected, that, for a time, I could not read. What a mine of truth and knowledge! what an ocean of love!

Friday morning.—Weak and feeble in body—a precious day, and the adversary is fled. The bed of sickness is almost always to me a pleasant spot, so that I rather covet than dread it.

Wednesday, May, 1838.—The adversary has been trying to shake my faith in everything. He first tried to distress me in regard to my temporal necessities,

When I told him that He who had given the best, will not withhold the meanest gifts, he whispered, He never has given you the best; you have the form of godliness, but not the power. I could only say, Well, if it be so, He can give now, and will do so to all who ask. But the tempter would not cease thus. How, said he, do you *know* there is any God, any Saviour, any Holy Spirit? This religion is all a delusion, a dream. I could only cry out, Ah! Lord, if the foundations be destroyed, what can the righteous do? Thou must fight for me. I wept till I was almost exhausted. I could not pray in *words*, but my heart prayed in groanings that could not be uttered. I read the tenth chapter of John, and in it heard my Saviour's voice.

Friday noon.—Our social prayer-meeting. Conversed about the "prayer of faith." I think there has been much error on this subject in the minds of a certain class of Christians. Not that we can have too much faith in God's promises; but we may have too much in our own *impressions.* God will give all that is *consistent with his glory.* I may be led astray; for I am in great danger from my old enemy, spiritual pride. Oh! when, when shall *self* be slain.

Evening.—I have feared lest darkness and apathy should again enshroud my mind. But light and joy beam upon me, and my cup runneth over. Everything around me is full of beauty—full of God. I almost fear to yield to the luxury of these moments, lest they should be delusions; yet I cling to them, and know I cannot work them up in my own mind. They are God's gift, and I may gratefully enjoy them. Saw Mrs. Knox a few moments; she is still in the land of Beulah.

January 11*th*, 1840.—The shadow of a great rock in a weary land. Thither I flee; if I perish, I perish there. Though all other graces seem dead, or dying, *faith lives*, hoping against hope, and is, I think, the stronger for all the efforts of the adversary to induce despair. Skeptical thoughts—when shall I be rid of them?

New Brighton, April 22*d*, 1845.—Still suffer from my attacks of chronic disease. Everything is pleasant here, yet I am often cast down, and my poor body and more burdened heart complain,

"I am weary, my father, of grieving thy love;
Oh! when shall I rest in thy bosom above!
I am weary, but oh! let me never repine,
While thy word, and thy love, and thy promise are mine."

October 13*th.*—Once more in New York. I have an *abode* now; I cannot call anything but heaven *home*. The past season has been one of pain, debility, and sickness nigh unto death. But,

" Strength is promised, strength is given,
When the heart by God is riven."

I am not grateful as I ought to be for prolonged life. *Sinfully*, I fear, I have longed to depart. But my kind and gracious Refiner still keeps me in the furnace, till my own will shall be wholly lost in his. I find it good to be brought low. When I can lie at Jesus' feet, and feel that he takes me to his bosom, oh! it is all, one such hour. To feel that others are called *to do*, while my vocation is *to suffer*—yet I can only say, Here am I, Lord; use me as thou wilt.

Friday, 30*th.*—I fear I sin by these earnest longings to depart and be with Christ; but at times it seems impossible to repress them. I have lately been so distressed with fears of the power and malice of Satan, and with such a sense of my own weakness, that I cannot but dread life. Dear Saviour! it cannot glorify thee that I should fall and wander; gather me safely into thy fold. Thy arms were around me this morning, and I wanted to die there. Here, in this world, everything is full of danger.

Union Square, *August*, 1847.—Am I not soon to be called home? Can this poor frame last much longer? And if not, am I ready? It is easy to talk of death with calmness when he is distant; but if he really comes to-night, can I meet him without fear? If death were the only messenger that calls me, I shall shrink; but if my loving Saviour " comes again to take me unto himself, that where he is, I may be also," I shall see no enemy, but the friend, loved and longed for. Saviour of *sinners!* Adorable name! Oh! my soul clings to it as my hope, my joy. If ever I attain to the piety of the early Christians, it must be by saying with them, " *We have known and believed the love that God hath to us.*"

November 22d, 1848.—I am waiting, with extreme anxiety, the tidings from Bombay, with little reason to hope that G. B. is still living; and, indeed, scarcely knowing what to desire. I would prove the sincerity of my friendship for him, by love and prayer for the heathen, whom he loved. I am quite giving up letter-writing, though I regret to do so. It sometimes seems mysterious that I should still be kept in this half-way existence, between life and death. Yet I know He is not frustrating his own work, but by this discipline is fitting me for future work, either on earth or in heaven. At times I can, indeed, be "joyful in tribulation."

Sabbath, December 17th.—My beloved husband's birthday. Oh, that I could obtain for him the gift of the Holy Spirit! He has gone to church, and I cannot but hope, that in this day of God's power, the work may reach his heart. Father mentioned to me, a few days ago, the subject of this day's sermon, and it is peculiarly applicable to him. Oh, that while my husband is listening, I may wrestle, like Jacob, and prevail, like Israel, though I go "halting" to my grave! I did plead for him; yet when he came from church, he was unmoved. He spoke of the sermon as remarkably fine; but oh, that was all!

Sabbath, December 31st, 1848.—Near midnight. I am thankful that I am able to be up, and alone, at this solemn hour, when the Old Year is passing away, and the New is coming in. The girls have gone to their "watch-night," and I wish to end and begin the year in prayer. Oh, that it may be a year of the right hand of the Most High! Whether it will be to me a year of sickness or health, pain or relief, life or death, prosperity or adversity, God will control every event, and make all things work together for good to them that love him.

> "Why should the children of a King
> Go mourning all their days?"

I would praise Him. Praise, praise Him, all ye people! I go to His throne, that these last and first moments may be employed in praising Him. Let the chain that binds the old and new year be kept bright by prayer and praise! The name of Jesus is a "thing of beauty and a joy forever." I begin another year, but I am weary of wandering, and still shrink from the snares and dangers that may be before me in a longer sojourn in the wilderness.

Monday, September 2d, 1850.—Yesterday was mother's and Dr. Edward's birthday. And shall we not rejoice for dear Edward, that prayer is no longer needed for him? Could I forget, on this day, the past season, when, fearing lest God had left him, we united our entreaties, with fasting and tears, on the return of his birthday, that, whatever it might cost of temporal weal, he might be saved from eternal death? And now that we can joyfully celebrate his new birth, and his reception into the glorified family above, may we not take courage and hope for the rest? The family are scattered: father and mother at Newport, and A. and A. G. and M. at Fire Island. I am anxious about Mr. Lee's decision as to business. He thinks seriously of going to California. I dare not advise. I am willing to go, if God directs our way. I know well that wherever he guides us we shall find peace, though we may meet with trials. If He would permit us to do something for his cause there, I would gladly go. Yet on some accounts it is very difficult to know the path of duty, and alas! I am not living so near to God as to be quick to discern the guidance of his eye. My Heavenly Father knows that I have begged and do beg him not to grant a single earthly good which he sees would be unsafe for us.

Sabbath, 29th.—On this bright and beautiful Sabbath morning, surely my Gracious Father will draw near to me. The spirit of grace and supplication I need more than all. Oh, prayer is not with me what it once was. Alas! that I must *look back*, instead of forgetting the things that are behind, and pressing forward! O my Saviour! let me not live to wander from thee! And to-day hear my feeble prayer for the gift of thy promised Spirit to the church and the world, that thy power may be made known, and thy name honored. When, when shall thy Kingdom come?

Monday, September 30th.—My fortieth birthday. Can it be that so much of my life is gone? And alas! to how little good purpose! Never did outward events and inward wants call upon me more earnestly to cry mightily unto my beneficent Father, the God of all grace, to bestow upon me a double portion of his Spirit. O my Father! again and again must I reiterate the cry, "If thy Spirit go not with me, carry me not up hence." Suffer me not to enter upon the new duties and trials that are before me, alone, without Thy constant presence and aid. Remember Thy word unto Thy servant, on which Thou hast caused her to hope. Oh, let this new year of my life begin with a new baptism of the Holy Ghost! I would be Thine, Thine alone, henceforth and forever. And oh, my gracious God! have I no record of thanksgiving for all Thy mercies? What shall I say when I contrast this day with the many days of bodily pain and anguish and seclusion that are past? Help me, O thou Giver of every good gift, to feel and testify my gratitude for Thy healing, restoring mercy. Oh, wretched one that I am, when shall I be delivered from the power of sin? This peevish, impatient spirit, I am ashamed of it, yet do not amend. If I were living daily in closer communion with Jesus, I should possess and manifest more of his meek, lowly, gentle, and loving spirit. My heart is sad and discouraged to-day. I feel that I need purifying in the furnace, ere I am meet for the inheritance of the saints in light; and yet I cry, oh, take me home, safe and sheltered from these foes without and fightings within! My kind, my patient Saviour! I come to thee. To whom else shall I go? Mystery of infinite love! my beloved is mine, and I am his.

Sabbath evening, October 13*th.*—" My sheep hear my voice, and I know them, and they follow me." This was the subject of the sermon this morning. Instructive and comforting as were all the services, my own heart did not respond with that warmth and fervor which I long for. To-day is the anniversary of my first communion, 19 years ago. And now all my dear sisters are gathered into the fold. Truly I can sing of mercies, abounding mercies, as I review these years. Dear mother was not with us to-day. I fear she may not be well again. When the ingathering of a family into our heavenly home *is begun*, surely we should look upon each other as more dear, more lovely. *One* is not, and all are advancing. Let us anticipate that blessed hour. But oh, my heart yearns over my *best beloved*, that he should still stay away. I must still hope, still ask.

Sabbath, November 3d.—Oh, the wonders of that love! Shall I not " take with me *words*, and return unto the Lord, and say unto him, take away all iniquity and receive me graciously, so will I render thee the calves of my lips?" How precious are the words of this Holy Book! How wonderfully adapted to our condition and wants! I need no other proof of its divine inspiration. It is better than all the arguments of the learned. And then the precious promise that follows, " I will heal their backslidings; I will love them freely." May I not be encouraged *to-day*, that the Gracious Spirit, the Remembrancer, has brought these words to my mind? Oh, thou God of infinite love! shall not my hard heart melt at such a message from thee? Let me take this " word in season " to-day, this portion, Benjamin's portion truly, and try to feed upon it, that I may " grow thereby."

Saturday, February 1st.—We are still at Bloomingdale. How beautiful are all God's works, each season, as it returns, bringing with it its own peculiar attractions. I have been out on the bank of the now frozen river, and among the leafless trees. Oh, how much those lose who never commune with God in the still scenes of the country! I have not been in town for a long while; and though I miss the society of Christian friends, and am uninterrupted by visits, I do not improve my solitude as I might. This is Walton's birthday; I hope to write to him. We have only heard of his arrival in Cuba; no particulars of his health. Poor Walton! trials weigh upon him. Would that he might flee to the only hiding-place, before the storm overtakes him!

February 20th.—I have been reading works of fiction. They are not profitable; yet I have not the courage to lay them entirely aside. I hope, if we go to Yonkers, as we now anticipate, that I may find in the church there some work to do. Every day and year, as it passes, shows me more and more of the love of God in his dealings with me in times past. Of late, I have felt very deeply, that the very events the world calls trials have been our greatest blessings. When I mingle with my more wealthy and fashionable friends in town, and see their general style of living, the pomp and luxury, the care and anxiety, the pride, the envy, and the emulation, and how all these things are eating out the heart of spirituality and heavenly-mindedness; and when I look within my own heart and see how very readily, if I could, I would enter into the same course, and even probably go far beyond it; I can see plainly the love that snatched me from the danger, by taking away health, and wealth, and children. And while I see the dangers of others, and gratefully acknowledge the wisdom and love that have hedged me and kept me from them, let me not forget that my own sins, the dark secrets of my own heart, the envy, the uncharitableness and pride, lurking under the mask of this seeming humility and unworldliness, are all open and naked before Him with whom I have to do. Oh, wash me thoroughly from mine iniquity, and cleanse me from my sin!

Sabbath, 23*d.*—Went to church and heard a most solemn sermon from father, from the words, "My spirit shall not always strive with man." It was, indeed, a word in season to my own soul, and to the church in general. While listening, my heart was filled with longing for the fulfilment of the one great "promise of the Father" upon the church and the world in all its fulness. Take not thy Holy Spirit from us; leave not this poor lost world, for which thou hast shed thine own precious blood; leave it not any longer under the dominion of thy foe, but claim thine own!

Sabbath, March 16*th.*—A stormy day, and alone at home. I have been much interested and absorbed in reading Lectures on the Book of Revelation, by Dr. Cumming, an English divine. It is very well written, contains a great amount of historical and other information, and his expositions are very plausible. I hope it has done me good; I must read it again. Should his views prove true, I may live to see the fulfilment of those promises for the fulfilment of which I have prayed; and then the time will not seem *so long.* But whether it be on earth or in heaven, that glory will be our joy. One thing is true, that if the Saviour come *now*, he will scarcely " find faith on the earth."

April 29*th.*—Alas! what shall we say? " Righteous art thou, O Lord, when thou judgest!" Another blow has fallen: dear Walton is taken from us, and we shall see his face no more. I cannot realize it. Again, as a flood of recollections rush upon me, our past affectionate intercourse, our hopes and fears and joys, my heart is oppressed, and I feel as though I would gladly die with him. I have been anxious for his soul, and cannot but *hope* that these months of solitary suffering were sent in mercy. Oh, what a power for happiness or misery is memory! How, even in this present, imperfect state, it can envelope us in darkness, or light! Many of my recollections of dear Walton are pleasant, but some cause me self-reproach. Had I been as earnest and importunate in prayer for him, as affectionate and watchful in my influence over him as I ought, I might now be rejoicing in a brighter evidence that he has entered into rest. His brother and the attending clergyman think he was prepared to die. Received a letter from his desolate wife. She had gone to New Orleans to accompany him home. She was unprepared for the unexpected blow, and learned the sad event from a newspaper. She has great confidence that all is well with him now. Since I read the letter which the Rev. Mr. Prime wrote to father, I have felt that we have good cause for hope.

Sabbath, 11th.—This has been a precious day. Father preached from the words, " He gave them their request, but sent leanness into their souls." It was a most solemn sermon, and I would search my own heart by it. I hope I can say,

> " Give what Thou wilt; without Thee I am poor;
> And with Thee rich, take what Thou wilt away."

Christ's prayer for his disciples, John xvii. ch., 17th verse, I desire to make the directory and model of my own. This is the anniversary of our dear little Mary's birth [their only daughter]. She would have been 18 years of age to-day. It seems hardly possible that so many years have passed. God has taken her from me, and it has drawn my heart from the joys and cares of a mother here, to that heaven where she dwells. Was much overcome in church by the recollections of dear Walton; the music brought him so vividly to my mind. It seemed that I could hear that delightful voice, and could not refrain from tears. Oh, is he indeed singing the song of Moses and the Lamb? Heaven! Oh, how dear is that home now! When shall I see its sinless joys, its loved inhabitants, the Lamb, the light and glory of all?

Sabbath, May 25th.—How beautiful is this green earth on a Sabbath day! There is a peculiar calm, still cheerfulness in all the sights and sounds of a scene like this, on this day of days. Oh, how full of God! and full of beauty, because he hath *blessed* this day and blessed this earth, on which the Saviour's blood has been shed, and made all these the types and earnest of a more beautiful world, and an eternal Sabbath. For the first time since Walton's death, I opened my piano and sang. I felt that while all God's works praise him, my voice also should be vocal with his praise; yet they were subdued joys; I could only give utterance to the words:

> "Thine earthly Sabbaths, Lord, we love,
> But there's a nobler rest above."

Sabbath, Oct. 11th.—It is our communion Sabbath. Mother had all her daughters by her side but Lizzie, and she, though floating on the ocean, was, I doubt not, with us in heart. We remembered her. It is a great privilege to be thus united as a family. But my heart sighed for our brothers and husbands. Samuel was much in my thoughts; oh, how it would have rejoiced my mother's heart if she could have seen *him* there with her. I have this day renewed my covenant with my Saviour, at his table. Twenty years! is it possible? and what have I done for Thee? And what a record is this twenty years of Thy wonderful forbearance and patient love!

Sabbath, January 4th, 1852.—A new year! Its first Sabbath, shall it be lost? I know my poverty, and that He counsels me to buy of him, without money and without price, all spiritual blessings. Give me, then, O Saviour! this blessing; a spirit of patient, fervent perseverance in prayer for myself, and Zion, and dying souls. I am thine by our consecration, and thine, I trust, by thine own sealing. Unworthy, negligent, guilty as I am, I cannot, cannot write myself *thine enemy*—an outcast! an alien!

"Jesus has loved me, I cannot tell why."

Went and heard father on the " Glory of Christ ; " a most interesting discourse, the closing appeals very solemn. I have missed three of the lectures ; and though I can obtain the manuscript, it is not like *hearing*. And I can say, *This Christ is mine!* What more do I want?

Friday, March 27th.—There is a renewed interest in religion in the city. A morning prayer-meeting in Dr. Adams' lecture-room, is so fully attended that they have been obliged to remove to the church. God is about to bless us once more ; and I will praise him even though my own soul remain like the dry fleece of Gideon, when all around is wet with the dew of heaven. *I am* blessed, if Zion prospers. "Pray for the peace of Jerusalem. They shall prosper that love Thee." Oh, *make* me to walk in the way of thy precepts. Was not, is not this thy new and better covenant—that thou wouldst *cause* us to walk in thy ways, and that we *should* not depart from Thee?

Monday morning, January 3d, 1853.—We have our neighborhood prayer-meetings here in Bloomingdale, and the prospect of getting up a new Presbyterian church. We are very much interested in it. I have a number of invitations to evening parties. I do not want to go to them. Yet those who invite me are professed Christians. What shall I do? I am not satisfied that it is right. The late hours, the luxury, show, and fashion, the immodest dances,—I think Christians should steadfastly set their faces against such things.

Sabbath, March 29th.—Behold, what manner of love is this!—this love, this unsearchable love, in adopting such a sinner as this into his own family! How shall I magnify him, love him, rejoice in him as I ought? I am so far from just views of his glorious character, and have such poor, low, and selfish thoughts, that I can only be silent at his feet. I let him look into my poor, benighted heart, and see the need there is for his light, and fill the longing desires he himself has awakened. I have been looking at this love to the whole family of the redeemed, in all ages, and through eternity. Oh, how great, how glorious it is! Oh, the depth! Can it be that this glorious Being is MY GOD! Let me veil my face and adore thee. I know that I have but begun to know, and desire, to feel after thee. Oh, to dwell in thee, to rest in thy love, in thy *holiness*, justice, power; to lose myself in thee! This is the truly blessed life, "hid with Christ in God." My heart longs for this repose. O my Saviour! this distance from thee, thou only source of all true rest!

Saturday, 20th.—I am still at Susan's, "Morning Side," as mother calls it. A beautiful spot. These movements in the Old World distress me. These rumors of war in Russia, Austria, and Turkey, are of deep interest, as connected with prophecy—the destruction of the Mussulman power, and the condition of Palestine. Our King is upon the throne, and will put all things under his feet. Oh, for the outpouring of his Spirit upon the church and the world! Our church edifice at Bloomingdale is going up rapidly and well. It is a temperance movement among the workmen.

Sabbath, 25th.—It is so pleasant to hear father again. I have been reading his "Bible not of Man." It is a most beautiful book. The arguments seem, to my mind, so very clear, simple, and convincing. They are such truths, as when once presented to the mind, we grasp and take possession of, as needing no other proof than their self-evident reality. I often think, if I should live to be old, I should want no other library than my Bible, and father's writings. Father preached from the words, "Thou hast dealt well with thy servant, according to thy word." I shall not easily forget the prayer or the sermon. Went to see dear Mrs. Guy Richards. Oh, how she had changed! Yet she is so lovely, so patient, and even cheerful, and rests so intelligently upon the Saviour, that the sting of death is taken away.

January 2d, 1854.—I trust I shall be enabled to devote the early hours of morning more faithfully to prayer and devotional reading. More of a spirit of *intercessory prayer*,—this is the one gift I crave on this New Year. The only true and blessed life is a useful one. I cannot do much in the giving of money or personal labor; I am the more bound to prayer, earnest and constant prayer. Spirit of all grace! wilt thou not consecrate me to this good work? I expect to go into Bond-street to-day. For many years after my marriage, I always was there at family prayers on the morning of the New Year. This week is preparatory to the communion, and this evening the prayer-meeting will be at Mr. Holden's; I shall stay in town and go. They think of appointing a series of prayer-meetings up town, from house to house. Oh, for more of the *power* of intercessory prayer!

Monday, 9th.—The services of yesterday were very precious; the sermon instructive and comforting. It was the plea of Moses for God's presence with his people through the wilderness, Ex. xxxiii. 16: " For whereby shall it be known that I and my people have found grace in thy sight; Is it not that *thou* goest with us?" The sermon I wish I could record. God's presence with his church in every age. Not now by miracles, but by his watchful providence, by his Holy Spirit, by the collected record of what he has done and has promised to perform. The Bible is the standing miracle now; the pillar and the cloud; the manna from heaven and water from the rock; the existence of the church in such a world as this is itself a miracle. I could not take in all the sermon at once. I would like to read it over and possess myself of all of it. Our Sabbaths seem to me better and better as father grows older, and I cannot but hope that he who blessed his youthful labors with the early rain, will give now the latter rain in his season.

Sabbath, June 19*th.*—Awoke in pain. I shrink from the apprehension of my old sufferings more than is right in one who so proved the power of God to sustain and comfort. I feel that I have wandered from my refuge, and may well dread the coming storm. My heart has been sad to-day.

"Nearer to thee, my God, nearer to thee."

Monday, 20*th.*—Went down to church yesterday morning, but was confined to my sofa the rest of the day. But I would suffer all, ten times over, rather than miss such a sermon. It was an hour and twenty minutes long, and nobody was wearied. It was on "the excellency of power," the three great powers of evil, the world, the flesh, and the Devil; and the three great powers for good, the power of truth, the power of the Spirit, and the power of prayer. Father's eye begins to fail him. His remarks yesterday, about his own labors, and the prospects of the church, were very touching; there were not many dry eyes in the assembly; for myself, I could not restrain convulsive weeping.

April 16*th,* 1855.—At Bloomingdale now for a week, alone. Almost every day last week, suffered greatly, and had none to attend to me. Yet it was not an unhappy week, for my heart was drawn especially to fervent pleading with God for the outpouring of his Spirit upon the world. I cannot but hope that he is about to do great things on the earth. I know it looks dark, but I have seen the promises, and am persuaded of them, and have embraced them; and his will and his time is mine. My dear, dear husband is still away in Tennessee, and I am heart-sick at this prolonged separation. I tremble when I think what a dreary blank this world would be to me, if he should be taken away; and how dependent I am upon his love.

Mr. Lee returned the 24th of April, and found me, on the morning of the 25th, at the dying-bed of dear Jane Adams. Just two weeks, almost to the hour, from our joyful yet chastened meeting there, the messenger of death, the *fearful railway*, struck him down, ten minutes after he had bid me good-bye for the day. He was brought home a corpse.

May 21st, 1855.—Blessed be the name of my covenant God, for a tranquil, submissive, grateful heart, though the heaviest calamity has fallen upon me. I am A WIDOW! a widow, yet *not comfortless*, not *utterly desolate*. My Saviour, God, has upheld me, from the first terrible moment when the tidings were brought to me. His power and love calmed my tossed spirit, and shed down an *irresistible* peace and stillness upon my trembling, breaking heart. For, oh! he was very dear to me. It was not, it is not insensibility that gives me this calmness and peace, this tranquil sleep at night, these peaceful awakings. It is not that any earthly help or hope comforts me, though all that human sympathy and aid can do are given me. But their love and care only make my heart yearn the more for those loving words, and tender cares and attentions, which, for twenty-five years, were never intermitted. Yet I can feel all this and be calm, for the love of Christ, that passeth knowledge, is mightier even than such floods of tender recollections. I am now at my sister Susan's, in Fourteenth-street. I cannot write more this morning, but wished to record the faithful mercy of my God, and his *power* to help and comfort.

Wednesday, May 23d.—Is it possible that it is only two weeks this morning, since that terrible blow fell upon me? It seems like years—as if all of life before that day was in the past, and belonged not to me, but to another person. Yet there is much in that other life; I would not forget it. Especially the two weeks after his return, and so many tokens to me that God was preparing his mind for this sudden death, that I treasure up every hour of our intercourse. We were together alone every evening at Bloomingdale, all the time. Oh! these floods of tender recollections! how could I bear them, if my wounded heart could not flee, every moment of anguish, to my strong Helper? He survived the blow from twenty to twenty-five minutes; was perfectly calm, and asked if they could not carry him *to his wife!* Oh! my precious one, why was I not there? The last act of his life was to raise his eyes to heaven, clasping his hands in the attitude of prayer; then he calmly closed his eyes, and they opened no more. He breathed only a very few times after this. And there was an expression of such perfect peace upon his countenance, till he was carried away from me to the tomb, that it seemed to speak to me more forcibly than words, that in calm trust his spirit had left its earthly house. It was a great blessing to my troubled heart.

June 2d—Seventeenth-street.—" He leads me to the rock that is higher than I." What time I am AFRAID—afraid of all my sorrows, I will trust in Thee. For an instant, the overwhelming floods seem rising to sweep away all love, and trust, and true submission; but it is but for a moment. His strong arm is around me. As a loving mother shields her terrified babe, he carries me in his arms and in his bosom, shielding me even from the sight or sound of the raging storm. He enables me to say, " He hath done all things well." I am wandering about; but I wish to remain in town, that I may be near the house of God, and go and hear father as long as he continues to preach, and before the operation on his eyes. I am anxious, too, to be near my parents.

Sabbath morn, June 3d.—This is a day of praise. How many Sabbath hours have I employed in singing the songs of Zion to my dear husband. He loved to hear me sing, though he could not sing himself. A hymn of McCheyne's, *Jehovah Izidkenu,* "the Lord our Righteousness," which I had set to music myself, he specially loved, and asked me to sing it the very Sabbath before his death. How much I miss my dear one on the Sabbath! None but God knows all that he was to me. Oh! the mighty power of the human heart to endure! and the mighty power of God's grace to sustain! I hardly dare tell to others the fulness of peace and rest I find in him. And then he makes my heart rest so gratefully in the assurance of his mercy to my dear one.

Sabbath, July 8th.—I am ashamed that I do not bear disappointment better. I have been looking forward for weeks to this July communion; once more to sit in my own seat in that corner there, where I first ate the bread and drank the wine; but I must give it up. I shall have many such lessons to learn. I say no more. My regrets and my tears this morning have much in them that is wrong, selfish, and impatient; though, I think, my chief desire was to meet my Saviour at his table, and go back, like Jacob, to Bethel, where God appeared to me at first. But "the blood of Jesus Christ his Son cleanseth from *all* sin."

CHAPTER IX.

THE SOUTHERN REBELLION.

The most interesting event of the age in which I have been permitted to live, is the formal secession of eleven States of this Union, constituting themselves an independent and sovereign Confederacy. With the exception of Southern jealousy of the growing power of the North, never were the prospects of these States brighter, and never had they so honored a name among the nations of the earth. But there was a root of bitterness in the Southern mind, deeply implanted by SLAVERY, and cherished by the indications that the sceptre was about to depart from that favored portion of the land which had swayed it so long.

The lessons of my youth, the associations of college-life, my intercourse with ministers from the Southern churches in our ecclesiastical judicatories, a personal inspection of Southern habits and the condition of the slave population, both in the cities and on the plantations, together with the bonds of domestic relationship, threw me outside of the ranks of *abolition*, and with those conservative influences which struggled to ward off the impending conflict. I did not then know of the *fixed purpose* of the Southern aristocracy to form a separate and independent government; nor of the existence of the "Knights of the Golden Circle," whose project was so artfully arranged for the overthrow of the Government. As early, therefore, as the year 1839, and subsequently in the year 1851, I preached and published two lectures, the object of which was to rebuke the abolition spirit of the North, and to assuage the apprehensions and mitigate the severity of Southern feeling towards the Northern churches. There were some considerations, humane in their character, which led me, even just before the eruption of the South, to espouse the Southern cause. I could not, with any tranquillity, contemplate the dismemberment of this glorious Union. Yet this was the great question; and how to avoid it, or parry the blow, was a matter for grave consideration. The Constitution of the United States recognized the existence of slavery; nor could the rights of the slaveholder be legally called in question. There is not a State in the Union that had not a *constitutional* right to be a slaveholding State. To deny this right to the Southern States was a violation of the Federal compact. And this was a just ground of complaint on the part of the South; the solemn compact was violated in a matter that was one of the material inducements to its formation. I would be slow to provoke the South to secession, if it could possibly be avoided.

In this spirit of conciliation I labored, in the pulpit and out of the pulpit; but it was all in vain. The North was bent on the abolition of slavery, and the South was bent on secession; there was but one alternative, and under the pressure, my views and my conduct were revolutionized. I could no longer defend the South; their appeal was to the bayonet, and I felt that we must meet the issue. That noble senator from Kentucky, Mr. Crittenden, had exhausted the resources of his own fertile mind and patriotic heart, in his efforts to reconcile the jarring elements; but the limit for argument and expostulation was past. Northern abolitionism was rampant; and on the accession of Mr. Lincoln to the Presidency, Southern jealousy became hatred, and that hatred became infuriate.

For several days I was in the gallery of the Senate, when the discussions took place that were preliminary to the conflict, and was never more desponding of the issue. Wigfall, of Texas, supported and excited by that artful statesman, Mason, of Virginia, directing his remarks to the Northern benches, repeatedly, and with unrestrained vehemence of voice and gesture, uttered the words, *We hate you! we hate you! we hate you!* and they made my ears tingle. It was during the angry discussion of that memorable morning, that a senator on the right of the presiding officer boldly declared that *reconciliation now is impossible. Gentlemen can specify no terms on which we will consent to remain in the Union.*

It may be recollected, that soon after the Act of Secession was passed by South Carolina, a kind and pacific circular, signed by a number of Northern ministers of the Gospel, was affectionately addressed to ministers and churches of the South, assuring them of our fraternal love and confidence, and entreating them to unite their prayers and efforts with ours, peradventure the horrors of this unnatural and fratricidal war might be prevented. But the melancholy fact must be recorded, that the ministers of the Gospel in the South were, if not the instigators, the great supporters of the rebellion, and that, without their influence, the political leaders must have abandoned their bloody enterprise. I cannot recall an instance in which so many good men have been so perfectly infatuated, so given over to blindness, and so mad upon their idols, as that which these well-known and beloved brethren themselves present. The fact is notorious, that the masses of the Southern *people* never gave their consent to the rebellion, and that on the church and clergy of the South, uniting their influence with their leading politicians, rests the responsibility of the war. The Rev. Dr. Palmer, of New Orleans, the Rev. Dr. Thornwell, and the Rev. Dr. Adger, and Dr. Lelland, of Columbia, South Carolina, and the Rev. Dr. Smyth, of Charleston, men of distinguished ability, and with talents fitted to control the popular will, gave utterance to views which not only justified and counselled the rebellion, but instigated and urged it with all the enthusiasm and vehemence of the pulpit, and all the weight of their personal and official character.

They threw themselves into the van of secession. The testimony of one of the generals in the rebel army was, that "Dr. Palmer's services were worth more to the rebel cause than a soldiery of ten thousand men." Bishop Polk, of Louisiana, was a major-general in the rebel army, and Dr. Dabney, of the Union Theological Seminary in Virginia, and from whom we had hoped better things, though in the early part of the rebellion he took strong ground against secession, and charged the heavy responsibility upon the religious portion of the South, himself became an adjutant in the army, and was upon the staff of Stonewall Jackson.

The manner and spirit in which our circular was responded to, will appear from the following examples, and they are but examples. One of them, dated Lagrange, Georgia, and signed by Robert Legare, after a dispassionate discussion of the whole matter, closes by saying, " If the day should come when the fell spirit of fanaticism shall be predominant in our General Assembly ; if it should show its head in the Boards of our church ; then the Presbyteries of the South will know how to act for themselves and for the church. Dismiss the idea that the people of the South do not understand their true position. If you have influence at home, exert it to prevent any attempt which may kindle the flames of civil war. Should this come, we will leave our wives and children to the care of our faithful domestics, and meet the enemy with what strength God may give us." Another, dated Louisville, Accomac County, Eastern Virginia, January 28th, 1861, and signed by Enoch Reed, of Aberdeen, says, " *The people* do not sympathize with you, and are in deadly hostility to our constitutional rights. This is what we *feel:* we are, therefore, driven out of the inheritance left us by our fathers, and are under the painful necessity of withdrawing from the Union. It is no fault of ours. The South forms a distinct republic, not of choice, but because she is denied her rights by the people of the North. Politicians, especially those of the North, are many of them disorganizers, and anxious to divide the Union. There can be no doubt that the leading members of Congress from the North are doing all they can, secretly, to sunder our Government. The *people* are duped. Will the people of the non-slaveholding States guarantee to the South her constitutional rights? If they will, all may yet be well; if not, then no power on earth can keep the South from forming a separate government; Maryland, Virginia, and all. And that is but the beginning. Two republics is not the end. New York city will be a separate government. She cannot lose the trade of the South. She will not humiliate, yea, and degrade herself so much as to play second fiddle to little Boston, and be tail-end to puritanical New England. Then the West will not relinquish the outlet to the Gulf; so not two republics, but many petty governments. Then, in a short time, aggression; then war; then anarchy; then some bold spirit, consolidating the whole into a despotism; and then farewell to human liberty and evangelical piety. May God, in mercy, help you of the North to heal the deadly breach! Alas! that it should come to pass just as the Hon. John C. Calhoun told me at his residence in South Carolina it surely would; his vision saw what we now feel."

Another response was made to our circular, enclosed in the following envelope:

"Roswell, Cobb Co., Ga., *January* 28, 1861.
"Rev. G. Spring, D.D.:

"Dear Brother: I send the enclosed to you, as the leader in the Address to Southern Christians, hoping that you will make that use of it which your Christian prudence will dictate. It is the expression of an individual, but he also thinks it is, in substance, the mind of most Christians in the cotton States. I have not sent it to a newspaper, but leave you to do that if you like. We are a *separated* people, and force cannot draw us together.

"May God lead you to stay the hand which would smite us.

"I am yours, sincerely,
"Arch. Smith."

The communication referred to is too long to be inserted entire. I insert the following extracts: "Roswell, Cobb County, Georgia, Jan. 28th, 1861. To the Rev. G. Spring and others: Brethren, I will answer your circular, in hopes that it may be one of many, and that it may have some influence on your minds. You speak of 'a system of misrepresentation' affecting the Southern mind. I think it very probable that you speak the feelings of your hearts, and that you have been moved by the misrepresentations of the Northern press, and have not had access to Southern newspapers to counteract them. There are the signatures of thirty-five of our brethren, some of whom we know by their works, and all of whom we love and honor for this same appeal. Is it rash in me to suppose, that not ten of your number 'have access to Southern newspapers, either religious or political? How few of your number have been recently among us, and become familiar with our feelings! You daily see or hear remarks from so-called Conservative journals, which speak not kindly of Southern society. Which of your children have not studied Moral Philosophy, as it appears in *Wayland*, and gotten light on the Scriptures, through *Barnes' Notes?* With us it is otherwise. 'We read the Southern and the Northern papers. There is scarcely a man of leisure, certainly not a merchant, who does not take one or more Northern political papers. How many, think you, of those you address, have studied in Northern school-books, have attended Northern schools and colleges, and mingled in social life repeatedly at the North? No, brethren, we are not led by such misrepresentations as you suppose; we have seen and *felt* the evil *growing* from the time we were school-boys at the North; we have watched the darkening cloud until we have seen that intelligent Christian patriotism has succumbed to fanaticism and demagogism. The whole Congregational church is against us; the Methodists and Baptists have severed and cast off their Southern brethren as unholy; and finally, in that church which we have looked upon as the strongest bond of union, we have a fire-brand thrown in the midst of us. We have surveyed the whole ground, and feel that the *wedge* is entered, and fixed by a giant's hand. The last blow is not struck, but we feel the last tie is giving way. The great difficulty is the SLAVERY QUESTION. And here our appeal is to the law and the testimony, and with a 'thus saith the

Lord,' our consciences are satisfied. And now, with rolling years, we only find increasing numbers against us, until, as allies with our enemies, a sectional majority has elected a ruler over us, who, to say the least, would not deny his hearty approval of their views, and allowed himself to be called the author of the '*irrepressible conflict.*' And can we be blamed for retiring to our reserved rights, and from such withdrawing ourselves ? We are not forcing our views upon the North ; we are not seizing their forts, and are not threatening invasion. We have kept our constitutional compact, and merely say, Let us go in peace! We have taken our stand. If this matter of secession be not of God, it will come to nought; but if it be, ye cannot overthrow it.

" Yours in Christ, An Elder in the Cherokee Presbytery, Georgia."

It is a bold issue, and we leave it in His hands who reigneth over all the children of men. It may be that, by this time, our Southern correspondents have some misgivings as to the righteousness and wisdom of their enterprise, and less confidence in God as helper. Whatever difference of opinion may exist in regard to the teachings of the Bible on the subject of slavery, two *conclusions* have been long since adopted by my mind, and by the conservatives at the North. *The one is*, that the whole system of *American slavery* is at war with the Word of God. Its immorality and licentiousness, its selfishness and despotism, its ignorance and *degradation*, its disregard of those domestic and social ties which the Bible so urgently enforces upon bond and free, and all of them sanctioned by custom, and most of them by law, cannot stand a moment before the searching test of God's Holy Word.

The other is, that *a system of slavery in any form* is incompatible with a Republican Government. They cannot long co-exist: there are no elements of elective affinity between them, but all the elements of suspicion, jealousy, distrust, strife, and war. Sooner or later, the one or the other must die. The slave-power must be overcome, or the Government must perish. With these convictions, I rejoiced in the election of Abraham Lincoln. The more I have watched his course and his measures, the more am I persuaded that an all-wise Providence has raised him up for this solemn crisis in the nation's history; that the God of our fathers has a work for him to do, and that that work will be accomplished.

I became the decided friend of the Administration. I knew that "to err is human," and that there might be measures adopted by it that were not faultless. But it required an eagle's eye to discern them. At home, abroad, in the Cabinet, and in the field, the Government had my confidence, as a citizen, as a minister of the Gospel, as an old man, and as a ruler in the house of God. In this latter capacity the Presbytery of New York appointed me their representative at the annual meeting of the General Assembly of the Presbyterian Church in these United States, which held their sessions in the year 1861, in the city of Philadelphia. There were present some members from the South, and more from the border States, and there was a strong combination of a powerful minority to shut out all discussion and all action upon the state of the country.

I was mortified at the state of feeling in brethren of high standing, and whose character and attainments gave them deserved influence. The following is an extract from the Minutes of the Assembly:

"Dr. Spring offered a resolution, that a special committee be appointed to inquire into the expediency of this Assembly making some expression of their devotion to the Union of these States, and loyalty to the Government; and if, in their judgment, it is expedient so to do, they report what that expression shall be. On motion of Mr. Hoyt, this resolution was *laid on the table,* by a vote of 123 to 102." After the result of the vote had been announced, Mr. H. H. Clarke moved to take this resolution up from the table, and on this motion called for the YEAS and NAYS. It was Saturday, the third day of the session; and during a discussion on points of order, it was resolved that "the resolution of Dr. Spring be taken up, and made an order of the day for Tuesday next." No action, however, was taken on this subject on Tuesday. On Wednesday, "Dr. Spring offered a paper with resolutions respecting the appointment of religious solemnities for the 4th of July next, and the duty of ministers and churches in relation to the present condition of our country; which, on motion of Dr. Hodge, was made the first order of the day for Friday morning next." In the interval between Wednesday and Friday, strenuous efforts were made by some members of the Assembly, and some who were not members—and by none more assiduously and urgently than by Dr. Boardman, of Philadelphia, who was not a member of the Assembly, but who, though a Northern man, had, from domestic alliances, strong Southern proclivities—to induce me so to modify my resolutions, as to be more conciliating to the Southern members. Much as I respected these gentlemen, I could not accede to their request.

On Friday morning, " the order of the day, the paper moved by Dr. Spring, was taken up, and Dr. Thomas moved to adopt it. Dr. Hodge proposed a substitute, and on the motion to adopt the paper, the discussion was continued to the time for closing the devotional exercises."

The Assembly adjourned, to meet at 4 o'clock, when " the unfinished business of the morning was taken up; the paper by Dr. Spring, and the substitute moved by Dr. Hodge. The discussion continued to the hour of adjournment."

On Saturday morning, the discussion was continued to the time of adjournment; and " on motion of Mr. Hamill, the unfinished business was made the order of the day for Monday next at 11 o'clock." On Monday morning the discussion was continued till the hour of adjournment; and on Monday evening " Dr. Hodge asked and obtained leave to withdraw the substitute he had offered for the paper of Dr. Spring," and another substitute was moved by Dr. Wines, and after some discussion, " a motion was made by Dr. Hodge to lay this whole business on the table."

The *yeas* and *nays* were ordered, and the motion

was lost by 153 nays to 87 yeas. On Tuesday morning, the paper of Dr. Spring and the substitute of Dr. Wines were referred to a special committee, with instructions to report in the afternoon at 4 o'clock. The Rev. Dr. Backus, of Baltimore, was moderator of the Assembly, and announced that committee as consisting of Drs. Musgrave, Hodge, Yeomans, Anderson, and Wines, ministers; and Messrs. Ryerson, Giles, White, and H. K. Clark, ruling elders. A resolution of Dr. Hall was also referred to this committee. A majority of that committee, eight out of the nine, made their report, which closes with the declaration, " That in the present distracted state of the country, this Assembly, representing the whole church, feel bound to abstain from any further declaration in which all our ministers and members, faithful to the constitution and standard of the church, might not be able safely and consistently to join."

Dr. Anderson, of California, faithful to the church and the country, offered a minority report, consisting of Dr. Spring's resolution, with a slight alteration. A motion was made to accept that of the majority, and the discussion continued till the hour of adjournment. On Wednesday morning the discussion was resumed, the question being on adopting the report of the majority of the committee, when, after discussion, it was "resolved that the final vote be taken this afternoon at 6 o'clock." Fatigue and debility had constrained me to leave the Assembly, and I was not present during these last discussions, nor at the final vote. The report of the majority of the committee was rejected by 128 *nays* to 84 *yeas*. The minority report of Dr. Anderson was then taken up, and carried by the vote of 156 *yeas* to 66 *nays*. It is substantially the paper originally presented by Dr. Spring, and is as follows:

"Gratefully acknowledging the distinguished bounty and care of Almighty God towards this favored land, and also recognizing our obligations to submit to every ordinance of man for the Lord's sake, this General Assembly adopts the following resolutions:

"*Resolved*, 1. That, in view of the present agitated condition of this country, the first day of July next be hereby set apart as a day of prayer throughout our bounds; and that, on that day, ministers and people are called on humbly to confess and bewail our national sins; to offer our thanks to the Father of Lights for his abundant and undeserved goodness to us as a nation; to seek his guidance and blessing upon our rulers and their councils, as well as on the Congress of the United States about to assemble; and to implore him, in the name of Jesus Christ, the great high priest of the Christian profession, to turn away his anger from us, and speedily restore to us the blessings of an honorable peace.

"*Resolved*, 2. That the General Assembly, in the spirit of that Christian patriotism which the Scriptures enjoin, and which has always characterized this church, do humbly acknowledge and declare our obligations to promote and perpetuate, so far as in us lies, the integrity of these United States, and to strengthen, uphold, and encourage the Federal Government in the exercise of all its functions under our Constitution; and to this Constitution, in all its provisions, requirements, and principles, we profess our unabated loyalty.

"And, to avoid all misconceptions, the Assembly do declare, that by the term, 'Federal Government,' as here used, is not meant any particular Administration, or the peculiar opinions of any particular party; but the central Administration, which, being at any time appointed and inaugurated according to the form prescribed in the Constitution of the United States, is the visible representative of our national existence."

This last paragraph was appended on the motion of the Rev. Dr. Edwards, of Philadelphia. Such were the resolutions which sixty-six members of the General Assembly of the Presbyterian Church made such efforts to neutralize and annihilate. I do not perceive how the resolutions could have been more conciliating, without being faithless to the country. I only wonder at myself that they were not more full and more stringent. Perhaps the registered sixty-six would vote for them *now*.

To give some idea of the different and opposite sentiments outside of the Assembly, the following communications are not irrelevant, the first two directed to me at Philadelphia.

"NEW YORK, 12*th May*, 1861.

"REVEREND AND DEAR SIR:

"I have conversed to-day with three influential

gentlemen of this city, in the Old School connection —two of them ministers. All say, it will do our body vast harm to *vote down* resolutions sustaining the Government. Do show the brethren how ruinous it must be to falter now in the expression of your loyalty. I write at midnight, at the instance of others, and of my own convictions.

"Very respectfully,
"FREDERIC G. CLARK."

"NEW YORK, 25*th May*, 1861.
"DEAR SIR:
"On my way to New York yesterday, I read, in an evening paper, a brief telegraphic account of the proceedings of the Assembly yesterday, in regard to your resolutions on the state of the country, and am even more amazed at the proceedings of yesterday than at those when the subject was first up.

"My dear sir, do stand *firm* in the position you have taken, and have the ayes and noes recorded, that we may see who the men are who are afraid to avow their attachment to the Government, lest they should offend Southern traitors. If your Southern members cannot vote for resolutions expressive of attachment to the Union, and a determination to defend and maintain it, is it not because they are in favor of subverting it? Is it not because they *do* sympathize with Jefferson Davis' government, and, in one way or other, labor to give it success?

"What a strange course has Dr. Hodge taken! No one knows better than he, that every prominent Southern minister is a *thorough-going* secessionist;

and how absurd to say, they are absent from the Assembly owing to providential reasons! They are maturing their plans of rebellion; of course, they cannot be with you. Providential! how enormous the perversion! Why should we be so tender of our Southern brethren? what are we to gain? Either the country will be permanently divided, or it will not; and more than twenty millions hold, with me, that it shall never be divided. Why should we, out of deference to the men, North or South, who want it divided, refuse to express our determination that it ought not, and shall not, be divided?

"You have taken the true ground; and those Northern men who *caucus* with the South now, and help to prepare and pass milk-and-water resolutions in place of yours, will be held to a fearful accountability.

"They will divide churches, and unsettle many a minister. I assure you, there is a strong feeling on this subject. For one, I frankly say I will try to make it stronger, if your resolutions should be voted down and the substitute be adopted.

"Very truly yours,
"D. V. McLean."

The following short note is anonymous, but has the post-office stamp of Louisville, Kentucky, with the date, September 27, 1861. It was doubtless written for my personal edification; it may perhaps amuse the reader.

"I suppose I ought to congratulate you. You

are doubtless happy that your friend, the devil, now rules supreme in our country. You have worked hard for him, and will get your reward. Beecher and Cheever must be in a glorious state; supremely happy in the contemplation of the bloody fields of battle, and starving women and children throughout the country. But, sir, a young devil must and will spring up, who will envy you and them the bloody feast you now enjoy so much, and will snatch the cup from your lips. The devil will reign only a thousand years; but your torments will not cease till time shall be no more. Remember—

"PHILADELPHIA GENERAL ASSEMBLY.

"General Order, No. 3.

"All teachers of Christianity shall be put to death.

"MILITARY NECESSITY."

There is a smack of the Southern pulpit in this. We have no objection that it should fall under the eye of the Rev. Stuart Robinson, or his faithful coadjutor, the Rev. Mr. Hoyte.

The question of *state rights* is not a novel one. There are such rights guaranteed by the Constitution, and well defined; but the right of secession is not one of them. Not only is it not granted, but implicitly denied by the very accuracy and exactness by which those rights are defined. Who does not see that the right of each State to secede from the Union at will is destructive of our national existence? Recognize this right, and we are no longer a nation. Southern secessionists have forgotten that it is a right expressly ignored by themselves, when the original thirteen States became an organized nation.

In the adoption of the FEDERAL CONSTITUTION, our forefathers had under consideration *four* different forms of government. The subject was attended with no small embarrassment, and was ably discussed, especially by Patrick Henry, James Madison, Edmund Randolph, and John Marshall, in the Virginia Convention in 1788; by Alexander Hamilton and Gilbert Livingston, in the Convention of New York during the same year; by the Rev. Dr. Witherspoon, in the Congress of 1776; by Charles Pinckney, at a meeting of the Federal Convention in Philadelphia in 1787; by Luther Martin, before the Legislature of the State of Maryland in 1787; and by Oliver Ellsworth, in the Connecticut Convention of 1788. One of the four propositions was that the *entire American people should be consolidated into one government, in which there should be no separate State governments, no State rights, and in which the existence of the States as such should be lost sight of and absorbed.* The objection to this arrangement was, that to support with vigor a single government over the whole extent of our territory, would demand a system of the most unqualified and unremitted despotism. Another plan was *to ignore all union, or association, and act as separate, disconnected, and independent States.* The objection to this arrangement was, that to reject all union, and act as separate and disconnected States, would be to make the separate States the prey of foreign influence and foreign intrigue on the one hand, and on the other to make them the victims of mutual rage, rancor, and revenge. The third plan was *to form two or more confederacies, which should be independent of each other.* In some aspects this appeared, at first sight, no uninviting arrangement, and had some advocates in the Convention which formed the Constitution. But upon close inspection it was thought unwise, and that it would be attended with great inconvenience and alarming danger. It was therefore *abandoned*, and with it *all right of secession.* The fourth arrangement, and the one finally adopted, was a *union of all the States under one Federal Government.* This was the arrangement advocated by most of the distinguished statesmen to whom I have already referred, and so ably illustrated by Hamilton, Jay, and Madison, in "the Federalist." It was thought the best government for the American people, giving, as it does, a minute attention to the interests of all the parts, and a paramount regard to the superior interests of the whole. This was the great principle on which the Federal Government was formed, and had it not been adopted, we should never have come into existence as a nation. The views of those who framed the Constitution were not limited by the North or the South, by the East or the West, but were formed on a larger scale, having no sectional preferences, and adopting the time-honored motto, E PLURIBUS UNUM.

This is the Constitution which was adopted by THE PEOPLE of these States—themselves the sovereigns—the sovereign people, thus binding themselves to one another and the world by solemn league and covenant; a Constitution the purest and best ever known to men; a Constitution which bound alike and concentrated the interests of every part of this extended republic, and secured peace and prosperity to the American States and the American people as a Federal Union.

The Constitution is not a *felo de se;* it makes no provision for self-destruction. The men who framed it, and the people who adopted it, never indulged any such idiot-dream. "No North, no South, no East, no West," is the language of our history from the beginning; it is the language of nature, uttered from the very physical structure of the land we dwell in; it is the language of Providence; it has been the language of hope and fear; it has been the language of peace; and now it is the emphatic language of war. The Southern States are slow to understand this; they have wandered too far from the principles of their fathers, voluntarily to return to the true path.

They have suffered long and intensely; they have been overwhelmed and well-nigh crushed; their physical resources and their moral power have been evaporating like the morning dew; and our prayer long has been, and shall be, that the God of nations would no longer turn their hearts to hate their Northern brethren, but rather stay the shedding of blood, and turn their captivity as the streams of the South. The North does not ask for political or civil preeminence; it only asks for that which it has never enjoyed; political and civil equality with the South. It asks only those considerations and regard which, in common with the South, are its blood-bought birthright. We give them proofs of loyalty, and we ask the same proofs from them. It is our firm purpose to give them, and, by God's help, to extort them where they are withheld.

We live under the empire of liberty and law, and we admonish them to take heed how they invade it. We are not prophets; we do not mean to be boasters. The crisis is too solemn, and the results of this transition state are yet too uncertain not to excite solicitude, and urge us to valor and to prayer. It is the religious sentiment of the North that stirs it. Truth gives its potency to the sword.

The North is in earnest, because the South is the enemy of freedom. Slavery seeks power. The motive forces of the age are against it; Christianity, literature, the arts, commerce, industry, are, for the most part, all on one side of the "irrepressible conflict."

I write the present chapter during this civil war, and I cannot well restrain my pen. It appears to me that the God of heaven is frowning upon princes, bringing down high looks, elevating the masses, and breaking every yoke. If wisdom is justified of her children, she will fall in with the leadings of his providence. I have been wrapt in joy when I have seen that he is honored in this conflict, and I am wrapt in painful contemplation when I have seen that he is forgotten, and that my countrymen are so prone to "trust in man, and make flesh their arm." "Let not the wise man glory in his wisdom, neither let the mighty man glory in his might; let not the rich man glory in his riches; but let him that glorieth, glory in this, that he understandeth and knoweth me, that I am the Lord which exercise loving-kindness, judgment, and righteousness in the earth; for in these things I delight, saith the Lord."

God rebukes national arrogance, and he will rebuke our arrogant self-complacency. There is a wisdom above the strategy and tactics of the warrior. God has his way of working; it becomes us to honor his providence, and, in grateful views of his supremacy, ever to remember that the race is not always to the swift, nor the battle to the strong. No human intellect can decide the fortunes of war; "time and chance happeneth to them all." By many an unthought-of incident, the God of heaven may disappoint human expectations, and make the warrior's face gather paleness. I confess to misgivings as to the result of our vain boasting. We have "made gold our hope, and said to the fine gold, thou art our confidence;" but riches profit not in "the day of wrath." It is the great sin of the American people, that *gold* is the *Moloch* of the land. The shibboleth of party rings through its halls; sworn legislators worship at its altars; and even *justice* pays tribute at its shrine. There is no government of the world which the God of heaven is so set on humbling, as the pride of man. It is a humiliating fact, that so little is known of God in a world where men and nations have so much to do with him, and he has so much to do with them. There is "a power above us;" and we may well give this truth an abiding lodgment in our hearts. A punitive providence is visiting us; and we may well believe that "verily, there is a God that judgeth in the earth." Our strongest hopes in this bloody conflict are in the fact that "judgment and justice are the habitation of his throne;" that he will plead our cause, because it is his own; that he cannot approve of the wrong-doing of the rebellious; and that he will "lift up himself, and render a reward to the proud." I do not know that history records a more criminal procedure, than this Act of Secession; so causeless, so rash, so ruthless, so suicidal, and in its treachery and spoils so unequalled in wickedness. I have confidence in the rectitude of our cause; and therefore I have confidence in the valor of our army, and *I have confidence in God.* If we give him the throne, he "will defend the right." He surveys the field at a glance; manifold as the agents and events are, they are under his eyes. His finger is upon the electrical wires, and he is directing and controlling the whole. His government is not the management of policy, but a government of principle and law. His language to rulers is, "Kiss the Son, lest he be angry, and ye perish from the way when his wrath is kindled but a little." This prince and Saviour is now going forth "in his majesty and in his glory, because of truth, and meekness, and righteousness, and his right hand is teaching him terrible things," and opening the seals of the book, which none could open but the Lion of the tribe of Judah. His purposes will not be accomplished without fearful judgments. The devil is come down in great wrath, because his time is short, and to gratify his malice and revenge against the Son of God.

This war is but an emanation of the conflict with the powers of darkness.

Invading violence must be overthrown by resisting violence. It came upon us unexpectedly; it was not known until it was felt; we found no relief in it but in the arbitrament of the sword. Nor have I any doubt that God has important purposes to answer by the American people and their present struggle. We are called upon to solve the problem whether or not liberty is consistent with law; whether or not we can be a free, and yet a governed, people; and whether or not, as a governed people, the descendants of the Puritans, the Hollanders, shall be a "byword and a hissing among the nations." We are deciding for or against free institutions; for or against governments, the corner-stone of which is *slavery*, or the corner-stone of which is liberty, with law, religion, and justice. Daniel Webster once remarked, that "human liberty may yet perhaps be obliged to repose its principal hopes on the intelligence and vigor of the Saxon race."

Let us not prove recreant to our trust. We are a Christian nation, and Christianity and justice are one. Bound, beyond all other lands, to the claims of civil and religious liberty, we may not hesitate between slavery and justice. We have but to let conscience do its office, and this question is settled.

This question settled, we rest upon principles which God approves, and are animated by hopes which he sustains. It is his cause we are advocating. He is our helper and our shield. Let us rally round the standard of union and peace—union first, and peace afterwards. The "Stars and Stripes" will then float over a land no longer burdened with the curse of slavery, but herald His advent who shall reign from the Northern lakes to the Southern Gulf, and "from Eastern coast to Western." These unbroken States, each in the enjoyment of its own rights, and of the common weal, will then go forward under the guidance of the cloud by day and the pillar of fire by night, and with no serried hosts burnished for slaughter. Inveterate asperities will be mitigated, popular passions will be assuaged, Christian magnanimity will forget the past, and the smiles of heaven will return to bless our disenthralled land. Our Government will be established on a more permanent foundation, and the people will be prepared for the last conflict with the Man of Sin, and the great battle that is to issue in the "cleansing of the Sanctuary" and the latter day of glory. The God of our fathers will be exalted on that day; and though we shall sleep in the dust, our children's children shall trace the destiny of unborn generations under the full-orbed glories of liberty and law, Christianity and justice.

There is one thought, on the subject of slavery, which I may not omit. Utterly rejecting the doctrine of human servitude, or the right of property and ownership in man, I would not be in haste to elevate the colored race to a position for which they are not fitted. I would not, from an enthusiastic attachment to "liberty and equality," violently thrust them into offices of trust and responsibility, or give them the elective franchise, until they are prepared for it. Their own welfare, and the safety of our own institutions, would, in my judgment, be imperilled by such a policy. I would make them *free*, but I would treat them as servants, and just as I would treat the white races from abroad, and in our own land, who seek and are fitted for no higher position. Let them go when and where they will, and enjoy all the protection of law; let them serve whom they will, and in the capacity which they themselves may select, and receive recompense for their labors; but let them not aspire to a seat on the bench, nor to the pulpit, *until their intellectual culture and moral qualifications shall have fitted them for these responsible positions.* "Wisdom is justified of her children:" the results will show that this is the true policy towards the colored race.

When *Christian* men and women are found among them, I would treat them with Christian love, which is "without partiality and without hypocrisy." I would treat them as "Paul the aged" would have Philemon treat Onesimus, not as a "slave, but above a slave, and a brother beloved." I would not assign to them the lowest place at the communion table, nor the highest, but a place where they are acknowledged as brethren and sisters in Christ. There is a beautiful incident in the ministry of the late Dr. John M. Mason which illustrates these thoughts. He was connected with the Associate Reformed Church, and then the pastor of the large congregation in Murray-street. Rachel Ferguson, a colored woman, advanced in years, well known in this community as a woman of exemplary piety, had long been a member of the church, and had been accustomed to take her place at the communion table in a retired spot, scarcely observed by the great body of communicants. At an early observance of this sacred festival, and after the prayer consecrating the elements, the Doctor rose from his seat at the head of the table, and with a solemn and dignified mien, walked the whole length of the broad aisle, down to the seat of Rachel Ferguson. All eyes were fixed upon him when he took Rachel by the hand, and led her up to a seat occupied by the more wealthy of the church, and, as he led her through the aisle, solemnly and tenderly repeated the following words: "For ye are all the children of God by faith in Jesus Christ. There is neither Jew nor Greek; there is neither bond nor free; there is neither male nor female; for ye are all one in Jesus Christ."

CHAPTER X.

THE SOUTHERN REBELLION SUPPRESSED AND PEACE RESTORED.

WHEN the chapter on the Southern Rebellion was written, I did not expect to see its close. Most unexpectedly, I have lived to see it broken and scattered; nor may I lay down my pen without recording my humble testimony in honor of that Providence by which it has been subdued, and peace restored to this bleeding land.

No nation on the face of the earth has greater cause for thankfulness to the God of heaven than the American people. From the early settlement of this country to the present hour, he has done more for us than for any nation now on the earth. Springing from no base and degenerate origin, and unlike the nations whose foundations were laid in ignorance, superstition, and blood, the American people trace their lineage to men of whom the world was not worthy. Great numbers of them were intelligent and religious men, sagacious and wise statesmen, and strongly attached to those Christian and literary institutions which are the glory of the land, and men, in principle and valor, qualified to lay the foundations of a great empire. They were no visionary theorists, but men of strong common sense. They were the friends of liberty, but the friends of law and order, and trained to activity and endurance. For almost a century we have been an independent and united people, and so enlarged, protected, and guided by divine Providence, that "a little one has become a thousand, and a small one a strong nation." And, under God, our national covenant is the foundation of our greatness.

Yet has the God of heaven a controversy with us. There was a worm at the root of this green and fair tree of Liberty, and so closely attached to it that its leaves began to shrivel, its blossoms were scorched, and its fruit decayed. To say nothing of our abounding sins as a nation, and of those varied moral causes which called for the divine judgments, the single *sin of* SLAVERY uttered its loud cry to heaven, and was enkindling animosity and division. Men began to talk of a separation of the States, and not a few of the idiot-dream of a peaceful separation, constituting a Northern and a Southern Confederacy. There were four millions of slaves in the Southern States, and though, through their power upon the ballot-box, the South had the predominant control of the country, they were not satisfied. In an evil day, the cockatrice-egg of secession was hatched, and broke forth into a viper. They hardened their hearts, they braced their nerves, they sharpened their swords, and the land shook and trembled under God's rebuke. A terrific cloud hung over us; we could no longer view it at a distance; blackness was added to the dark shade, and tears and blood were added to our sighs. The men of influence in the border States, and the few in the South who sought the integrity, the safety, the interest, the peace of the nation, raised their admonitory voice, but raised it in vain. Without any just ground of complaint against the Government, and after the public acknowledgment of the leaders of the rebellion that it is the best Government in the world, and with their recorded *oath* to support it, they struck the blow that has resulted in their destruction. When we cast our eye towards that once genial and sunny land, we see it in ruins and deluged with blood. It has a melancholy history, written by the sword, the bayonet, and the flames. Uncounted treasure, and the blood of not less than two hundred and fifty thousand of our fellow-men, have been sacrificed to this long-meditated and accursed plot of treason, designed to shiver the Republic and blot out the nation's name.

But it was not yet to become all chaos and ruin. In the wise counsels of Providence, the men who created the storm that they might float into power on this sea of blood, have been overtaken by the tempest, and themselves made to drink blood, for they are worthy. The desolation that has swept through the South; the busy and smiling activities of social life that have disappeared from those bright skies; the pursuits of learning and science that have been abandoned; the Sabbaths that have everywhere been desecrated, and the sanctuaries that have been turned into hospitals and prisons; the dearest sympathies it has turned into perpetual antagonism and apprehension; the deep foundations of law and order which it has broken up, all tell us that this rebellion has been the portal to calamities which cannot be repaired until the existing generation of the South has passed away. This war has been no fiction, and, as an old man, I desire that my own views of the causes and objects of it may be thus known to those who come after me. It is amusing to hear some persons attributing it to Northern Abolitionism; when the historical fact is patent to the world, that it was projected by the "Knights of the Golden Circle," twenty years before Northern Abolitionism was thought of. It is, indeed, most astounding to hear that arch-traitor, Jefferson Davis, appeal to the civilized world, and affirm that the war and the consequences of it, are not to be attributed to the South. *To whom*, then, I demand, are they to be attributed? *Who* waged the war? *Who* with rebel lips and rebel armies bid defiance to the powers that be, and are ordained of God? *Who* stealthily appropriated our national treasure, our forts, and arsenals, and armories? *Who* arrayed the first battalion, fired the first gun, drew the first blood, and for four years continued their atrocious depredations by sea and land? Whatever the South may think, all the world knows that their position is of their own choosing, and it is the natural result of their armed resistance to law and government. It is their own atrocious resistance to a government whose protection and varied blessings they shared in common with the North, and, so far as regards governmental patronage, were its chief beneficiaries. The United States Government did nothing more than they ought to have done—than they must have done without suspending the operation of law and justice, conniving at all the atrocities of revolt, and consenting to the subversion of all government and the disastrous misrule of anarchy. We were shut up to the issue of government or no government.

This great question the God of heaven has decided for us. He gave us the strength of principle and the strength of nerve to meet the exigency. The corrupt propensities and passions of men, their overbearing and aristocratic superciliousness, their love of power and their grinding oppression of the degraded slave-population, have received their deserved rebuke. Because the Lord God omnipotent reigneth, the devices of the crafty have been disappointed, so that their hands cannot perform their enterprise. When Grant and Sheridan and Sherman drew their *cordon militaire* around the armies of Lee and Beauregard and Johnson, the God of Israel looked from the cloud and troubled the hosts of the rebellion, broke up their confederacy, scattered their combinations, and made the wrath of man to praise him. He was "wonderful in counsel and excellent in working," when, as he called Moses from attending to his pastoral vocation on Horeb, to be the leader of his ancient people through the wilderness, he called Abraham Lincoln to be the leader of his American Israel through this great and terrible war. It was a wonderful providence, which fixed its eye upon this unpretending citizen in the far distant State of Illinois, to "stand in the gap and make up the hedge," which seemed to require a Marlborough, a Napoleon, a Wellington, or even a Washington, to occupy. He was "the right man in the right place." The people had known something of him; he was the favorite of his native State, and in her legislative councils had developed such qualities of mind and heart, and intuitive perception and correct judgment, as gave him commanding influence. When elevated to the honorable distinction of a seat in the Senate of the United States, the policy and the destinies of his country, the sources of its prosperity and greatness, and the principles inwoven with its existence as a Republic, found in him an intelligent and warm-hearted advocate. When a still more honorable distinction awaited him, and the national voice called him to the highest and most responsible office in the land, his discretion and firmness, and the clemency of his benevolent heart, showed him to be the fitting head of a self-governed people. And when this gloomy and prolonged war chafed and irritated the minds of the nation, and defeat and victory alternately attended the march of our armies, and many a standard-bearer fainted, and suffering and danger fomented animosities, and fanned the flame of discord, and the hesitating friends of the Government became its open and avowed enemies; there was no such tranquillity to the fears of the timid, no such opiate to the jealousies of party, no such resistance to the arts of the designing, as the heart and head of Abraham Lincoln. He filled this responsible sphere with an energy, a promptitude and disinterestedness, that made him the hatred of his enemies, and the joy, the glory of his and the nation's friends. From first to last, in the selection of his Cabinet, and in the appointment of men who were to control the battle-field, his object was single. It was to save the country and rescue it from invasions engendered in hate, nourished by the love of power, its proud temple built on the corner-stone of slavery, its walls indented by the lash of the task-master, and discolored by the blood of the slave. He lived to see the contest closed, and the nation restored to the blessings of returning peace.

But the joy that thrilled the heart of the nation had scarcely begun to find utterance, and the generous shouts of victory had scarcely reached its outer borders, before the startling telegram announced that this beloved man, the nation's chief, had fallen by the pistol of the vile assassin. He had but just entered upon his second career of glory, when disappointed ambition, desperate in its madness, and bent on "rule or ruin," struck down its victim in the person of our Martyr-President. It was a dastardly crime, and seemed to be the only thing wanting to sever the rebellion from the respect of its last advocate and defender. Language fails to depict the hate, the revenge, the madness, of the hellish deed in the heart of that accursed assassin. We had neither crown nor sceptre, nor any of the spoils of royalty to be numbered among the trophies of his fury; but we had a stable government which his fatal grasp endeavored to destroy. Let his name perish, and rot, like a dog's carcass, in his defiled grave.

We never knew Mr. Lincoln until the day on which he fell. His dawn was gradual, and never culminated to its meridian until the hour of its sudden and portentous eclipse. We deplore his fate; but his work was done. That beloved form is now but a wasting tenement of clay; but that precious dust is consecrated by a nation's tears. I well remember the day when Washington died, and the nation wept; but I never knew such absorbing grief as burst from the national bosom when Lincoln fell. The marts of business were still as the grave, and the whole land was draped in mourning. None rejoiced but the prince of darkness, and the fiends that nourished this rebellion, and, with deep and dark intrigue, concocted this diabolical crime. It is no marvel that distant nations are appalled by such a deed as this, and that in this plotted assassination they begin to discover the spirit, the *animus* of the Southern revolt. O my country! well may you weep. Israel wept at the death of Moses, and again at the death of King Josiah. England wept at the death of the Princess Charlotte, and France at the death of the Duke of Orleans; but they never wept, and we never wept, but once before, as we weep now. Yes, O my country! well may you weep. "How is the beauty of Israel slain upon thy high places!" England's Queen and the Emperor of France may well breathe their sympathies across the ocean to this mourning land. Ye sons and daughters of servitude, well may you weep at the grave of Lincoln! I rejoice to witness these civic honors thus paid to his memory, and that thus flow in from distant shores. Yet he knows them not. He hears not the funeral knell, nor the cannon's thunder, nor the eulogies of the press, the pulpit, and the forum. He sleeps to awake not until the heavens be no more. And there stands the promise, "Them that sleep in Jesus will God bring with him." Though we are forbidden to inquire into his religious emotions at the last moment, for it was but a moment, yet we know enough of his character to believe that he lived and died a Christian.

Would that the sad tale could be here closed. There is reason to fear that our Martyr-President was the victim of a deep conspiracy, well understood and approved at Richmond, if not concocted, by the Cabinet of the revolt. We do not assert that it received the seal of its *chivalrous head;* that Jefferson Davis was privy to it, and its responsible adviser, though his position unfitted him to strike the blow. A kind Providence has now made him our captive. "In his iniquity, his *heels* were made bare." The prophecy was literally fulfilled, "In thine iniquity are thy *skirts* discovered." He has paid dear for his chivalry. Instead of being hailed, as was predicted in the English Parliament, "the founder of a nation," he is remembered as its would-be destroyer. His very subjects, awakened from their delusion, have awoke only to reproach him. He sowed the wind and he has reaped the whirlwind. No amnesty could save him; no act of oblivion swept deep enough to blot out his infamy. No appeals for mercy ought to stay the claims of even-handed justice. Should the proud and boasted career of this worthless leader be closed on the gallows, no veteran armies would weep at his funeral. Even faction might be silent; it would not be safe for it to pay any kind of devotion to his memory. *Jefferson Davis* is but another name for indelible infamy.

It is a kind Providence that has deferred his trial until now, when the triumph of conquest is subsiding into the magnanimity of the conquerors. Justice still frowns upon the rebellion, and demands the punishment of its leaders. But our nationality is saved, and we can afford to be magnanimous. While I hope that the leaders of the rebellion will be forever disfranchised, I still hope that, in the exercise of a sound discretion, the Government will see fit to extend to them all the lenity which is consistent with the welfare of the nation. Times have altered; the South has altered; the spirit of the North has altered; there has been suffering enough; no man calls for blood now. Our "erring sisters" have seen their error, and all we ask of them is to return to their first love. One thing is obvious, and that is, if we remain a prosperous, peaceful, and happy people, *we must treat our Southern friends with kindness*. The demon of secession cast out and purged of slavery, we ask of them nothing but loyalty and confidence. We would be glad to see their prominent clergymen free to acknowledge that bitter experience has taught them that, honest as they were, they were mistaken in their views, and that they had no right to take arms against the Government. We can welcome them as brothers, and forget the past. Yet the thought may not be repressed, that it is a fearful heresy, that there is no sin against God in political crimes. Moral character is inseparable from citizenship. Christ's kingdom cannot prosper where the first principles of civil government are ignored. Revolution may be justifiable; causeless and hopeless rebellion never. "If the foundations be destroyed, what can the righteous do?"

This mad Confederacy demolished, let us give

thanks to the Almighty Ruler, that our national integrity has been preserved, and the land been delivered from a prolonged and bitter conflict, and restored to safety and peace. All honor to our victorious armies! All honor to the wisdom and justice of our Government! Above all, all honor to the God of heaven! It would be a dangerous error, and fatal delusion, if, dazzled by the lustre of our victories, we forgot Him who "maketh wars to cease." Now that the storm is over, give honor to Him who "ruleth the raging of the sea, and stilleth the tumult of the people." He governs the world, and has spoken to the rebellious the sentence of retributive justice. He will not delegate his authority or his power to creatures, nor will he allow them the triumph and glory which belong to him. If we have the wisdom and the valor, the will and the power, they are all from Him. The grave of Lincoln will testify against us; our own prayers, and tears, and vows of patriotism, will testify against us, if we so demean ourselves as to be forsaken of the God of our fathers. Our heads will soon lie low in the dust; and if we are recreant to our trust, better Christians and better patriots will come after us, who will learn to ascribe all the glory to Him to whom it belongs. This is our only appropriate triumph. When the last vestige of this rebellion is blotted out, and its last murmur silenced, let us sing with Israel's millions on the banks of the Red Sea, "The Lord hath triumphed gloriously!"

CHAPTER XI.

THE PRESS AS WELL AS THE PULPIT.

It would be no small relief to the writer of these sketches, if the present chapter had fallen into other hands. The services of the pulpit have been the great labor of his life; but, with very few exceptions, his publications from the press were first issued from the pulpit. They enter largely into his personal history; nor can that history be at all full and complete without giving some account of them. Though embarrassed by some delicacy in so doing, he here presents them, and in the order of time in which they made their appearance. They are as follows:

A Sermon on *Faith and Works*, preached before the New York Widows' Society, published in 1811.

A Sermon entitled *Something must be done*, preached on the last day of the old year in 1815; it reached a fourth edition.

Essays on the distinguishing Traits of Christian Character; published in 1815. This volume reached the ninth edition; it was republished in the French language by the Tract Society of Toulon, and also, through the bounty of Mr. E. K. Corning, by the American Tract Society, for gratuitous distribution.

A Sermon on the *Doctrine of Election*, published in 1816, and republished by the New England Doctrinal Tract Society.

An *Oration* on the death of Dr. Dwight, the President of Yale College, in 1817.

A *Brief view of Facts* in relation to the formation of the New York Missionary Society of Young Men, in 1817.

The *Life of Samuel J. Mills*, in 1820, reprinted in Scotland, and also at Andover.

A *Tribute to New England*, before the New England Society, in 1821.

A *Sermon* before the American Home Missionary Society, in 1823.

A Tract on *The Sabbath a Blessing to Man* in 1823, reprinted in modern Greek and in the Italian language.

A *Sermon on the death, and an address at the grave*, of Rev. Philip Melancthon Whelpley, in 1824.

The Discriminating Preacher, a Sermon at the ordination of Rev. Carlos Wilcox, in 1824.

The Excellence and Influence of the Female Character, a Sermon, in 1825.

An *Address of the Executive Committee* of the American Tract Society, in 1825.

The *Internal Evidences of Inspiration*, in 1826.

A *Dissertation on the Means of Regeneration*, 1827.

Moses on Nebo, a sermon on the death of Rev. J. S. Christmas, 1830.

Tribute to the Memory of Jeremiah Evarts, 1831.

God's Judgments righteous, a Sermon on the day of Fasting and Prayer, during the Cholera, 1832.

An *Address to the Theological Students at Princeton Seminary*, 1832.

A *Dissertation on Native Depravity*, in 1833.

Hints to Parents, in 1835. Reprinted in London.

The Extent of the Missionary Enterprise, a Sermon at the annual meeting of the Congregational Union of England and Wales; printed in London, 1835.

Annual Sermon before the American Board of Commissioners for Foreign Missions, at Utica, in 1835.

The *Power of Sin*, a Sermon, in 1837.

Sermon on *Christian Knowledge*, introductory to the Murray-street Lectures, in 1837.

Death and Heaven, at the funeral of Dr. Griffin, 1837.

An *Address before the Mercantile Library Association*, in 1837.

A volume of Miscellanies, entitled *Fragments from the Study of a Pastor*, in 1838.

An octavo volume, entitled *The Obligations of the World to the Bible*, in 1839.

God the Governor of the Nations, and *The New Sepulchre*, two Sermons on the death of Pres. Harrison, 1841.

The Danger and Hope of the American People, a Thanksgiving Sermon, in 1843.

The Saviour's Presence with his Ministers, at the opening of the General Assembly at Louisville, in 1844.

A Dissertation on the Rule of Faith, in 1844.

The *Attraction of the Cross*, in 1846; republished in London.

The *Bible not of Man*, in 1847; published by the American Tract Society, and the Religious Tract Society of London.

The *Bethel Flag*, short sermons to Seamen, in 1848.

The *Power of the Pulpit*, in 1848.

Strictures on the Princeton Review, in 1848.

The *Mercy Seat*, in 1850; republished in Scotland.

First Things, in two volumes, in 1851.

The *Glory of Christ*, in two volumes, in 1852.

Address before the New York Female Bible Society, in 1853.

The *Contrast*, in two volumes, in 1855.

Triumph in Suffering, at the funeral of Rev. Dr. Spencer, 1855.

Closing Sermon in the Old Brick Church, in 1856.

Opening Sermon in the New Church, in 1858.

Sermon at the *Installation of Rev. Dr. Hoge*, 1859.

Sermon on the *fiftieth Anniversary of my Ordination*, in 1860.

Sermon on the *Death of Mrs. Spring*, in 1860.

Sermon on the *Death of Horace Holden, Esq.*, in 1860.

The *Mission of Sorrow*, 12mo.; published by the American Tract Society, and perpetuated by an individual, in 1862.

Sermon on the *Southern Rebellion*, in 1862.

Pulpit Ministrations, 2 vols. octavo, in 1864.

A Sermon on *Influence*, in 1865.

These *Reminiscences*, 2 vols.

The above series embraces 22 volumes, octavo.

The commendatory notices of some of these publications, both from the American and British press, I may not speak of, except to say that they have been sufficiently gratifying, and have encouraged me in seasons of doubt, fear, and depression. The Dissertations on the "Means of Regeneration," and on "Native Depravity," and the work on the "Power of the Pulpit," have called forth serious discussion from abler pens than my own, but I have seen no reasons to alter my views. The Dissertation on the "Rule of Faith" has troubled one of the feebler advocates of Romanism at the West, and I can only recommend to him to read it again. I did not expect the attack on the "Power of the Pulpit" from the source from which it came—the Biblical Repertory. The "Strictures" upon it from my own pen were deserved, and I am happy to know that they have received the approbation of my brethren, all of whom are the friends of Princeton, and some of whom have more than a personal responsibility in the direction of its affairs. The Rev. Dr. McGill, in a letter to myself, under date of October, 1849, writes, "We expect to circulate all your books, not excepting the 'Power of the Pulpit.' That review of the reviewer has been torn to tatters by the many readers to whom I have loaned it; and by the testimony of all, you are right in the impression that 'Princeton is answered.'" Before I published the Strictures, I gave an outline of them to a clerical brother, in whose judgment I have great confidence, and solicited his opinion as to the wisdom of the course I thought of pursuing. He replied, under date of January, 1849, as follows:

"My Dear Brother:

"Your work, the 'Power of the Pulpit,' I have read with much interest, as did my family; and aside from the gratification it has afforded, we hope we are not unbenefited by the perusal.

"I am the less able to give you an opinion touching the expediency of *publishing* your Strictures on the Princeton Review, as I have not seen it, and am led to infer its character only from your remarks upon it, and from a too mild rebuke it receives in the 'New Englander,' said to be from the pen of Rev. Tryon Edwards. One needs to be in the Presbyterian church, or, at least, familiar with its condition and influences, to know how far it may be expedient to set forth such a document as your Strictures. You have treated the reviewer with caustic severity, but not, as I judge, unjustly. In this region the sentiment is entirely with you, and you need no vindication, either from your own pen or another's. All with whom I have conversed, condemn the review as one-sided and unfair. The reviewer has manifestly made a false issue, and few, except the prejudiced or the envious, will be found to sustain him. The article in the 'New Englander' is generally, as to its spirit, commended. It expresses one thing with sufficient plainness—that your position is not, as they at Princeton would affirm, one of hostility to theological seminaries. No man who reads your book would discover such a sentiment there, except he were predetermined to find it.

"As to the question you suggest, I hardly know what to say. There is a class of feelings which I share in common with many, that would prompt me to approve and desire the publication of your Strictures. But a better knowledge of all the circumstances might alter my opinion; and I am the more inclined to cherish the doubt, because of your own hesitation. If the way were in every respect clear, I think the eldest son of Dr. Spring of Newburyport would not falter. May it not be a monition from the God of peace that you should content yourself with shaking off the venomous beast into the fire?

"Truly yours, —— ——."

I will not here repeat, nor anticipate, the remarks elsewhere thrown out, on Dr. Taylor's review of the Dissertation on the Means of Regeneration. The review of the Dissertation on Native Depravity " by a Presbyterian," whether clergyman or layman I do not know, and professing to give " a critical, philosophical, and theological view of the whole subject," makes it matter of regret that it had not fallen into the hands of Dr. Goodrich & Co. before their courteous discussion in the "Christian Spectator." We are not surprised that it had the patronage and endorsement of Rev. Dr. Brownlee, for most egregiously did it need to be upheld by a weightier arm. A kind, charitable man, Dr. Brownlee, thus to dispense his favors in time of need! The reviewer aims to be witty, yet there is no fun in him. He aims to be learned, by the frequent repetition of great names; yet he gives no specification of their views. He aims at literary merit, and Dr. Brownlee says of him, that he does " not know of any critical production from an

American press, of late, which possesses so much real merit," and that "his style is as elegant as his argument is acute;" yet the review shows an obvious want of scholarship, and no want of bad grammar. The reviewer did not learn his rhetoric either in an English or American university. He aims to be logical, yet his review is wanting in method and in perspicuity of reasoning; it is a chaotic mass, without beginning, middle, or end. He highly commends the author of the Dissertation as a man "calculated to shine in didactic theology," and at the same time affirms that his writings indicate false, and evasive, and empty reasoning." He aims heavy blows at the New England theology, and intimates that the prevalence of the Hopkinsian doctrines has led to Socinianism and the decline of vital piety; yet he admits that the "principles of Dr. Hopkins' system are evidently Calvinistic." I know of no writer who is so entirely ignorant of the theology of New England, as the reviewer. As to his argument, it is an utter misrepresentation of my views in the Dissertation. I have nowhere said that "actual, personal sin is against a *known* law;" on the contrary, I endeavored to show, at some length, that "sin may and does exist where there is *no knowledge* of the law," and that "sin does exist where men are not conscious at the time of committing it, that it is sin." And I quote the declaration of our Lord, "He that *knew not*, and did commit things *worthy of stripes*, shall be beaten with few stripes." Nor have I, as the reviewer represents, anywhere denied the doctrine of original sin, but endeavored to show, throughout the Dissertation, that it is the doctrine of the Bible. The argument of the reviewer from the analogy between the world of matter and the world of mind, only confirms the position which it was the object of the Dissertation to establish. The reviewer says that "no man but Dr. Spring ever believed that conscience is a *faculty* of the soul." Let him consult the writers on intellectual and moral philosophy, and he will find that Dr. Spring's views are by no means singular. The Edinburgh Encyclopedia says, "Conscience is that principle, power, or *faculty* within us, which decides on the merit or demerit of our own actions." Reid speaks of it as "this *power* of the mind which we call *conscience*, or the *faculty* of distinguishing right from wrong." Stewart calls conscience "the moral faculty." Butler calls it the "principle of reflection, a *faculty* natural to man as a moral agent." Witsius says, "conscience is wont, in the sacred writings, to be set forth as a faculty of man." Ames, in his Medulla Theologica, quotes Perkins, a strict Calvinist, as calling it a "natural power or faculty." Edwards calls it "a faculty." Emmons calls it "a *distinct faculty* of the mind, that enables us to discover the moral quality of actions, that gives us a sense of moral obligation, and that approves what is right, and condemns what is wrong, in our moral conduct." Dick says, it is "that *faculty* which distinguishes right and wrong in actions, approves and disapproves, and anticipates the consequences, whether good or evil." The reviewer thinks that conscience is an *act* of the soul, and not a faculty. And how does this distinction bear upon the argument? The Dissertation nowhere affirms that conscience is a dormant, but that it is an acting, faculty, and that it belongs to the soul of an infant. If the reviewer will have it that " native depravity is not *moral* depravity," and that " moral corruption is the fruit of natural corruption," that " natural is born and moral is acquired," we leave him in his alliance with Pelagius and Whitby; but never let him again claim allegiance to the " Edwardean School." The Dissertation contends that native depravity is a moral evil, a sin, and not a mere natural evil, as the reviewer affirms.

Several of these publications were republished in England and Scotland. The Evangelical Magazine, published in London, has the following notice of the " Attraction of the Cross."

" 'The Attraction of the Cross; designed to illustrate the leading truths, obligations, and hopes of Christianity. By Gardiner Spring, D.D. New York: 12mo. pp. 334. Tract Society.'

" The visit of Dr. Spring, his sermons and speeches, some dozen years ago, are remembered with pleasure by a numerous class of our readers. Few Americans ever made so deep an impression on an English audience. The fact of his visit has ever since prepared the way for the successful republication of whatever has emanated from his pen; and we cannot doubt that this last, the largest and by far the most valuable of his productions, will meet with a hearty welcome."

The Scottish Guardian, Glasgow, speaks thus of the " Mercy Seat."

"'The Mercy Seat; thoughts suggested by the Lord's Prayer. By Gardiner Spring, D.D. Edinburgh: T. & T. Clark, 1850.'

"Many excellent expositions of the Lord's Prayer have been given to the world. In the present work, Dr. Spring, of New York, both expounds the import and spirit of the Prayer as a direct appeal to the mercy-seat of Heaven, and uses it as a series of texts, for the illustration of many highly important doctrines of revealed religion. The book is a truly excellent one. It is characterized by orthodoxy of sentiment, precision of thought, and animation of style. A few of the highly-wrought passages are rather deficient in simplicity and grace, but, on the whole, the composition, by its vigor and beauty, corresponds to the solid thought and noble views in which the treatise abounds. The author takes occasion, in connection with the petition, 'Forgive us our debts, as we forgive our debtors,' to denounce war in very emphatic terms; and we confess that, with the qualification which he himself introduces towards the close of his discussion, we cordially assent to the general view which he propounds. If his description of the horrors of war be neither so finely wrought as that of Robert Hall, in his finished sermon on the subject, nor so full of stirring enthusiasm as that of Chalmers, in his discourse on 'Universal Peace,' it resembles both in its fidelity of statement and in its tenderness of feeling."

I hope I may be allowed to add, that the London Tract Society not only transmitted to me a kind and complimentary letter, but a handsome collection of their printed volumes, in " testimony of their regard for the valuable accessions " I had " made to Christian literature."

The following communications, expressing the approbation of the writers, of the publications to which they refer, were as unexpected as they were gratifying.

"MALTA, *July* 28, 1829.

"TO THE REV. DR. SPRING, New York:

"REVEREND AND DEAR SIR: I take the liberty of forwarding to you the tract on 'The Sabbath a Blessing to Mankind,' in the Italian and Modern Greek languages. Where these languages are spoken, the Sabbath is scarcely known, except as a day for gayety and hilarity—a day bearing a much greater resemblance to the noisy mirth of our Fourth of July, than to the stillness and solemnity of our Sabbath days.

"This tract will probably be widely circulated, especially in Modern Greek. It will probably be read where Apollo and his brother Bacchus were once worshipped—where once stood the temples of Diana, and Neptune, and Hercules, and where once were consulted the oracles of Jupiter, and Venus, and Mercury, and Juno; will probably be read on the summits of Parnassus, and at the foot of high Olympus, at the fountain of Castalia, and by the famous river Helicon, on the classic shores of the Hellespont, in the ancient Peloponnesus, and in the provinces of Thrace and Macedonia; will, in short, be read by the descendants of Plato, and Xenophon, and Demosthenes, of Archimedes and Pindar, of Herodotus, and Sappho, and Homer, and Orpheus, and many others celebrated in classic story.

"Should it be instrumental in bringing a *single* individual to give suitable honor and reverence to the Lord of the Sabbath, in purifying *one* heart, and in directing *one* inquirer into the path of life and salvation, it will do what all their writings could never achieve. Should it, like the salt of the prophet ' cast into the spring of the waters,' be the means of purifying and healing the land; and, by promoting morality and a knowledge of God and of true religion, be the means of personal holiness and of national prosperity, it will be remembered with emotions of unspeakable joy when ' their remembrances shall be like unto ashes,' and all the proud monuments of their genius and art shall be buried in obscurity and oblivion.

"This tract will probably be hereafter published also in the Armeno-Turkish language. It will, I doubt not, be accompanied by your prayers, that, wherever sent, and in whatever language, it may, under the direction of the great Head of the Church, be a blessing to ' many peoples and nations,' and even to the generations yet unborn.

"With affectionate salutations, yours truly,
"W. GOODELL."

"NEW YORK, *October* 22, 1839.

"MY DEAR SIR:
"I return my grateful acknowledgments for the

present of your volume, on 'The Obligations of the World to the Bible,' and I should have done this agreeable duty the sooner, if I had not wished to read the work previously, and thoroughly to understand it. You may judge of the attention and fidelity with which I have perused the volume, when I assure you that I have made notes (my usual course in all thorough reading) containing the substance and most striking passages of every lecture. I now beg leave to say, that they are written with great neatness, simplicity, perspicuity, and energy of style, and exhibit everywhere profound and accurate research bearing upon the comprehensive theme. I admire your fervor and your strength, and I hope you will excuse me when I add, that the volume cannot fail to impress every Christian reader with the evidences of deep piety and elevated and glowing devotion. I was very much struck with the aptitude and force of your abundant Scripture quotations; and with the eloquence and fervency of your illustrations; and with the solidity and excellence of the conservative principles which you have drawn from the Bible, and which are so necessary to sustain and improve the social institutions of mankind.

"Though I cannot say I assent to every remark you make, and to every doctrine you advance, yet I most cordially agree with the work considered in the whole, as an entire performance; and I believe it to be eminently calculated to recommend the truth, study, and inestimable value of the Bible to the head and heart of the general reader, beyond any work of the kind I ever perused.

"Accept of my best wishes for your health and perseverance, and believe me to be,

"With the highest respect and esteem,

"Yours, etc.,

"The Reverend Dr. SPRING."

"CARROLL COLLEGE, Waukesha, Wis., *July* 27, 1864.

"REV. DR. SPRING:

"REV. AND VENERATED FATHER: I have just been reading your '*Power of the Pulpit*,' and, although unknown to you, I feel constrained from my sense of obligation to thank you, in the only way I can, for giving such a book to the public and the rising ministry.

"Though called to preside over the dubious fortunes of an infant literary institution in the great Northwest, I have not lost my interest in the pulpit. The minister of Christ should aim to be a *preacher*. As Herbert so beautifully says, 'His pulpit is his throne.'

"I have read many books on preaching and the ministry, but none which has so stimulated and quickened me as 'The Power of the Pulpit.' You have spoken earnestly and eloquently, and your words have the more weight as coming from one who has himself been for so many years one of the most distinguished ornaments of the pulpit in this or any country. They are to be envied who have had the singular good fortune to be associated with you in the pastoral office. As a young minister, I can conceive of no greater earthly privilege or advantage. Would that the days might return when the younger ministry might enjoy the benefit of the experience and counsels of their superiors.

"May your life and services be long spared to the church.

"With grateful and filial reverence, I am, dear sir,
"Your servant in Christ,
"W. ALEXANDER."

"REV. DR. G. SPRING:

"A deep sense of obligation prompts me to address you. An Israelite feels you have exacted from him and his whole people the homage of their profound respect for the noble and generous tribute you have rendered to the intellectual superiority and grandeur of the ancient Hebrews, in your admirable work on the Obligations of the World to the Bible. He feels convinced that the man who entertains the opinions you do of the Old Testament and its *time-worn guardians*, is no enemy to the Jews. He believes you sincere when you declare, as the Apostle did of old, 'That you are a debtor to the Jew.' Would that all Christians acknowledged as much!

"He believes you will agree with an Israelite that preceding generations have not lessened the debt, but rather increased it: unmerited aspersions, obloquy, and persecution, could not have been the means to subtract anything from this constantly accumulating claim. Let us fervently hope that the day is soon at hand when all religions will acknowledge its justice, and that the present age, which has done so much to repair the injuries inflicted by its predecessors, will atone for the past to the Hebrew people.

"Do you not see how strangely we are rooted like a rock in the midst of the dashing billows—imperishably preserved amid the fall of empires and dynasties?

"If the great promise of the national restoration is to be fulfilled, and which is believed by all Jews, the means by which Christianity may vindicate its claim to justice, and cancel the *obligations* due and yet unpaid to the Jewish people, is in their own power. Christian benevolence, liberality, and brotherhood, are yet to accomplish the high and prophetic destinies of the Hebrew people. The noble efforts made by Christianity to diffuse the Bible are beyond all praise. The Israelite feels a deep and abiding interest in your labors. He considers that Christianity is yet to be a pillar on which the Kingdom of David will rest for support and protection in the latter days. He thinks the Christian church will be found the most active in reëstablishing the foundations of Zion, and, united to the temple, go hand-in-hand in spreading the knowledge of the Lord from isle to isle, to the uttermost ends of the earth.'

"Can you, then, censure us for believing that the maintenance of the national faith—community of sentiment, religion, and laws, among the Jews in all climes and nations—preserves the materials wherewith to reconstruct the body politic, and to bring back the dispersed tribes, actuated by one soul and moved by one impulse, to the possession of their long-lost heritage?

"The descendant of David is still to be recognized

by the characteristics which distinguished the minstrel-king: impassioned energy, poetical enthusiasm, and vivid imagination, belong peculiarly to their character. The very attachment of the Israelite to his national faith carries with it an air of grandeur not entirely unmingled with a romantic tinge. The rich casket which the minstrel-monarch bequeathed to his people in such marvellously splendid gems of musical and poetical composition, is still cherished by them as the dearest relic of the national glory.

"An Israelite trusts that the enlightened and benign spirit you have brought to the investigation of the philosophy of the institutions of Moses, may be carried still farther in examining the writings of the Hebrew sages who flourished in Spain during the Augustan age of Jewish literature. He thinks your attention would be deeply attracted by the depth of learning, purity of sentiment, elevation of thought—in fine, by all that could interest a man anxious to penetrate into the history of the ancient people.

"An Israelite offers no apology in making this communication. Gratitude, duty, and feeling, crowd together to offer their voluntary homage to the author of the 'Obligations of the World to the Bible,' and he considers both Jew and Christian ready to meet on common ground when such sentiments are the index of the public mind. Yours, most truly, I."

Such communications as these made me "thank God and take courage." They are the crowning expressions of God's goodness to one sufficiently unworthy.

CHAPTER XII.

FAMILIAR LETTERS.

The following letter, from the President of the College of New Jersey, relates to that remarkable young man referred to in Chap. II. of Vol. I., *Mr. Periam*, whose name I am gratified to rescue from oblivion, if it were only for my father's attachment to him.

COLLEGE OF NEW JERSEY, PRINCETON,
May 25, 1865.

"REVEREND AND DEAR SIR:

"It appears from the triennial catalogue of our college, that Mr. Joseph Periam was graduated here in 1762, and that he became a tutor in the college in 1765, and resigned his position the following year; that he was reappointed in 1767, and continued in this office of a tutor until 1769.

"In a life of the Rev. Dr. S. S. Smith, the seventh President of this college, by the Rev. Dr. Beasley, the following mention is made of Mr. Periam:

"'During his residence in Princeton, as an undergraduate, he had been consigned, more especially, to the care of Mr. Periam, who had rendered himself distinguished in the institution and in his country, by a profound acquaintance with mathematics and natural philosophy. Accustomed to the study of abstract sciences, Mr. Periam, it appears, had not confined himself exclusively to the cultivation of the branches which it was his province to teach, but had extended his inquiries to metaphysics also, and became infected with the fanciful doctrines of Bishop Berkesley, which consist, as is generally known, in denying the existence of a material universe, and converting every object of the senses into a train of fugitive perceptions. How this professor, who had been habituated to the hardy pursuits of mathematical and inductive philosophy, could have brought himself to embrace such a visionary theory, a theory so repugnant to common sense, and rather an object of ridicule than of serious consideration, it is difficult to explain, unless it be upon the principle, that having been accustomed, in those departments of science which he cultivated, to require the most conclusive proof of everything before he assented to its truth, he so far misconceived the subject, as to imagine that he must have arguments drawn from reason, to convince him of the existence of an exterior world, before he would admit the reality of it; and this surely is an evidence which nature would deny him, as she rests the proof of it solely and entirely upon the simple testimony of the senses. However this may have been, certain it is that Mr. Periam had address and ingenuity enough to infuse the principles of the Bishop of Cloyne into the mind of Smith; and he began seriously to doubt whether there were in the world such real existences as the sun, moon, and stars, rivers, mountains, and human beings. So sincere and zealous did he become at this time in the maintenance of immaterialism, and so confident of the proofs by which it was supported, that he was ever ready to enter the lists in a controversy on the subject.' * *

"'Mr. Smith, although captivated at first by the specious fallacies of the Bishop of Cloyne, had too much sober sense and penetration to be held in bondage by the silken chains of such a fantastic theory. Dr. Witherspoon arrived from Scotland, and bringing with him, we are told, the recently broached principles of Reid, Oswald, and Beattie, furnished him a clue by which he was conducted out of the dark labyrinth into which he had been betrayed by Bishop Berkeley and his disciple, Professor Periam. From the cloudy speculations of immaterialism, he was now brought back to the clear light of common sense.'

"'The above extracts furnish all that is said with respect to Mr. Periam's views and teachings, by Dr. Beasley, in his life of Dr. Smith. This Life is prefixed to two volumes of Dr. Smith's sermons, published in 1821, by Potter & Co., of Philadelphia.

"With the highest respect, yours,
"JOHN MACLIAN.

"Rev. Dr. SPRING."

It was remarked, in the early part of the first volume of these reminiscences, that I was in the habit, on the anniversary of my birth, of addressing an affectionate and dutiful letter to my much-loved and honored parents. On the return of that anniversary after their decease, I wrote to my brother Samuel, at East Hartford. *That* letter, for several reasons, I should have been glad to have inserted here, but it was destroyed by the fire which consumed his house, his library, and *all* his private papers. I have, however, preserved his reply to it; it is as follows:

"EAST HARTFORD, *February* 28, 1855.

"MY VERY DEAR BROTHER:

"Your kind and fraternal letter, written on your 70th birthday, gratified more than it surprised me. It was a welcome and refreshing token of that love of which I have already had so many proofs, and gave me additional reason to bless the God of providence and grace for his merciful allotment to me in my parentage, and all its collateral advantages and hopes. It has not escaped your discernment, that although but few years (between seven and eight only) have marked the difference in our ages, I have been prone to regard our relation as almost a parental and filial, rather than a fraternal one. The eldest son in a family is, I believe, not unfrequently destined to bear somewhat of this honorable responsibility, while, as an offset to the influence and authority it gives him, he must sometimes forego the gratification which might result from a more intimate, though possibly burdensome, familiarity. I have lost much in not being more unreserved and confiding with you, and yet I have found it well-nigh impossible to divest myself of that restraint which something, more than the mere distance of years, must have imposed. Let me hope that this embarrassment will be obviated during the little time we shall either of us be permitted to remain here. I would still, as heretofore, look up to you for counsel and example, and would hope to derive no little comfort from your more mature experience, and more extended, because in many ways more elevated, field of observation; but I would nevertheless love sometimes to come near your heart, forget my inferiority, and talk with you on paper, or face to face, as a brother who shares some mutual obligations and some common hopes.

"Truly, my dearest and most honored brother, you have reason to be grateful for the goodness that has continued your life through so many years, and that has crowned it with so many and so rich mercies. We, who love and honor you, have often given God thanks for his signal kindness to our father's house. Not one of us living but has reason to bless him for having made us the children of such parents; and you of all of us have, if I err not, the most abundant occasion to thank and praise him for the fidelity, the solicitude, the prayer, and, more than all, the *faith* of them both, but especially of that godly mother. Oh! what answers to prayer have been given in your person, your family, your congregation, your public labors, your official station and influence, and the promise of extended usefulness when your lips must be closed, and your pen laid aside! I have it not in my heart to envy you one of your well-earned honors. I could wish them multiplied many, many fold, for I know that you lay them all at the feet of the Saviour, and that any accumulation of them would only add lustre to his abounding grace. Should my own life be spared, I trust yet to see that God has more to accomplish through your instrumentality, and to find additional reason to 'glorify Him in you.' But suffer me to say, Be careful, my brother, you may plan more than 'threescore and ten' will admit of accomplishing. The partial failure of your sight, which is news to me, and distressing news, is admonitory. You ought not to write a sermon a week. Though you find comfort and pleasure in the exercise, I fear it will be too expensive a service. Better employ an amanuensis, than impose a burden against which prudence and skill enter their protest.

"In ten days, if I live, I shall reach the age of sixty-three years, thirty-three of which have been spent, how imperfectly you well know, in the service of the best of Masters. Often I have fainted by the way, many times been discouraged, and never have I done with my might what my hands have found to do. A feeble body, an ill-disciplined mind, and an inconstant heart have been my great burdens. I have been made to possess the iniquities of my youth. Still I have loved my work, and God has, in great condescension, given me some success in it. I have enjoyed, though altogether undeserved, the confidence and affection of the three congregations to which I have ministered, and in my present station, where I have just entered my twenty-third year, I do not know that I ever stood more highly than I do to-day. For these things it becomes me to be grateful, and yet the very view I thus take ought to fill me with shame. Numerous sins and imperfections stare me in the face, and I find no relief but in a daily application to the blood of sprinkling. My attachment to the humbling doctrines of the cross every year's experience has confirmed, and I rest upon them with more peace and confidence, for my own poor soul, than ever. In my family I have to record the loving kindness of God. All my daughters are hopefully pious, one of them the wife of a beloved minister, and the others useful as God gives them opportunity. My health droops; and if there is one spot brighter than all the rest in my religious experience, it is that this circumstance gives me no uneasiness. I look forward with hope and pleasure, though I trust not with impatience, to the close of my pilgrimage. I would fain die daily. Of death as an event I have no fear. God has graciously given me this victory. My dear family I can peacefully leave with his providence. The worldly circumstances of all of them are good, better far than if they were rich; and if I could see them all taking refuge in the Ark, my cup of joy would be full.

"Again, then, dearest brother, I thank you for your letter. It is a cordial to my spirit. I am mindful of its closing injunction.

"As ever, your affectionate brother,
"SAMUEL."

The following is addressed to my family, and dated at sea:

"SHIP LONDON, *at sea*, long. 32° 32', lat. 46° 16',
August 8, 1822.

"MY DEAR SUSAN:

"You will perceive from this date, that the day

on which I am writing is one on which I have cause to dwell with very many solemn and tender thoughts. It is the anniversary of my ordination. Twelve years ago this day, I was publicly set apart to the work of the holy ministry. Time flies. Perhaps the most and the best of my time and my work are over. 'To me, who am the least of all saints, is this grace given, that I should' for twelve years 'have preached the unsearchable riches of Christ.'

"The last I wrote you, closed with a narrative of some of the incidents of my voyage, up to the last Lord's day. On the morning of that sacred day I rose very early, with the hope of some enjoyment in the devotions of my state-room. Nor was I altogether disappointed. I rejoiced in the Sabbath. It is a day marked with the same discrimination by us at sea, as by you on shore. Late on Saturday evening, I carried forward to the seamen a little treat of eatables, and covered the top of the bundle with Mr. Payson's excellent address; observing, when I gave it into their hands, '*Now, my lads, keep a sharp lookout for the cover.*'—'*Aye, aye, sir!*' was the reply; and the next morning they sent a formal deputation to me into the cabin, thanking me for the bundle, and saying that they had *all* taken good care to read the cover! Our seamen, most of them, reverence the Sabbath; though I do not know that any of them are pious. One reads his Bible, another a tract, another is willing to converse on religious subjects, and all seem pleased to attend public worship. The Bethel-flag was hoisted at ten, when our quarter-deck was constructed into a very convenient little church, and

at the tolling of the ship's bell we all assembled, to
unite our homage to the great Ruler of the sea and the
dry land. It was a precious service. I find it best
to preach on these occasions without notes, and at this
season God gave me some liberty with the poor seamen.
I spoke from Job xxii. 21. I endeavored to
show them that sailors, as well as other men, were ignorant
of God; to instruct them what it was to be
acquainted with him; to present the present and future
benefits of this holy acquaintanceship; and to
urge the duty upon *them* as their present and indispensable
concern. At the close, I told them I loved
seamen; that I had a brother who followed the seas;
and as I drew aside the curtain of poor Lewis' history,
I saw they hid their faces. Some covered them
with their hats; some put them between their knees;
some bent them over the quarter-railing; and some
looked alternately on the deck, at me, and at each
other, while the big tears rolled uninterruptedly down
their hard and weather-beaten cheeks. I tried to
make them feel that they had souls; and God grant
that they may feel it, before it is too late. I felt
quite happy in the whole of this service. It was delightful
thus to acknowledge God on the deep waters.
I felt greatly privileged, here, in view of the rolling
ocean, almost infinitely extended before my eye, and
the bending heavens, which seemed not reluctant to
hear the voice of our praise and supplication, to testify
the Gospel of the grace of God before a collection
of neglected and generous-minded seamen. The
thought entered my mind, while engaged in the service,
that it was a blessed privilege to bear my testi-

mony for God and his holy Sabbath, here, on the wide seas. In the afternoon Mr. Broadway, a local Methodist, preached; and I must say, he is a *John Bull* of a preacher. What pity that men who need to be taught what are the first principles of the oracles of God, should undertake to teach others. Our American Methodist brethren would hardly have included him in the apostolic succession. We spent the evening in the after-cabin, in a very pleasant family way. We find the dews very heavy; otherwise the evenings are incomparably fine on deck.

"If I frequently repeat the remark, that the sailing and the weather are beyond our anticipation pleasant, it will be because I have occasion to do so. We have not had an unpleasant breeze, or an unpleasant sea, since we embarked. I should judge our passage bears a strong resemblance to a passage on the Pacific Ocean. I do not know that there is an hour in which we should have been unsafe in a ship's jolly-boat. Had we selected our weather, and winds, and seas, expressly for a sail of pleasure, we could not have hit upon a milder sea, or sweeter breezes. We are not without prayer on board the ship; but I conclude we have been followed by the breath of prayer from other sources, as we are now about half across the Atlantic. What a world of waters is this by which we are surrounded! We have seen nothing but sea and sky, since we lost sight of the Highlands; and we seem, hour by hour, penetrating seas and skies, which immeasurably recede.

"On Monday, we awoke to the same cheering view and prospect. The seamen say, they never knew so pleasant a passage across the Atlantic. We are not sailing rapidly, but glide along at the average rate of one hundred and fifty miles per day. To-day, we were all very much interested in catching a *dolphin*. He had followed the ship a number of hours, and at length fell into the snare. It was a beautiful, nay, a splendid fish, reflecting alternately all the colors of the rainbow; and I could not but pity him, when I saw the ragged irons pierce his body, and mangle his beautiful form. You must know, there is no small degree of this cruel business going on on board a ship. I was a little surprised, when I learned that we had actually shipped a *butcher!* The squealing of pigs, the bleating of sheep, and kids, and the cackling of the whole feathered tribe, have become almost as familiar as the breathing of the wind. We have a park for our deer, a sty for our swine, a lawn for our sheep and goats, a coop for our fowls, and a knife and stomach for them all. Not, indeed, for all *at once;* for then we should be dragging about John Bull's belly.

"About twelve o'clock the succeeding night, we fell in with the ship *Spartan*, from St. Petersburgh to New York. I had letters prepared to send by her, but as we were sailing in opposite directions, and quite rapidly, I had no opportunity of throwing them on board of her. I must not forget to tell you that we had a good view of the grampus whale. A number of them were playing at a little distance from the ship. The sea 'boiled like a pot' before them, and foamed in playful undulations, as though obedient to their word. * * *

"And now, my dear Susan, I must close this long and tedious letter. I have half a mind to throw it into the sea, it is so much fitter to be devoured than to find its way to your pure eye. And yet I will send it, and even protract it till I have finished the sheet. It is certainly well enough for a man to creep out of the 'little pin-hole' of early associations and early habit, if it were for nothing else than to find that he himself is much smaller, and the world much larger, than he had imagined. I confess I have perceptions of the magnificence of the world I inhabit, to which I have been, hitherto, a stranger. I feel like a very little thing, confounded and overwhelmed in this world of mystery—this ocean of immensity. The more I survey the extent of this sublunary creation, the more is my heart enlarged, as well as my thoughts expanded, by the view. I can scarcely look at these wonders of the ocean without discovering, every day, something that is new, and in each discovery beholding new arguments for my admiration of the living Deity. I know I have often surveyed the scenes which this voyage has spread before me, with an ardent eye, and I hope I have sometimes done it with an adoring heart.

"But I weary you, and only subjoin the signature of an affectionate husband.

"GARDINER SPRING."

"SHIP LONDON, *at sea*, lat. 49° 23′, long. 12° 48′,
"*August* 14, 1822.

"MY DEAR SUSAN:

"I hope this is the last letter I shall have time to

write before we are in sight of land. We have been sailing so rapidly for a few days past, that I think we *must* be not far from some coast. A famous pilgrim in Walter Scott's Kenilworth remarks, 'If I were to travel only that I might be discontented with that which I get at home, methinks I should go on a fool's errand.' Though very few ships have traversed the ocean superior to the London, and though everything on board is as domestic and comfortable as it can be, I can assure you, I am in no danger of being discontented with home.

"My last brought us up to the 8th. On the following day we had a fair wind, which continued mostly through the night. The whole day was occupied in reading. The 10th was Saturday; and during the whole day, we were running from seven to ten knots directly on our course. Our ship rides it over the swelling seas in a very proud and lordly style. The *lord mayor* (for that is the ship's figure-head), must have had his face washed to-day. Towards evening we were all much interested for a poor wandering bird, which fluttered, trembling and faint, around the mainmast, and at length alighted, as though she were glad to find a resting-place for the sole of her foot. Our ark is so peaceful and happy, that a dove would be scarcely tempted to fly from us.

"There is nothing like home, my beloved wife and children; there is nothing like home on Saturday evening. All seem conscious that the Sabbath is approaching, and appear to be predisposed for serious conversation and religious duty. But this does not constitute it *home*. When the sun sets at home, the confusion and bustle of the week subside into the wonted order and silence of God's own consecrated day. We assemble around our domestic altar, and there is no spot so precious to a parent's heart as *such a spot*. I thought of you on this evening, and fancied I saw you all assembled, to read God's holy Word, and sing his praise, and call upon his name; and I could not but feel that there is no such sacred harmony of song, as I thought I heard, when you and our dear children began to sing. I could almost hear you; and as, now and then, a note seemed to fall on my distant ear, I could scarcely suppress my voice from uniting in the supplication,

"Dread sovereign, let my evening song
Like holy incense rise."

But these sweet winds deceived me. It was no such sound that I heard, but the echo from a heart that would fain have thrown back the Alleluia, and commissioned the winds to waft it to the ear of those I love. Precious evening! Enjoy it, endeared family. Endeared partner of all my cares and mercies, enjoy it to the full. And ye, beloved children, be not strangers to the joy of a family so often and so cheerfully consecrated to God. I, too, enjoyed it here. I did not forget who has said, 'When thou passest through the waters, I will be with thee; and through the rivers, and they shall not overflow thee. When thou walkest through the fire, thou shalt not be burnt, neither shall the flame kindle upon thee; for

I am the Lord thy God, the Holy One of Israel, thy Redeemer.'

"After a fine run through the night, we were once more ushered to the light of the Lord's day. During the preceding twenty-four hours we had run upwards of one hundred and eighty miles. At ten o'clock, the Bethel-flag was hoisted, and the bell rung for public worship. I preached from Galatians iii. 24, and the seamen paid the most respectful attention. Some, who evidently disliked the arrangement for religious services when first introduced, seem to like it well enough now. I adapt my discourses chiefly to the sailors, and make them very short. Our whole service occupies no more than an hour and a quarter.

"In the afternoon, Mr. Broadway preached from Heb. ii. 2, much after the old sort. With the hope that before another Sabbath we should be on shore, I alluded to to-day's opportunity, as not improbably the last Sabbath service we should enjoy together. I was gratified, when, a little after, one of them came, and said to me, 'Pardon me, sir, and won't you preach to us in the *Downs?*'—'I don't know how that will be, my good fellow,' replied I.—'But won't you go back in the ship with us, sir?' said he; 'it is the mind of all *of us*, that you should go back with us, sir.'

"I have not rendered myself odious to the sailors, if their treatment of me be any criterion of their true feelings. I took the opportunity to talk with the man at the helm a little to-day, and he seemed to think religion of more importance than the world, and eternity more valuable than time. This Sabbath was not, in some respects, so pleasant as the last. The wind was almost too fresh to hold divine service on deck. We had a fine breeze, sending us away from you at the rate of eight, nine, and ten knots per hour.

"Monday morning presented a little interruption to our pleasant weather. It was more or less squally the most of the night, and during the day the skies lowered. But the wind was in our favor, and wafting us on at a great rate, I assure you. On Tuesday the weather was still squally, but in our favor still. On Tuesday afternoon and evening we were running down our longitude very rapidly, and looking out for a *blow* before morning. Nor were our apprehensions groundless. On Wednesday morning, early, I was awoke by a great bustle on deck. The convulsive tossing of the ship, the whistling of winds through the cordage, the occasional blast of the captain's speaking-trumpet, all confirmed me in the belief that we were just encountering a gale of wind. I went on deck as soon as I could climb the companion-way, and the ocean was in a foam. It seemed as though the ship flew on the wings of the wind. I had great confidence in the skill of our commander, but it was greatly increased by this short blow. The gale increased till we were obliged to take in most of our sails, and even then we scudded over the surface at the rate of ten and twelve knots. Our ship is truly an excellent ship. As I stood and saw her moving with such stateliness through the dashing billows, I could not but admire that general law of a wise Providence that gives so much security to such a frail bark amid such dangers. The gale lasted about five hours, during the three last of which, the sea became so much agitated that it was truly a sublime sight. I never felt more calm and cheerful. Our only anxiety was, lest it should continue till we came too near the land. But, happily, the clouds dispersed about noon, and left us a pleasant though rough sail the remainder of the day.

"Towards evening we hove the lead, but found no soundings. We are all looking out for land, and hope to see it to-morrow. How easy it is for God to blast our prospects! But I feel happy to leave the events of the voyage with him, and in the sweetness of this sentiment, once more subscribe myself your affectionate husband,

"GARDINER SPRING."

"FULTONHAM, MUSKINGUM CO., O.
"REVEREND AND DEAR FATHER:

"Your goodness, I know, will pardon the seeming intrepidity of a *personal* stranger in thus addressing you.

"I am a young, inexperienced minister of the Gospel, and, in order to fit myself for my pulpit duties (humanly speaking), I have been for the last few weeks reading 'Miller on Public Prayer,' 'Bible not of Man,' 'Power of the Pulpit,' etc., etc. This last work has made such an impression on me, that I cannot refrain from addressing its distinguished author, and ask of him a favor.

"Oh! when I read that the pulpit had power,

and of the elements of that power, and agents of that power, etc., it seemed to me wonderful that ever God let such a *poor, ignorant sinner* as I am be the honored channel of this power. Oh! I wept and prayed over my unworthiness and God's goodness. But why, oh! why, my dear father, did you still seem to implicate yourself when showing the duties of a minister of Christ? This was awfully *discouraging* to me! Oh! if *you* fall short of doing your duty as an ambassador of Heaven, where am I? Alas! alas! poor me.

"Don't think I am finding fault; no, no: I bless God that he ever put it into your *heart* and head, to write such a book, on such a subject; and when I read Dr. Payson, I then think I find the reason of Dr. Spring's complaining of his own remissness in duty.

"You will think me flattering. But no, no: God forbid that such a poor, ignorant, unworthy worm as I, should attempt such a thing! Yet I must say *that book* has led me to the fountain where I hope to drink until I become wise unto salvation.

"Oh! to think you expect soon to *die* and be with Jesus; and that *I* must stay here, in this cold, unfriendly world, and 'fight the fight of faith!' yet I will not repine. May God give me grace to '*know* and *do* his will.' Oh! if I could only *have a double portion* of *your* spirit! to take such a high and Godlike view of the pulpit, its power and truth; then I *could* preach; now I cannot. It seems I ought never to go into the pulpit. Who am I, or what is my father's house, that I should stand between the living and the dead? I feel ashamed of myself; yet I wonder at my success. I was licensed to preach April 19th, 1849; was ordained April 9th, 1850; have two charges, 'Deerfield,' and 'Uniontown,' Zanesville Presbytery, Synod of Ohio. Since I commenced my labors, sixty-five have united with my charges, and the good cause seems to prosper. Uniontown was organized November, 1848, with nine members; we have now thirty-seven, and a fine house erected and paid for, in which to worship. Yet all this gives me little personal comfort whilst I *feel* my own ignorance and weakness.

"The favor I ask of you is to pray for me, and at some time, when you have leisure, address me a letter of *advice*, and, if possible, encouragement. You say, 'go to Jesus;' I do, in my weak way; but I want *you* to go for me also; oh! I want *all* ministers to pray for me; nay, I want the Christian world to pray.

"Oh! would to God I had the mantle of Chalmers or Miller! what, then, could not I do? Oh! father, I ask thy prayers and thy blessing. One line of your own hand and pen I do crave, before you die and go to heaven. I often wish I had written to Dr. Miller and gotten a line of advice *direct* from his hand, before he left us. But now he's gone home to his Father, I'll never see him. You must soon be there; and if I had a letter from you to look at, when laboring in God's harvest-field, methinks it would do me good.

"I have never seen, nor do I know *personally*, any of the great men of our beloved church. I was educated at West Alexander, Pa., under Dr. J. McClusky, who is my uncle. I was raised in *poverty*, yet, I trust, in *piety*.

"But I must close. I suppose I shall *never* see you here on earth: in heaven I hope to meet you. May the Lord Jesus bless you, and go with you through the evening of life, comfort you in the night of death, and receive you home to glory.

"Please address,
"W. M. FERGUSON,
"Fultonham, Muskingum Co., O.
"Dr. G. SPRING, N. Y."

"PARIS, *March* 23, 1835.
"*To the Young Men belonging to the Congregation worshipping in the Brick Church:*

"MY BELOVED YOUNG FRIENDS:

"At our last interview in Hudson-square, at the house of our esteemed friend, Mr. Lord, I engaged occasionally to address you from some portion of this distant land. I sit down this morning to redeem this pledge in part.

"My voyage, as you have probably heard from some members of my family, was in every view prosperous. Seventeen days and a half brought us to the mouth of the Seine, and in less than three weeks from the day on which I left my native shores, I arrived in Paris, and was pleasantly situated in the chamber where I am now writing.

"The ocean charms me. I know not which the most to admire, the sea, or the dry land. The vast, immeasurable ocean appears full of God. It was, I assure you, very precious for me to feel, when flying over its waters, that though I had taken the wings of the morning, and dwelt in the utmost parts of the sea, yet *God was there.* I can give you no better idea of the *vastness* of the ocean, than by telling you that we traversed an horizon of forty-five thousand square miles without seeing a single sail, and that, though hundreds and thousands were traversing the same seas. Often it seemed as though a few more miles, and we should certainly see the shore; and yet we travelled on, and travelled on, and pursued our way, day after day, and no signs of land, or human being, appeared. I used not unfrequently to say, *Who knows where we are?* No being but One; no, none in the universe but One.

"I found the advantage of being on board a temperance ship. Everything was quiet, everything comfortable, everything safe, everybody punctual and industrious; there was a place for everything, and everything was in its place. But though the life of a common sailor is not an unhappy life, I wish I could say it is not a *degraded life.* Seamen must be a different class of men, before the world can be converted to God. What can be done for seamen? Ought not a heavier and more active impulse to be thrown into the efforts of our countrymen for the intellectual and moral elevation of this useful class of men?

"Since my arrival in Paris, I have been occupied in delivering my letters of introduction, which, I assure you, is no small task. I am under many and great obligations to my friends in New York for having secured for me so much attention of the most valuable kind. I am not a little indebted to the courtesy of the American ambassador here, which I the more cheerfully mention, as in this particular I have heard him frequently criminated by Americans, both in Paris and the United States. I find that his impression is decidedly that there will be no war between France and the United States. Yesterday I was introduced by him to the sittings of the Chamber of Deputies; my card gave me access to the seat occupied by the diplomatic corps, so that I had every opportunity of hearing and seeing all that I could desire. But there was no such thing as *hearing*. I never saw a body of men so regardless of all mutual courtesy as the French Chambers.

"Of the moral state of Paris I can say little. There is less of form, state, and civility, than under the reign of Louis XVIII., eleven years ago. It is easy to see that the Parisians mean to have a popular government, and, at the same time, that they are not prepared to enjoy it. I know not all the causes, but the fact is, that the Protestantism of Paris is almost as bad as its Romanism. There is not, probably, much true religion here. There are some English, and a *few*, very few Americans, who let their light shine. But there is a miserable jealousy, in the minds of the English, of American Christians and their influence, which greatly disheartens our dear American brethren who are here. There is, however, a little salt, to keep this fermenting mass of iniquity from universal putrefaction. Last Saturday evening I attended a little prayer-meeting in a private family, that refreshed me, and reminded me of home. There were about twelve persons present, all Americans but two, and those Scotchmen. Besides preaching to about one hundred Americans and a few English on the Sabbath, I heard two of the Protestant ministers, and a part of a sermon from a Roman Catholic. I find I can understand the French language much better, when *spoken from the pulpit*, than when uttered in the rapidity of private conversation. The young men who visit Paris would do well to omit no opportunity of attending public worship, if it were for no other reason than to secure the *very best* opportunity of becoming acquainted with the French language.

"You perceive that I have but just entered on my tour. I can scarcely persuade myself that it is only a month to-day, since I attended the last prayer-meeting with my beloved people. And if time flies thus rapidly, I shall soon, if the Lord will, see them again. Nor is there any portion of them I shall more joyfully salute, than those to whom I address this hasty letter. There are high obligations resting on the young men of the present generation—obligations which, I am confident, my young friends, that are felt by all *of you*. May you feel them more and more! And may the Lord of the whole earth grant that you may not feel them in vain!

"The next letter I am permitted to address to my friends in America, must be to the church. I shall write to your little circle again, as soon as I can find time. In the mean time, permit me to say, that I write at snatches, and in much haste.

"Still remember me, as you yourselves are remembered by
"Your affectionate pastor,
"G. Spring."

"Paris, Rue de Rivoli, No. 28, *April* 2, 1835.
"*To the Session of the Brick Presbyterian Church:*
"Very Dear Brethren: There is no medium of addressing the beloved church with which I am connected, at once so proper and so pleasant, as those beloved men with whom I am officially associated. I write while many revel, and many sleep; but I love to feel myself in the act of correspondence with you, if it were only for my own sake, and to remind me that though I dwell in a far-distant land, the distance neither diminishes my affection for you, nor my obligations to you. Daily do I think of you, and daily do I pray for you; I have, more than once, had occasion to remark, that the signal kindness of God towards me and the dear child that is with me, is sufficient evidence to my mind that we have not been forgotten in those seasons in which you have had near access to the throne of mercy. I know I owe it not a little to your kindness that everything smiles around me; that both foreigners and my own countrymen regard me with so much attention and benignity; and that I have so many opportunities of doing good, among a people where I expected so few.

"I have not been idle since I have been in Paris. Two pulpits have been, very politely, offered to me; one of which I feel it a privilege to occupy every Lord's day. I mention it with gratitude, that the

Rev. Mr. Wilkes, an English clergyman, and the Rev. Mr. Mines, of our own country, who every alternate Sabbath occupy the same church, have both insisted upon my occupying their places as long as I remain in Paris. My congregation is increasing; is composed of Americans, English, and French; and I cannot but hope that *some* good may be done in the name of our Lord Jesus. Here, amid the sin, and folly, and atheism of France, I am permitted to utter the same glorious truths which I have so often preached to my people at home.

"Of Paris and of France I can at present say but little. Paris appears to me to be a city of idleness and sin. It is difficult for a stranger to understand how its splendor and luxury are supported, because he does not see industry enough to procure even the common means of subsistence. Even the common people and the poorer classes appear devoted to loitering and pleasure. Paris is, indeed, a splendid city; but in conversing, this morning, about its splendors, with a lady of distinction, she remarked, with emphasis, '*O Monsieur, Napoléon a sacrifié la France à Paris!*'—'Oh, sir, Napoleon has sacrificed France to Paris!' The moral state of this city is, indeed, a lamentable state. Ignorance of God, ignorance of the Bible, self-gratification and licentiousness in a thousand forms, united with desecrations of the Sabbath, such as fill the mind with grief and horror, are a faint description of this guilty metropolis. I have been forcibly struck with the thought that the inhabitants scarcely know the difference between right and wrong; scarcely know *what it is* to sin against God;

scarcely know that there is *such a thing as sin* in the universe. I do not see that they have any standard of moral conduct, none but their own convenience, none but the laws of courtesy and honor. Paris is a Pagan land; and if I mistake not, it will even be more difficult to evangelize France, than though it were merged in all the darkness of Paganism. Christians in the United States are not aware how much is to be done for nations that are nominally Christian—nay, for large portions of Protestant nations—before the world will be converted to God.

"Protestantism in France is not what I have been in the habit of considering it. I knew it was in a measure corrupt, but not to the extent in which I actually find it. I do not think that the Romanists, as a body, have much confidence in the Roman religion. But the mischief is, that when thinking men throw off the bonds of Romanism, they relapse into infidelity. And it is very natural they should do so; for who, that knows nothing of the religion of the Bible except what he has learned from the absurd dogmas and the ridiculous usages of the Romish church, would not reject the whole system as a fable? The mass of the Catholics in this country, therefore, are so latitudinarian in their views, that they look with indifference upon the Protestants, and give them this negative countenance—that is, they do not oppose and persecute them. No; *true religion* in France finds its most bitter and unwearied enemies in Protestants themselves. The Protestants of this country are high Arians, if not absolute Socinians. There are now three hundred and fifty-eight Protestant *pastors* in France, besides their few vacant churches. But there are comparatively few among them all who love and obey the truth. France has every opportunity of religious advancement under the present king, but she is bound by the chains of her own iniquity; and the few faithful men in her churches are called to contend with difficulties which are truly disheartening.

"And yet there is a little leaven in France. In Paris I have found some excellent men. But they are under the control of English influence—influence which owes its power only to the fact that it has acquired it by long residence among the people; and, I must say, influence which, while it means well, and did well fifteen years ago, now looks with a jealous eye on everything which it does not originate, and is actually neutralizing the efforts of some of the best men in France, without their knowing it. Yes, there is a little leaven in Paris. I love these men, though I perceive they have been taught to be afraid of the influence of the American churches. I have to-day attended, in company with them, a very delightful exercise. It was a religious service conducted by the evangelical pastors for the purpose of ordaining and setting apart to the work of the sacred ministry Mr. François Daumas, of Paris, and Mr. Henry Homes, of Boston, the former a missionary of the Evangelical Society of Paris, and destined to the south of Africa; the latter a missionary of our own American Board, and destined to Turkey. It was a sweet season. There were eight American clergymen present, who were all requested to assist in the laying on of hands. The

Rev. Dr. Codman and myself were present as the representatives of the American Board. The Rev. Mr. Grandpierre and the Rev. Mr. Monod conducted the exercises. It was like the dew of Hermon, and like the dew that descended upon the mountains of Zion, when the Lord commanded his blessing. Mr. Monod said to me, at the close, taking me by the hand, ' This is good. I love to see our American and our French brethren thus mixed up together.'

"I have just alluded to the presence in Paris of a number of American clergymen. Among them is our beloved friend, the Rev. Dr. Macaulay, of the Murray-street church. He is in miserable health, and obviously not improved by his tour. I am near him, and see him almost daily.

"In relation to the prospects of war, the belief here is, that the French Chambers will pass the law indemnifying the United States, by sixty or seventy majority. I think we need not fear disruption.

"I shall probably remain in Paris until the 1st of May, and then, with all expedition, set my face towards London. The Paris Bible Society meets on Friday, the 1st of May, and the British and Foreign Bible Society on the following Wednesday; so that I will take the mail on Friday evening, rest in Calais on the Sabbath, and reach London, with God's favor, on Monday following.

"I close this letter at a sufficiently late hour. You will receive it as the familiar epistle of a pastor to his flock. Still give me, my dear people, an interest in your prayers. I hope to hear that the Lord is with you of a truth. I am quite contented for the present, and the more so, the more I find to do for the cause which I trust we all love.

"Peace be with you, and grace from Him who is the great Shepherd!

"Your affectionate pastor,
"Gardiner Spring."

"Paris, *April* 25, 1835.
"*To the Young Men worshipping in the Brick Church:*

"My Beloved Young Friends:

"If you have received my last communication, you have some just conception of the crude and desultory nature of my correspondence; which, if you have the patience to read, I ought surely to have the patience to write.

"The city of Paris is truly a marvellous place. The more I see and learn of the Old World, the more do I love the New; and the more do I admire the wisdom and goodness of the all-wise Disposer of human affairs, in establishing the government and churches of our beloved America, at a great remove from all the principles of human society as they are developed here. I have been five weeks in France; and I assure you, I know not how to speak of it—I know not what to *think* of it. It is a sort of chaos; it is without form, and must long remain so, unless the influence of the Gospel is felt to a degree which can scarcely be hoped for, for a great while to come.

"All tastes may be gratified in Paris; and this, perhaps, is one reason why such a motley population crowds this splendid metropolis. The man of business finds here everything to gratify his love of business and money; for here are the products of every age, and clime, and art, and one constant scene of activity and bustle. The man of literature has everything to excite his curiosity, and gratify his thirst for knowledge; for here are the literati of the world; here are institutions venerable for age, and distinguished for their researches; here is the dust of kings; here are the curiosities of the world; here are the relics of ages that are gone by. The man of taste has everything to attract his eye, please his ear, and fascinate his imagination; for in natural scenery there is here everything to charm; in splendid altars, there is everything to fill the mind with awe; here are pompous ceremonies, verdant gardens, and richest orders of architecture; here the canvas glows, the marble speaks, and the harp, and the organ, and the viol, in sweetest concert and solemn harmony, vibrate with a grandeur and exactness, as if moved by some secret machinery within. The man of pleasure has everything to tempt, ensnare, and satiate a luxurious, epicurean, and even grossly sensual mind; for here are gayety and dissipation, here are scenes of enchanting beauty, and here is a moral sense which feels no responsibility, and fears neither man nor God. The man of fashion may here see and be seen to his heart's content, with none to rebuke him for his vanity, or remind him that the lily of the valley is more admired than he. And the man of piety—what shall I say *of him?* Ah! he surveys a wilderness; he sees a field of labor not less interesting, and I will say not less arduous, than that which attracted the heart of Brainerd towards the wigwams of the savage, or the mind of Paul towards Rome. And even the man of leisure, and these are not wanting here, finds in this metropolis enough to occupy his time, without feeling that his time or employment are a burden. Here are wealth and poverty, power and subjection, piety and impiety, in strong contrast, and forming a state of society in many respects very peculiar, and in some inexplicable. I have seen regal splendor, and never did I wish less to be a king; I have seen military parades, and never did I wish less to be a hero; I have seen worldly greatness, and never did I wish less to have the world as my portion. I have returned to-day from visiting the royal palace and the richly-wooded gardens of Versailles; it was amid the verdure and bloom of the dawning spring; it was probably the most splendid spot this world has to exhibit, and I could not but turn away from it and say, *Is this all this world can give?* It was beautiful—it was exquisitely beautiful, and I enjoyed it exceedingly; I have no doubt I enjoyed it much more than its royal owner; but what was it? *Vanity*—truly, it was vanity! My people, my family, the church, the chapel, my hopes, my Bible, were more to me than all.

"I intimated, in my last letter, that the age of infidelity in France had passed away. But I was mistaken. Infidelity is still the crying sin of France. Never, perhaps, has it been more universal than it is now. You find it among all classes of men, from the most exalted to the most humble; from the chair of the philosopher to the bureau of the merchant; from the lecturer at the Sorbonne to the shop of the artisan; and from the palaces of the rich to the cottages of the poor. From learned men, and men who styled themselves the thinkers of the world, it has descended to the mass of the people, where it has taken root, and become, as it were, naturalized. It is found among those who have never read anything, never studied anything, and never knew anything, and who are infidels by instinct. It is amusing to hear the boot-black, the driver of a cabriolet, and the filthy market-woman, talk of their infidelity! The people are essentially an irreligious people. In the journals of the day, in all the organs of public opinion, in all the acts of the nation, you find nothing—nothing which indicates a belief in a Providence, a God, a day of final account. Ladies swear, and *Mon Dieu!* is as common from the lips of a well-bred lady presiding at her dinner-table, as it was twenty years ago from the quarter-deck of an American merchantman.

"There is, if I mistake not, also a *restiveness* in this community, which is like the troubled sea. It resembles a man in a fever. It has an excited pulse, an excited skin, and deranged organs of digestion. It is a diseased people. Nor do I regard this existing characteristic of the French people without solicitude. They appear to me to have a state of mind that is ripe for anything, and that can be controlled only by the sword. There is a general disquietude, which strikes deep into the foundations of human society. Indeed, society seems to have no foundations. And how can it have any? There is nothing believed, nothing loved, nothing durable and strong. Ambition, egotism, distrust, suspicion, and discontent form the picture of Paris. And yet, this is a strange community; for in the midst of all this, every one seems to be happy! To my eye, Paris is an anomaly in the history of man.

"And hence the frequent tottering of the throne, the revolutions, and the blood. And hence the spectacles, the amusements, the holidays, the shows, and all the chapter of public entertainments, often supported by the crown, to keep up and gratify this excited state of mind, which, if not otherwise occupied, would break out in rebellion. And thus it is that the people dream, while tyrants forge their chains.

"But I will not weary you any longer. Of the objects and men whom I have seen, I cannot speak. The next week is the week of the religious anniversaries here, at three of which I have been desired to take part in conducting the exercises. If I can find time, I shall, in my next, give some account of them *to the church*. I leave this for England, God willing, on the 1st of May, where I shall be more occupied, and have less time to write.

"I remember you daily, as a most interesting part of my spiritual charge. The Lord of all the earth bless you, my young friends, pour upon you his Spirit, and make you useful in the church and in the world!

"Your affectionate pastor,
"GARDINER SPRING."

CHAPTER XIII.

THE NINETEENTH CENTURY A PRACTICAL AGE.

As such, as an age of great energy, purely practical, the nineteenth century stands first and foremost of all epochs since the beginning of time. Perhaps no age abounds more in those influences, those active tendencies, which shape the character and fortunes of the human race. We except one age—when imperial Rome was at the height of her greatness; when the limits of her empire were almost coincident with the limits of the then known world; when from the Atlantic to the Euphrates, from the wastes of Africa to the northern seas, her will was law to the nations; when all the learning that the ancient world could transmit to us, had nearly completed its course; and when, in a corner of the imperial dominions, in an humble village of Syria, the God-Man was born, a legislator, a priest, an instructor, whose teachings were ultimately to sow the seeds of inquiry and progress, in a word, to impart to mankind all that was worth learning in religion and in morals, and to proclaim those principles which have proved the germ of all that mankind has since achieved, worthy of honor and remembrance; principles which have had for their result the civilization of Christianity. This first century of our era was incomparably the most potent in its influence upon the destinies of the world.

The fifth century was unquestionably a marked era in the world's history, when the barbarians of the North invaded the empire of the Cæsars, and overthrew the edifice reared by the labor, valor, and genius of ages. Europe, even at the present day, feels the effect of this irruption in all its institutions, civil, military, and legislative. But while the northern hordes overthrew the arms and overturned the civil structure of Rome, they yielded to her arts, they bowed to her superior civilization, they were awed by the pomp and majesty of her religion. Rome, vanquished, subdued them in her turn; they kneeled at her shrines, became the lambs of her fold, and trembled in submission before the crozier of her bishops.

It was well that it was so. These northern barbarians infused new life into the veins of the southern people, and it was only under the auspices of a pure religion, and thus invigorated, that western Europe was able to resist the fiery fanaticism of the Moslem. The eastern empire was without this renovating influence, and fell before the Ottoman arms, and remains a subject people at the present time. It was to the adoption of the Christian faith by the victorious Northmen that we owe it, that the civilization which we possess is not the civilization of the Mahometan, of the Druid, or of the Scandinavian, as the march of victory might have decided. But the religion of Rome, although pure in its origin, was becoming corrupt and debased. The stream at its fountain-head had been as crystal; but at this distance from its source, it flowed with less purity. The ministers of the church no longer strove to elevate, but to debase, the minds of the people; no longer sought to enfranchise, but to enslave, human thought; suppressing free inquiry, obstructing progress, debasing morals, and subjecting the human mind to the shackles of dogmas and ceremonies which were neither truths nor symbols. They perverted their mission. It was truth, but they made it falsehood; and instead of enforcing the precepts of the Gospel, they exhausted theological inquiry in contriving devices by which they might be evaded. But all this was soon to be changed.

The fifteenth century anticipated, as it were by four hundred years, the practical spirit of the nineteenth. A discovery was made, which, in process of time, was to sweep away all these corruptions from more than the half of Europe, and to open the way to liberty of thought and free inquiry. The art of printing was discovered; the press sprang into existence, and the shackles upon the human intellect dropped as if by magic. Thought became free! the Reformation arose; and man stood again, like Moses, face to face with his Creator, with no media of priests, of masses, and beads, but with Jesus Christ the great Mediator alone between them.

The eighteenth century was the age of intellectual and scientific development. Newton, Leibnitz, La Place, Clairaut, Euler, Descartes, and a host of others, explored the recesses of nature, and intellect advanced with rapid strides. The course of the stars, the earth's form and weight, the composition of its particles, were all investigated; water was analyzed, light was brought under the prism, and divided into parts; magnetism and electricity were evolved by chemical and mechanical processes, the atmosphere was weighed and measured, the animal and vegetable world was ranged and classified. The progress in moral and political science was scarcely less remarkable. The laws of mind were scrutinized, the rights of man to liberty, freedom of speech, and equality before the law, were loudly proclaimed and boldly advocated. Never was there seen such a host of intellectual giants. But the sciences were studied for the sake of scientific truth alone, abstractly, and without regard to utilitarian results. Studied, as studied by Newton, Galvani, Volta, and only so studied, they would have been without the slightest practical utility to mankind. Their scientific progress was unequalled in the history of learning. Their intellectual efforts were marvellous, but were without a definite, practical object. Their discoveries, with all their interest for the learned world, were without interest for the masses. Still they were the seeds of a future harvest.

The nineteenth century dawned, and the seeds sprang up into trees, foliage, and fruit. During the present century, a different spirit has attended the advances of science. Utility has marched hand in hand with intellectual progress. The nineteenth century is no age of shams, it is no age for the vagaries of astrology and alchemy; no one would in this age spend years in searching after the philosopher's stone, or the elixir of life, or voyaging, chivalrously, to discover the fountain of youth. The shams of spiritualism and animal magnetism are but charlatanism and jugglery. The characteristics of the present age may be fairly stated as the spirit of free inquiry, great practical energy, power of public opinion, and force of public conscience. The grand discoveries of the eighteenth century have, in the nineteenth, been applied to ameliorating the condition of society, to augment its well being, to multiply its comforts, to add to its enjoyments, to facilitate social and commercial intercourse, to diminish space and expand time. Newton analyzed light; Daguerre and Talbot have given us the daguerreotype. Volta, Galvani, and Franklin, eliminated by different processes that subtle fluid which, in its various forms, is found to be a marvellous force in nature; Morse, turning their investigations to practical account, has given us the electric telegraph. Watt discovered the wonderful powers of steam; Fulton and Stephenson have given us the steamboat and locomotive. This statement may not bear a rigid scrutiny into every minutia of date. The two centuries, with their modes of thought and action, coalesce as it were near their limit of contact. But the facts here presented are sufficiently accurate for the purpose of this retrospect; sufficiently accurate to establish the character of the two epochs.

The present age, also, is one in which there seems to be something like a public conscience, a moral feeling in the breast of all civilized nations of what is right and wrong. In the nineteenth century there could be no massacres of St. Bartholomew, no dragonades as under Louis the Fourteenth, no cruelties like those of Alva in the Netherlands. There is, in this present century, a public conscience, stronger than ever existed before. If the phrase *vox populi vox Dei* had ever more than a semblance of meaning, it has it in this our nineteenth century—the voice of God speaking in the breast of the people—an all-pervading conscience pulsating in the heart of the world.

So, too, the practical spirit of the present century shows itself in its Christianity. The great contests for the truths of the Bible, the great battle with Infidelity, was, as we have before seen, fought and won in the seventeenth and eighteenth centuries; and with the exception of German rationalism, and the assumptions of natural science, few call in question the authenticity and inspiration of the sacred records. So, likewise, the essential doctrines of the Gospel are no longer the subject of elaborate disputation. The age of metaphysical discussion has gone by. It has done its work, and is superseded by a less philosophic, but more active Christianity. The Christianity of the present age is essentially practical in its nature; it is the Christianity of active benevolence. It sends the Gospel to the heathen, it diffuses widely, almost universally, copies of the Holy Scriptures; it is a Christianity of mission schools and mission churches, of a generous solicitude for the spiritual well-being of seamen as well as landsmen; and in all these great works of benevolence, there is a union of the various religious denominations. The worth of Christianity is now brought to the test of its works. It was known always by its precepts; it is now known by its fruits more than ever before.

And in the development of the great characteristic of the age, this country has borne a not unworthy part. In its numerous agricultural implements, in its labor-saving machines in general, in the rapidity and extent of its telegraphic communications, it is unsurpassed. In naval architecture it was once foremost upon the ocean. Its rivers now swarm with floating palaces, unequalled in the world. In the late sad war, which has resulted so gloriously, it has left no mean record. This nation had been at peace for nearly twenty years, and was unused to the paraphernalia of war. It had been sneered at often, by the unwise, as a selfish, trading, over-reaching people. But when summoned to the contest in defence of the government and civil liberty, though staggered at the outset, it soon showed what material it was made of. And it was summoned by an enemy as gallant and inventive as itself, though inferior in numbers and mechanical appliances; yet the war was conducted with no want of energy, and to no inglorious issue. Its military roads, its military telegraphs, its commissariat, its corps of engineers, its sanitary and Christian commissions, its private hospitals, its freedmen's bureau, testify to its capacity to deal with any emergency.

With a comparatively small navy, likewise, and scattered over distant oceans, it has, under the pressure of the crisis, and in an incredibly short space of time, created a navy which, for power, offensive and defensive, is unequalled by that of any other nation. And if, as has been said by an eminent writer,* an English line-of-battle ship could have destroyed the Roman and Carthaginian fleets combined, it may with equal truth be affirmed that an iron-clad of our navy, of first-class magnitude and power, could have scattered the combined fleets with which Nelson and Villeneuve contended for the mastery of the seas.

This is, perhaps, no place to speak of the great men who rose to a level with the occasion, but their names are neither few nor of slight mark in military annals. For much that has been done during the war, the nation readily acknowledges its indebtedness to its citizens of foreign birth; but no foreign nation may share in the honor they have attained. It is the custom of this Republic to absorb into its own fame the meritorious deeds of those to whom she has given an asylum, and to assimilate their glory with her own.

* Lord Macaulay, we think.

CHAPTER XIV.

THE PAST AND THE FUTURE.

SINCE the days of my childhood, Washington—Adams—Jefferson—Madison—Monroe—the younger Adams—Jackson—Van Buren—Harrison—Tyler—Polk—Taylor—Lincoln, have been numbered with the dead. The great statesmen of our Republic, its eloquent orators and jurists, have passed away. Otis—Lee — Dayton — Livingston — Ames—Morris—Hamilton—Jay—King—Randolph—Rutledge—Quincy—Pinkney—Ellsworth — Gore — Harper — Marshall—Clinton — Giles — Tracy—Dexter—Story—Burgess—Sergeant —Wirt—Clay—Hayne—Webster—Calhoun—Everett, and their compeers, names memorable in American history, have no longer a place in our halls.

In Great Britain, George III., George IV., and William IV., kings to whom distant lands paid tribute, have, during my day, paid the last tribute to the exacting destroyer, Death.

The horrors of the French Revolution, the death of Louis XVI., the reign and death of Napoleon, the restoration of the Bourbon dynasty, under Louis

XVIII., Charles X., and Louis Philippe, have all taken place during the same period.

I have been witness to the changes in the British possessions, not only in North, but Central and South America, in the West Indies, and in Asia and Africa.

I look back to the city of New York as it was in 1810, and, though it now contains a million of inhabitants, well remember that its population was then estimated at less than one hundred thousand. Its northern limit was Canal-street; its eastern, the Collect and Stuyvesant's meadows; its western, the Collect and the grounds of Mr. Glover and Col. Varick. The wealth and splendor of the city were then below the City Hall, and on the lower part of Broadway and State-street.

I well remember the names of many of the large *capitalists*, such as Jacob Le Roy—Cornelius Ray—Robert Lenox—William Bayard—Archibald Gracie—Matthew Clarkson—William Edgar—Henry Rutgers—Henry Remsen—Richard Varick, and Henry A. Coster. These are honored names; and I take leave to insert them as a token of respect to *honest* men and the merchant princes of our metropolis.

Outside the class of retired capitalists, and the *most distinguished in active business*, were John Jacob Astor—Jonathan Little—Nicholas Fish—Isaac Clason—Matthias Bruen—Abraham and Jacob Barker—Boorman & Johnson—Clendenning & Adams—Gideon Lee—Higginson & Dodge—the Lorillards—J. & S. Ward—Philip Hone—Goold Hoyt—N. & G. Griswold—J. & G. De Peyster—Hoffman & Glass—Haggerty & Austin—Boggs & Thompson—

Najah Taylor, and others; all of whom have deceased except Mr. Taylor, whose name and character remain an honor to the business community.

The *learned professions* have shared the same fate. Of the *Ministers of the Gospel* during this period, the Rev. Dr. Livingston—the Rev. Dr. Abeel—the Rev. Dr. Knypers—the Rev. Dr. Broadhead—the Rev. Dr. Schureman—and the Rev. Dr. Christian Bork occupied the pulpits of the Dutch Reformed church. In the Presbyterian church, were the Rev. Dr. Rodgers — the Rev. Dr. Miller — the Rev. Dr. McKnight—the Rev. Dr. Milledoler—and the Rev. Dr. Romeyn. In the Scotch church, were the Rev. Dr. Mason—the Rev. Mr. Forrest—the Rev. Dr. McLeod—and the Rev. Mr. Hamilton. In the Episcopal church, were Bishop Provost—Bishop Moore—the Rev. Dr. Beach—Dr. Howe—Dr. Hobart—Dr. Harris— Dr. Bowen—Dr. Lyell — and Rev. Cave Jones.

The retrospect of my own Presbytery is melancholy, even to sadness. To say nothing of two other Presbyteries in the city, and of those connected with the New School Presbyteries, no less than *sixty-one* of my beloved and honored co-presbyters of the mother presbytery, are registered on our records as having finished their course since I became one of its members. When Miller—Romeyn—Spencer—McLelland—Alexander—Potts, and Phillips fell, the sad bereavement bore witness to the grief of thousands, and the waning lustre of our pulpit ministrations. I can truly say, with Richard Baxter, " Oh, how great a number of holy persons of my acquaintance, of exemplary lives, could I name, that God hath taken to himself." The memory of the just is blessed. It was the wish of St. Augustine, that when Christ came to call him by death, he might find him *aut precantem aut predicantem*. It was thus that some of these beloved brethren lived and died. Some of them were men of valor for God's truth, and could say with St. Chrysostom, *Nil nisi peccatum timeo*—" I fear nothing but sin." They practised what they preached, and their lives were a practical demonstration of the truth and power of the Gospel. That noble man, I. S. Spencer, *primus inter pares*, was called to conflicts; nor have I ever known a man who could with stronger propriety say with Luther, *Mallem ruere cum Christo, quam regnare cum Cæsare:* I had rather fall with Christ, than reign with Cæsar.

Of the gentlemen who occupied the *Medical Profession* when I came to the city, and during the ten succeeding years, with the exception of that patriarch of the profession, John Augustine Smith, not one remains. They were Dr. Post—Dr. Edward Miller—Dr. Seaman—Dr. Akerly—Dr. Rodgers—Dr. Kissam—Dr. Anderson—Dr. Bailey—Dr. Barrow—Dr. Borrow—Dr. Birch—Dr. Boyd—Dr. Mitchel—Dr. Bradhurst—Dr. Hosack—Dr. Miner—Dr. Nelson—Dr. Pascalis—Dr. Gilbert Smith—Dr. Tillary—Dr. Van Beuren—Dr. Watts, and Dr. Watson. It has often been an affecting thought to me, that those masters of the healing art who have attended my own family, Dr. Edward Miller—Dr. John R. B. Rodgers—Dr. Gilbert Smith—Dr. Alexander Stevens—Dr. Ansel W. Ives, and Dr. Edward Spring, whose fidelity and skill have rescued so many others from the grave, have gone to the land of silence, while so many of their patients remain in all the glow and bustle of the world.

The *Bar of New York*, in the year 1810, and the ten years following, was rich in learning and eloquence, accomplished in liberal as well as professional acquirements, and cultivated a high sense of personal character and dignity. Chief Justice Kent presided over the Supreme Court. The Court of Chancery was administered by Chancellor Lansing, but until the succession into it of Chancellor Kent, was very limited in its business, and its Bar was almost a private body. In the Supreme Court, Chief Justice Kent embellished his judicial course by great elegance of literary acquirement, and a spirit of truly domestic morals. His associates, Thompson—Spencer—Vanness, and Yates, varying greatly in their style of mind and learning, yet were all, by common concession, men of the highest character and merit, having everything which ennobled the character of a judge. During the latter part of this ten years, Jonas Platt was elevated to the Bench, in place of Kent, who was made Chancellor, and added to the dignity of the body by learning and private worth equal to that of his most honored associates. The Bar over which this Bench presided, had for its leaders, taking precedency in age, Richard Harrison—Abraham Van Vechten—Jonas Riggs, and John V. Henery. They truly represented a profession from whom learning and personal dignity, pure character, and accomplished education were justly expected, and which they furnished.

Among their associates, and of no less merit, were Colden—Hoffman—the two Radcliffs—Peter A. Jay—John Wells—the Ogdens, and somewhat their junior, Daniel Lord. Emmet had joined the profession, taking refuge from the revolutionary politics of Ireland, in a welcome, honored, and useful career in New York, a city which he adopted as his home. He heartily cherished it, and adorned it with very varied and professional learning, and with an eloquence second to none in the country from which he emigrated. Other gentlemen, all of pure character and high merit, from time to time added themselves to the number. George Griffin emigrated from Pennsylvania, and became immediately distinguished. Gardinier, from the country—Riker, the Recorder—Samson, a refugee with Emmet—E. W. King, of our own city—Anthon, and Baldwin were distinguished members of the bar, and added to its weight and influence. The Bar of the city was also strongly supported at this period by associates from the country, all men highly cultivated, and of great worth. *Elisha Williams*, and Martin Vanbeuren, of Hudson—Oakley, of Poughkeepsie—Gold, of Utica—Storrs—Ruggles—Hopkins, and Talcot, then coming into notice, the two Duers—Marcy—Betts, and Hermanus Bleecker illustrated the same period of the profession. I look back in my early history upon the Bar of New York, as a class of men who were an honor to the city and the State. In this enumeration the name of *Elisha Williams*, the father of the present Mrs. Spring, deserves more than this hasty notice. Chancellor Kent says of him, " He excited my esteem, admiration, and friendship, and they continued to grow with his growth and his success during the whole course of his distinguished and very celebrated career. There was no person at the Bar that had more devoted and affectionate friends." The New York Bar, and the Bar assembled at the term of the Supreme Court, at Utica, spoke of the wonderful effects of his intellect, and of the power of his imposing eloquence, the fearlessness and the generosity of his noble nature. At the meeting of the New York Bar, Judge Oakley said, "We can all unite in admiring his powerful intellect, his brilliant wit, and matchless eloquence. I speak of him as I knew him, as a lawyer whom few excelled, and as a true-hearted and liberal-minded man, to whom there was no superior." Mr. Griffin said, "A stranger would scarcely have been in company with Elisha Williams, without being aware that he stood in the presence of a remarkable man. I was associated with him in his last professional effort in this hall; when, like the clear, setting sun, he shed upon the horizon he was about to pass forever, the full and gladdening radiance of his matchless eloquence." At the meeting of the New York Bar, Judge Oakley offered the following resolution: " Resolved, That in the death of the late Elisha Williams, we deeply feel the loss of a respected and beloved brother, who was alike an honor to the profession, and an ornament to society, for the kindness and urbanity of his manners, and the sincerity, generosity, and benevolence of his heart; for the undeviating honor of his professional and private life, and the rich intellectual treasures which distinguished him, as well by their profusion as by the prudence with which they poured forth at the call of professional duty and private friendship."

The State was safe in taking from such men its magistrates, and placing them as examples, as well as efficient ministers of justice. They were mostly promoted to judicial seats. They were warm in their political principles, and may be truly said to have represented the education, principles, and spirit of an era not repeated in our history.

"Death loves a shining mark." With two or three exceptions they are no more. "We see that wise men die." All professions, lay and clerical, amid all the fluctuations and responsibilities of their career terminate in the grave. We would do honor to their character in inscribing their virtues on the urn which contains their ashes. Statesmen, jurists, physicians, preachers, the rich and the poor are alike the trophies of the inexorable destroyer.

As from this retrospect I look to the congregation under my pastoral charge, I am constrained to say, "Help, Lord, for the godly man ceaseth, for the faithful fall from among the children of men." Where are the men who greeted me with such cordiality and promptitude in the days of my youth, and in seasons of toil, and solicitude, and apprehension, gave me their love, confidence, and coöperation? Where are the godly women whose influence and prayers gave me courage in despondency and cheered me as I went on my way? Where is the congregation that called me to the pulpit I have so long occupied? There remain but *four* of them among the living, and these in the infirmities and helplessness of age. I have stood at the dying-bed of parents, of children, of grandchildren, of great-grandchildren, and in one instance of children of the fifth generation, who were baptized by these hands. The fathers, where are they? and the children, do they live forever? "Man at his best estate is altogether vanity. All flesh is grass, and the goodliness thereof is as the flower of the field."

There have been great changes among us since I first assumed the responsibilities of the Brick Church. From a population of less than a hundred thousand, our city has increased to somewhat more than a million. It has extended its boundaries from Canal-street to Central Park, and from "The Collect" to Bloomingdale and Yorkville.

To have some just impression of the rapid advance in the commerce of the city, we may advert to the following facts. The regular communication between New York and Liverpool was enterprised in the year 1818, by Isaac Wright and Son, Francis Thompson, Jeremiah Thompson, and Benjamin Marshall. They established a line of Packets, consisting of four ships, to leave each port on the first of every month. Many doubted the success of the enterprise; but the proprietors redeemed their pledge to the public, and were amply rewarded. They increased their ships to eight, when two other lines of four ships each were started by other firms, making in all sixteen ships, one departing every week. A few years after this two lines of four ships each were started for Havre, and two lines for London, all of which were successful—making together thirty-two large ships, running regularly between Great Britain, France, and the United States, besides others regularly in the trade. In 1838, the *Steamer Sirius* reached New York from Liverpool; and in the afternoon of the same day, the Great Western, 1350 tons, arrived from Bristol in fourteen days. I well remember the excitement produced by the arrival of these steamers. The celebrated Dr. Lardner had, as he thought, *demonstrated* that no steamer could ever cross the Atlantic. But the work was done. The Sirius and the Great Western departed in company on their return passage and were gaily escorted to Sandy Hook by an immense fleet of every description, and bearing thousands of spectators.

There has been a large increase in the number of our churches. I am not able to state with accuracy the number between 1810 and 1820. In 1785 there were only *nine*, and the increase was very gradual. In 1845 there were *one hundred and ninety;* in 1850 there were *two hundred and twenty-six;* in 1855 there were *two hundred and eighty-three;* in 1860 there were *three hundred;* and now, in 1865, there are *three hundred and ten*. In twenty years, the Roman Catholics have more than doubled the number of their churches, and the Jews more than trebled. The Presbyterians now have *fifty-eight;* the Dutch Reformed *twenty-two;* the Episcopalians *sixty;* the Methodists *thirty-eight;* the Baptists *twenty-nine;* the Congregationalists *four*, and the Unitarians *three*. There are more than three hundred benevolent institutions in our city, whose re ceipts, the present year, amount to nearly three millions of dollars. Including all denominations, and those without pastoral charge, there are now in the city four hundred and eleven Clergymen. The Free Academy, the New York University, the Theological Seminary of the Episcopal Church, and the Union Theological Seminary, have all risen to eminence under my own observation. The Temperance Reform, the Anti-Slavery movement, the associations for the religious instruction of Seamen, the Juvenile Asylum, the American Female Guardian Society, the Home of the Friendless, and the various Industrial Schools, are all the offspring of the present age. The great work of City Evangelization, including its fifty-four City Missionaries, and the New York Association for Improving the Condition of the Poor, the Greenwood Cemetery, and the Central Park, are among the striking and beautiful novelties of our own days.

It does not fall within the range of these pages to furnish even an outline of the *progress of literature and science* during the present century. I entered College in the year 1800; at that time there were but three professors; now there are more than thirty. When I advert to the terms of admission at that period, and to the prerequisites that are now demanded; when I contrast the number of students, professors, departments of instruction and extended course of study at the present time, with the limited instruction then imparted; I see evidence of progress that does honor to our institutions of learning, and that tempts me to feel that I lived fifty years too soon. The Greek language and literature, the Latin, the French, the German, and the oriental languages and literature occupied a small space compared with that which they now occupy. *Webber and Day* no longer limit the investigations in the exact sciences, nor is *Enfield* the *ultima thule* in Natural Philosophy. Ancient Geography, History, Political Economy, and the English Classics were matters of individual enterprise, rather than academic instruction. Natural science, especially in its application to the arts, was then in its infancy; now it is verging to matured manhood. The departments of Law and Medicine were scarcely known even as appendages to the course of instruction; now they form, if not an integral part of the course, an appendage which the exigencies of the age require. The strides have been rapid, from the ordinary culture of 1800 to the high culture of 1865. The very controversial literature of this period has given rise to a course of instruction that better bears the test of experience. It is not in my heart to depreciate the instruction of former days. There were scholars then that have proved themselves the adornment of the learned professions. They have been men of valor in the Pulpit, at the Bar, in the Senate House, and at Foreign Courts; but they were men who, if they were taught less, learned more; and who, not a little indebted to their persevering industry, while they have stood abreast with the improvements of the age, cheerfully congratulate their favored successors upon enjoying a more commanding starting-point.

In the preceding chapter we have furnished some illustration of the practical character of this nineteenth century. The age of thought is preliminary to the age of action. Former ages have been emphatically the ages of thought and investigation in all the departments of knowledge. They brought out great truths and principles. They treated largely of the grounds of human knowledge, and furnished systems of philosophy in mental, moral, and natural science. But they were satisfied with the discussion of principles; their philosophy led them no farther. The great leaders of thought, men like Locke, and Bacon, Butler, Reid, and Brown, possessed great vigor of intellect; but it was reserved for men of a later age to show the practical utility of their speculations and give them their appropriate influence upon the character and well-being of their fellow-men. Sir Isaac Newton, the father of modern science, did little more than lay the foundation of those scientific discoveries which are the glory of the age in which we live. We carry those investigations into practice. The same is true of Chemistry, and all the departments of natural science. This is the great characteristic of this nineteenth century. The halls of legislation indicate it; the Pulpit, the Bar, and the Schools of Medicine indicate it; the merchant, the mariner, and the agriculturist, as well as the varied forms of domestic economy, and the enjoyments of social life, each in its place and measure furnishes a practical history of those principles which form the groundwork of human improvement. They are alike applicable to the arts of peace and the art of war. Principles are valuable only as they are useful. Metaphysical subtleties that cannot be reduced to practice, the contemplations of the cloister, and amassed treasures of learning, are of no sort of use unless employed to some good end.

There are other characteristics of the present century which give it a marked place in history. The fondness for innovation—the spirit of free inquiry—an enlarged and catholic liberality, frowning upon all that is sectarian and contracted—the increasing power of public opinion—the obvious tendency to the elevation of the masses, are all characteristic of the age in which I have been permitted to live. But more than all, it is the age of action, of theories reduced to practice; of excitement rather than thought; of facts, experiments, and business, rather than the construction of theories. In this respect, the Christianity of this age is more like the Christianity that was illustrated in "the Acts of the Apostles." It is an active, a diffusive, an earnest Christianity; not, I would hope, that it loves principles less, but that it loves them for their practical influence.

When, with this thought in view, and from this retrospect, we lift the curtain from the future, we have more hopes than fears. The series of events that rushed upon us towards the close of the Southern Rebellion, was marvellous beyond a parallel. One of the daily papers of this city, published at the close of the war, contains the following paragraph:

"There is not in the history of any nation so thickly studded a page of great events as that which may be written of the past six months in the story of this war—events which have crowded so fast upon each other that, when we regard their magnitude and their results, we are almost bewildered. First there was the magnificent success of Sherman in Georgia and South Carolina; then followed the fall of Wilmington; then the victories of Grant and the capture of Richmond. Speedily came the surrender of Lee and his whole army; next the surrender of Johnson; then the capture of Mobile. Next, the sad event, the assassination of the President, followed almost immediately by the shooting of his murderer. Then Dick Taylor surrenders his army; and last, not least in great events, we now have the capture of the arch-conspirator, Jeff. Davis. A remarkable chapter of history truly, for six brief months to develope."

The results of these clustering events cannot now be measured. The discovery of the Mariner's Compass, the invention of the art of Printing, the practical application of steam to the mechanic arts, the facility of locomotion on land and sea, and the Magnetic Telegraph, have scarcely exerted a greater influence on the civilized world, than the results of this subjugation of the revolting States. The history of the world has been decided by a few great battles. The conquest of the land of Canaan by Joshua—the triumphs of Alexander the Great—the successful invasion of Rome by the Northern barbarians—the thirty years' War in Europe between Rome and Protestantism—the battle of Waterloo, the battle of Saratoga, and the battle of Gettysburg, open channels of thought, and have given impulse to effects which are felt in all lands. They are thoughts and principles which are embodied in *facts*, and have given rise to new social organizations, new laws and agencies, that are destined to renovate the world. Who does not see that the tendencies of Divine Providence, no longer limited to the overthrow of the Feudal System, and the annihilation of Baronial power, are well-nigh invariably, as before intimated, towards the elevation of the masses? Even despotic Russia feels its power, and aristocratic England is moved from her foundations, and France and Austria, so long the bulwarks of absolutism, fear nothing so much as the growing supremacy of the people. The success of our arms in the late conflict has established the fact that the people are the government. And this single fact is destined to renovate the world. Give the people intelligence and Christianity; let "knowledge with strength of salvation be the stability of our times," and the light of brighter suns will soon dawn.

Not more true is it that the past fourscore years form an important period in history, than that they furnish no doubtful tokens of *progress*. They are preliminaries to some new and unwonted impulse to the human mind, to human governments, and to Christian churches, and especially in our land. We have been disciplined in the furnace. God's way is in the sea, and his path in the mighty waters; but it is his prerogative to bring light out of darkness. He giveth not account of any of his matters. Oh, the depth of the riches both of the wisdom and knowledge of God! How unsearchable are his judgments, and his ways past finding out! The wheels of Providence are high, and move fearfully; but "the living creature" is in the midst of the vast and complicated machinery. There is no problem so difficult but he is working it out, and the result will show that he is wise in heart, as well as mighty in strength. The future is a sealed book, except where the seals are broken by the revealing Spirit. God's plans are large. After not a little inquiry, I am by no means satisfied that the predicted and long-expected Millennium is near at hand. Some future events are clearly revealed to us; and among them, the power of Rome, the great corruptor and enemy of Christianity, "The Man of sin," the "Mystery of iniquity," the head of the great Apostasy, "Babylon the great," never the spouse of Christ, but the "mother of harlots, and abomination of the earth." It becomes a Christian and free people not to sleep over her subtle invasions. She exists in growing power in this favored land. She is grasping for dominion; and, with all her professed attachment to our free institutions, is even now setting herself to convert them into instruments of her control. I have more *concern* for the religious and civil liberties of these States, from this source, than from any other and all other sources. What a few coming years will disclose, is not for human foresight to predict. The "Lion of the tribe of Judah" alone is able to open the leaves of this sealed book. This one thing is strongly impressed on my mind, that the ministers of the Gospel, of every name, and the churches of our ascended Lord, with all their characteristic peculiarities, were never so imperatively called on to merge the less in the greater, and present an unbroken front to the advancing foe. Just now are days of triumph; only let them be turned to good account, in preparing for days of trial. Not long after I am in my grave, my children, and my children's children, may be called to the conflict, and I hope to the overthrow of Antichrist. Stand fast, ye descendants of the Puritans. Put on the whole armor of God. Quit you like men. I have no fear for the final issue. Satan cannot go beyond the length of his chain. His end is nearest when he has done his worst. The greater his power for a time, the more complete will be his overthrow, and the more gloriously will the Son of Man be enthroned. Notwithstanding our fears, we have buoyant hopes for this land. The marvellous dispensation of a wise Providence towards our fathers—the large effusions of his Holy Spirit upon our churches—his blessing upon our arms, and the restoration of peace after this fearful war—the result of the sad catastrophe in the assassination of our Martyr-President—thus cementing the bonds of our National Union, are all indications of the Divine favor. They open to us a bright career of usefulness and honor among the nations. The single fact that 800,000 citizen soldiers have been disbanded within a few months, and have returned to the occupations of peace, a fact unparalleled in the history of the world, speaks volumes for our future history. The past is rich in lessons of experience, and rich in the promise that while "the lofty looks of man are humbled, and the haughtiness of man is bowed down, the Lord alone shall be exalted in that day." The Lord alone: for whom nations live, and to honor whom is their true dignity, the crown of their ambition, and the fulness of their joy. The Lord alone: the motive and the object of the nation's hope, and the vital power of those eternal truths which support his throne, and are destined to make earthly governments like his own. The Lord alone: with whom is no fearlessness of heart, no inconstancy of purpose, and no emotional instability, but, at an infinite remove from human weakness, human imperfection, and human passions, is the same, yesterday, to-day, and forever. The Lord alone: without whose centralizing energy, the kingdoms of this world dissolve away into as many separate parts as they have separate interests to pursue. The Lord alone: the great centre of the universe, around which regenerated nations revolve, and, in the unsleeping care of universal providence, preserving each in its appropriate sphere, enjoy the prosperity and repose that are equal to their desires. Dominion is with him, of him, and through him; and to him are all things, and to him be glory forever!

THE END.

www.ingramcontent.com/pod-product-compliance
Lightning Source LLC
Chambersburg PA
CBHW060945230426
43665CB00015B/2067